The Peter F. Drucker Foundation
for Nonprofit Management

The Peter F. Drucker Foundation for Nonprofit Management was founded in 1990. Named for and guided by Peter F. Drucker, the acknowledged father of modern management, its mission is to "Help the social sector achieve excellence in performance and build responsible citizenship."

The Drucker Foundation holds the following beliefs:

- A healthy society requires three sectors: a public sector of effective governments, a private sector of effective businesses, and a social sector of effective community organizations.
- The three sectors are interdependent, but each is, and must be, autonomous.
- Each sector has its own mission and its own tasks. Each requires its own competencies. Each needs to concentrate on what it does best.
- The mission of the social sector and its organizations is to identify the needs of the spirit, the mind, and the body of individuals, the community, and society, and to mobilize the energies and resources of the individuals within society and the community so that they can be put to fruitful work to satisfy these needs. It is also the mission of this sector and its organizations to create for the individuals within society and the community a meaningful sphere of effective and responsible citizenship.
- Finally, in American society at the present time, the social sector is the one that has the greatest potential for healthy growth and offers the greatest opportunities for contribution, but it also is the sector that faces the greatest challenges.

Through the provision of educational opportunities and resources to leaders of social sector organizations, the Drucker Foundation aims to inspire and enable those leaders to realize the full potential of their organizations. It pursues these goals through the presentation of conferences, video teleconferences, and the annual Peter F. Drucker Award for Nonprofit Innovation, as well as through the development of management resources and publications for nonprofit boards, staffs, and volunteers.

For More Information: If you would like more information on the Drucker Foundation and its programs and publications, or if you would like to support its work with a contribution, please write, call, or fax the Foundation at the following address:

 The Drucker Foundation
320 Park Avenue, 3rd Floor
New York, NY 10022-6839
Telephone: 212-224-1174
Fax: 212-224-2508
E-mail: druckerf@ix.netcom.com

The Leader
of the Future

DRUCKER FOUNDATION
FUTURE SERIES

The Leader
of the Future

New Visions, Strategies, and Practices for the Next Era

FRANCES HESSELBEIN
MARSHALL GOLDSMITH
RICHARD BECKHARD
EDITORS

Foreword by Peter F. Drucker

Jossey-Bass Publishers • San Francisco

Substantial discounts on bulk quantities of Jossey-Bass books are available to corporations, professional associations, and other organizations. For details and discount information, contact the special sales department at Jossey-Bass Inc., Publishers.
(415) 433-1740; Fax (800) 605-2665.

For sales outside the United States, please contact your local Simon & Schuster
International Office.

T⬥F Manufactured in the United States of America on Lyons Falls Pathfinder
Tradebook. This paper is acid-free and 100 percent totally chlorine-free.

Library of Congress Cataloging-in-Publication Data

The leader of the future : new visions, strategies, and practices for
  the next era / Frances Hesselbein, Marshall Goldsmith, Richard
  Beckhard, editors.
     p. cm.—(The Drucker Foundation Future Series)
  Includes index.
  ISBN 0-7879-0180-6
  1. Leadership. 2. Strategic Planning. I. Hesselbein, Frances.
II. Goldsmith, Marshall. III. Beckhard, Richard, date.
HD57.7.L418   1996
658.4'092—dc20   95–38959
                                                  CIP

HB Printing   10 9 8 7 6 5 4 3 2 1   FIRST EDITION

Contents

90570

Foreword

Not Enough Generals Were Killed

I have been working with organizations of all kinds for fifty years or more—as a teacher and administrator in the university, as a consultant to corporations, as a board member, as a volunteer. Over the years, I have discussed with scores—perhaps even hundreds—of leaders their roles, their goals, and their performance. I have worked with manufacturing giants and tiny firms, with organizations that span the world and others that work with severely handicapped children in one small town. I have worked with some exceedingly bright executives and a few dummies, with people who talk a good deal about leadership and others who apparently never even think of themselves as leaders and who rarely, if ever, talk about leadership.

The lessons are unambiguous. The first is that there may be "born leaders," but there surely are far too few to depend on them. Leadership must be learned and can be learned—and this, of course, is what this book was written for and should be used for. But the second major lesson is that "leadership personality," "leadership style," and "leadership traits" do not exist. Among the most effective leaders I have encountered and worked with in a half century, some locked themselves into their office and others were ultragregarious. Some (though not many) were "nice guys" and others were stern disciplinarians. Some were quick and impulsive; others studied and studied again and then took forever to come to a decision. Some were warm and instantly "simpatico"; others remained aloof even after years of working closely with others, not only with outsiders like me but with the people within their own organization. Some immediately spoke of their family; others never mentioned anything apart from the task in hand.

Some leaders were excruciatingly vain—and it did not affect their performance (as his spectacular vanity did not affect General Douglas MacArthur's performance until the very end of his career). Some were self-effacing to a fault—and again it did not affect their performance as leaders (as it did not affect the performance of General George Marshall or Harry Truman). Some were as austere in their private lives as a hermit in the desert; others were ostentatious and pleasure-loving and whooped it up at every opportunity. Some were good listeners, but among the most effective leaders I have worked with were also a few loners who listened only to their own inner voice. The one and only *personality trait* the effective ones I have encountered did have in common was something they did *not* have: they had little or no "charisma" and little use either for the term or for what it signifies.

All the effective leaders I have encountered—both those I worked with and those I merely watched—*knew* four simple things:

1. The only definition of a *leader* is someone who has *followers*. Some people are thinkers. Some are prophets. Both roles are important and badly needed. But without followers, there can be no leaders.

2. An effective leader is not someone who is loved or admired. He or she is someone whose followers do the right things. Popularity is not leadership. *Results* are.

3. Leaders are highly visible. They therefore set *examples*.

4. Leadership is not rank, privileges, titles, or money. It is *responsibility*.

Regardless of their almost limitless diversity with respect to personality, style, abilities, and interests, the effective leaders I have met, worked with, and observed also *behaved* much the same way:

1. They did not start out with the question, "What do I want?" They started out asking, "*What needs to be done?*"

2. Then they asked, "*What can and should I do to make a difference?*" This has to be something that both needs to be done and fits the leader's strengths and the way she or he is most effective.

3. They constantly asked, "What are the organization's *mission* and *goals?* What constitutes *performance* and *results* in this organization?"

4. They were extremely tolerant of diversity in people and did not look for carbon copies of themselves. It rarely even occurred to them to ask, "Do I like or dislike this person?" But they were totally—fiendishly—intolerant when it came to a person's *performance, standards,* and *values.*

5. They were not afraid of *strength* in their associates. They gloried in it. Whether they had heard of it or not, their motto was what Andrew Carnegie wanted to have put on his tombstone: "Here lies a man who attracted better people into his service than he was himself."

6. One way or another, they submitted themselves to the *"mirror test"*—that is, they made sure that the person they saw in the mirror in the morning was the kind of person they wanted to be, respect, and believe in. This way they fortified themselves against the leader's greatest temptations—to do things that are popular rather than right and to do petty, mean, sleazy things.

Finally, these effective leaders were not preachers; they were *doers.* In the mid 1920s, when I was in my final high school years, a whole spate of books on World War I and its campaigns suddenly appeared in English, French, and German. For our term project, our excellent history teacher—himself a badly wounded war veteran—told each of us to pick several of these books, read them carefully, and write a major essay on our selections. When we then discussed these essays in class, one of my fellow students said, "Every one of these books says that the Great War was a war of total military incompetence. *Why was it?*" Our teacher did not hesitate a second but shot right back, "Because not enough generals were killed; they stayed way behind the lines and let others do the fighting and dying."

Effective leaders delegate a good many things; they have to or they drown in trivia. But they do not delegate the one thing that only they can do with excellence, the one thing that will make a difference, the one thing that will set standards, the one thing they want to be remembered for. *They do it.*

It does not matter what kind of organization you work in; you will find opportunities to learn about leadership from all organizations—public, private, and nonprofit. Many people do not realize it, but the largest number of leadership jobs in the United States is in the nonprofit, social sector. Nearly one million nonprofit organizations are active in this country today, and they provide excellent opportunities for learning about leadership. The nonprofit sector is and has been the true growth sector in America's society and economy. It will become increasingly important during the coming years as more and more of the tasks that government was expected to do during the last thirty or forty years will have to be taken over by community organizations, that is, by nonprofit organizations.

The Leader of the Future is a book for leaders in all sectors: business, nonprofit, and government. It is written by people who themselves are leaders with proven performance records. It can—and should—be read as the definitive text on the subject. It informs and stimulates.

The first section of this book looks at the future of organizations and examines the role of leaders in the emerging society of organizations. The second part of the book gives vivid accounts of today's and tomorrow's leaders in action. It then turns to look at leadership development strategies, and it concludes with some powerful personal statements from effective leaders.

This is a book about the future. But I hope that it will also be read as a call to action. I hope that it will first challenge every reader to ask, "What in my organization could I do that would truly make a difference? How can I truly set an example?" And I hope that it will then motivate each reader to *do it*.

Claremont, California   Peter F. Drucker
October 1995

This book is dedicated to volunteers

*To the millions of people who donate their time
and effort to help make others' dreams come true*

*To our authors who donated their time
and effort to help make this dream come true*

Preface

This is a book about the future—the future quality of our lives, our businesses, our organizations, and our society—and the leadership required to move us into the exciting unknown. With every day that passes, the beginning of the next century nears. Some of us will edge into the twenty-first century warily, clinging to the past as much as possible. Some will back into the future with trepidation. Some will walk confidently into the future with a tool kit packed full of plans, charts, and blueprints only to find that the tools that have been packed don't quite meet the needs of a new destination. Some of the risk takers among us will take flying leaps into the unknown and cast their lot with fate. The leaders who ultimately will be successful in shaping the future are already scanning far beyond the horizon. This book is for them.

Looking beyond the known requires new mind-sets, new eyes and ears. To help today's executives and managers fathom the future of leadership, we have gathered the best ideas of an amazing array of the best authors, practitioners, consultants, academics, and philosophers. Each author offers a special perspective on leadership and a unique glimpse into the future. Some build upon lessons from yesterday; others note trends and project tomorrow. Together they represent a treasure trove of insight and knowledge. We hope that as you read this book, the visions of its authors will enrich and expand your vision of the future.

We have divided our exploration of the leader of the future into four parts: "Leading the Organization of the Future," "Future Leaders in Action," "Learning to Lead for Tomorrow," and "Executives on the Future of Leadership." These parts have been chosen in a somewhat arbitrary manner. We deliberately gave the authors a free hand, and our revisions have been only minor. The authors are all experts in their own right, and we wanted you to hear their views in an unfiltered form.

This is not a book that needs to be read cover to cover. It can be read one chapter at a time, starting anywhere in the book. Our suggestion is to begin with the authors who interest you most (who may well be the reason you bought this book) and then branch out to authors you may not have been exposed to in the past or who describe views you may never have considered.

Peter F. Drucker, who is the acknowledged father of modern management, opens the book with his foreword, "Not Enough Generals Were Killed." The foreword is a distillation of Peter's years of observation on leadership and ends with a challenge for the reader. He notes, "Leadership must be learned and can be learned—and this, of course, is what this book was written for and should be used for."

Part One, "Leading the Organization of the Future," examines the unique qualities required to lead in a different kind of organization—the organization of tomorrow. We can already see how rapidly accelerating technology, global competition, and changing demographics are creating new types of organizations that were not even imagined a few years ago. The chapters in this part show how changing organizations will require changed leadership.

The authors in Part One represent the mix of thinkers who are helping to create tomorrow's organizations. Charles Handy is one of the great, revolutionary philosophers in the field; William Bridges has been years ahead of his time in forecasting the "de-jobbed" organization; Sally Helgesen has pioneered work in new organizational structures; Gifford Pinchot invented the term *intrapreneur* and is a leading thinker on innovation; Peter Senge is the key thinker on the learning organization and is coordinating breakthrough efforts in reinventing organizations; Edgar Schein has long been a world authority on organizational culture and development; John Work is an expert in the field of diversity in the work force, which will become an even more critical topic in the next century; and Ken Blanchard has effectively translated the requirements for effective leadership into language that has had a positive impact on millions of people.

Part Two, "Future Leaders in Action," describes the actions, skills, and strategies that leaders will need to sustain a competitive advantage in tomorrow's fast-paced world. The authors include educators and consultants who have worked with many of the world's present leaders and who are helping to train the world's future leaders.

Rosabeth Moss Kanter is an innovator in describing the transitions required to make successful new-age organizations a practical reality; James Kouzes and Barry Posner have done leading-edge work in analyzing "once-in-a-lifetime" success stories; James Heskett and Leonard Schlesinger are thought leaders at Harvard Business School who are active in creating high-performance cultures; Frances Hesselbein (former CEO of the Girl Scouts of the U.S.A.) is widely regarded as one of America's premier leaders; Richard Beckhard is an authority on organization development and change management who is helping both major organizations and family businesses change for future success; Judith Bardwick has been consistently ahead of her time in studying the changes that have shaped today's organizations and predicting the ones that will shape tomorrow's; and David Noer has analyzed both the costs and the benefits of life in a totally ambiguous reengineered world.

Part Three, "Learning to Lead for Tomorrow," focuses specifically on the area of leadership development. The authors in this part describe some of the how-to's in getting from where leaders *are* to where they will *need to be*. These authors are all people who not only have talked about development but actually have helped to develop the leaders in hundreds of major organizations.

Stephen Covey has successfully applied learnings from age-old concepts in a way that can positively affect people's lives tomorrow; James Bolt designs executive development efforts for many of the world's most forward-thinking organizations; Caela Farren and Beverly Kaye are innovators in the areas of career planning and non-traditional, future-oriented career paths; Richard Leider is currently developing new approaches to life planning and self-leadership that are designed to fit tomorrow's "virtual" world; Douglas Smith is a respected thinker on teamwork who has a great view of leadership from the "side" and the "bottom" as well as the top; Dave Ulrich is the world's authority in designing human resource systems for the future; Warren Wilhelm is currently in charge of leadership development for one of America's most admired corporations and has led development efforts in several others; and Marshall Goldsmith is an international expert in designing customized feedback, training, and development systems that help organizations create future leaders.

In the concluding part of the book, "Executives on the Future of Leadership," "real-world" executives share their personal reflections and views on leadership for the future. The executives selected for this part include representatives from a cross-section of organizations.

Alex Mandl and Deepak Sethi (AT&T) are working to change a *huge* organizational culture that is making the transition from approaches that worked well yesterday to a process that will ensure success tomorrow; Alfred DeCrane, Jr., (Texaco) is leading a cultural change in an organization that has overcome old ways and incredible obstacles to achieve success and create value; William Steere (Pfizer) faces the challenge of leading one of America's most successful organizations into the future in a field, health care, where radical change is the only certainty; William Plamondon (Budget Rent a Car) is leading a cutting-edge cultural change in a midsized organization that is in the process of establishing a new identity; C. William Pollard (ServiceMaster) and Steven Bornstein (ESPN) are two visionary leaders who have helped grow major businesses out of ideas by being able to successfully read future trends. Anthony

Smith is a consultant who works not only with Steve Bornstein and ESPN but with McKinsey & Co. and several other trend-setting organizations. Sara Meléndez (INDEPENDENT SECTOR) and George Weber (International Red Cross/Red Crescent), two of the brightest executives in the social sector, are helping to meet social needs at a time when government is less and less able to help.

One challenge that we as editors give to you, our reader, is to be open to new ideas. Take the best from each article and apply what you have learned to your life. Weigh the views of the authors against your own ideas about the future. Question your assumptions and decide what changes you need to make to effectively lead in the future.

We have done our best to provide you with the latest thinking from many of the top minds in the field. Your challenge is to apply what you have learned to make a positive difference in the organizations and the people that you influence. Our goal is for you to become one of the effective leaders of the future and to serve as a role model for others.

The History of the Project

The Leader of the Future is truly a labor of love. The original idea was conceived by Marshall Goldsmith, a member of the Drucker Foundation board. After reviewing a list of leading consultants in the field of executive development, Marshall called Frances Hesselbein and said, "Wouldn't it be great if we called our friends and associates and asked each of them to write a short piece on the leader of the future?" Marshall and Frances found the concept appealing for several reasons:

1. The world is changing so rapidly that even ideas presented in the recent past seem dated.

2. Many thought leaders have written books but not concise articles representing their latest thinking.

3. Many leading thinkers are executives or consultants whose ideas are shared with major organizations but not the general public.

4. A book assembling original articles on this topic by so many thought leaders had never been written.

The project presented many challenges. The key thought leaders in the field of leadership are incredibly busy and incredibly successful. Why should they devote their valuable time to be "one of many" when each is a "star" in her or his own right? How could they be compensated for their services when the amount of compensation, for most, would be inconsequential compared to their earnings as consultants, authors, or executives?

As it turned out, almost every thought leader in the field has a positive quality that may be even more important than being extremely intelligent—he or she is extremely generous. The solution was simple: let the authors and editors *donate* their efforts (and the proceeds of this book) to a worthy cause. In this way, the state of the art in leadership thinking could be communicated to a wide range of readers, and many worthwhile human service organizations could simultaneously benefit from the effort.

Frances Hesselbein is currently the president of the Drucker Foundation, which is dedicated to providing the latest thinking in leadership, management, and innovation to leaders of organizations in the nonprofit social sector, the private sector, and the public sector. Frances, Peter Drucker, and the Drucker Foundation board of governors and board of advisers were already donating their time to help social sector organizations receive the best possible leadership and management educational opportunities and resources.

Frances enthusiastically agreed to be coeditor of the book and suggested that Dick Beckhard be the third coeditor. Dick is a member of the Drucker Foundation board of advisers, and he had served as coeditor of a widely acclaimed series of books on organization development. He suggested that the project be expanded beyond a *book* to become a *series of books* on important topics related to the future, such as the organization of the future and the community of the future. The series would be called the Drucker Foundation Future Series.

The three editors began to call their friends, and the results were amazing. Almost everyone who was asked to write an article *did* write an article. In fact, most of the authors expressed gratitude for being given the opportunity to participate. The few thought leaders who were unable to participate had very valid reasons for not getting involved and expressed a desire to participate in future books in the series.

The incredibly positive responses by Charles Handy and Rosabeth Moss Kanter were indicative of the group's reaction to the project. Charles said, "It would be a pleasure. When do you want it?" Rosabeth's comment was, "You can't publish this book without me!"

The first article to be completed was by Jim Heskett and Len Schlesinger of the Harvard Business School. The second article was submitted later that day by Bill Pollard, chairman of ServiceMaster. The quality of these two efforts gave us positive expectations that the articles would be superb.

Peter Senge spoke for many of the authors when he noted that only a small percentage of people who buy books on leadership actually *read* the books that they have purchased. He noted that many books in the field are simply too long for busy executives to read and digest. He liked the concept of presenting ideas in a concise format that people could read a little at a time and noted that this format might have a greater impact on large numbers of readers.

The challenges faced by Judy Bardwick were typical of those faced by most of the authors. How could she crowd this assignment into an already overbooked schedule of consulting, speaking, writing, and travel? She accomplished this feat by writing at night and on the weekends. Her dedication to volunteer service is representative of all those who have contributed chapters to *The Leader of the Future*.

Acknowledgments

To each author who has contributed to this project, the Drucker Foundation (and the voluntary social sector organizations it serves) can only say, *Thank you!* We appreciate the donation of time and effort that you have given to make your best ideas available to leaders in all three sectors and to help make our world a better place.

We would also like to thank the authors who submitted articles that were not included in this volume. Many of these articles will be valuable additions to future volumes in the series.

Saul Bass, of Bass Yager & Associates, America's premier designer of organizational logotypes, has earned special appreciation. He contributed the design for the Future Series logo. The letter "D" with an elliptical and dynamic sweep evokes the excitement and adventure we find in the future.

Rob Johnston, vice president of the Drucker Foundation, provided editorial and operational guidance on this project. He reviewed manuscripts, communicated with authors and editors, and shepherded the book to completion. Pat Rose, of Keilty Goldsmith, contacted contributors and potential contributors, provided traffic control for manuscripts, and was the West Coast contact for the editors. Alan Shrader and the team at Jossey-Bass deserve special mention. They have been incredibly patient in working around the schedules of busy authors. They have also been very helpful in editing and organizing input from many sources into one book.

Finally, we would like to thank you, our reader. All proceeds from this effort will be directed toward helping voluntary social sector organizations make a positive difference in communities around the world. By purchasing this book, you may be benefiting our world in two ways: (1) by becoming a more effective leader who can help your organization better meet the challenges of the future and (2) by helping voluntary organizations build a community and a better society for us all.

The Drucker Foundation Future Series: Where Do We Go from Here?

In editing *The Leader of the Future*, we have asked for, and received, some very valuable suggestions. Many of the ideas that we received are included in this book. Others will be reflected in future volumes. Al DeCrane, CEO of Texaco, was shown our original list of authors and challenged us by saying, "This is a great bunch of *thinkers*. Where are the *doers?*" His input led us to change the mix of authors and to add several practitioners and executives—including *him!* Deepak Sethi of AT&T said, "I have heard of all of these folks before; where are the new, young innovators who will be creating the ideas of tomorrow?" This statement led us to start on a new volume of the series, which will include articles by innovators. George Weber, calling from Geneva, noted that *The Leader of the Future* was too heavily weighted toward Americans. His input has caused us to ensure that future volumes will represent a stronger sample of thinkers from outside the United States.

Our goal for the Drucker Foundation Future Series will be to provide you, our reader, with the latest and best thinking in the world on the future of leadership, organization, change, and innovation. We will do our best to practice what we preach by continuing to innovate and improve with each volume. We also commit to continuing to use the proceeds from each volume to help voluntary organizations meet the ever-expanding challenge of human need.

October 1995

Frances Hesselbein
Easton, Pennsylvania

Marshall Goldsmith
Rancho Santa Fe, California

Richard Beckhard
New York, New York

A Personal Note

The Drucker Foundation owes Marshall Goldsmith, the key editor of this book, its deepest gratitude for more than five years of financial, intellectual, and emotional support. He has been a regular contributor to our conferences, and a moderator and session leader at them; he is a member of our Board of Governors; and he is the parent of *The Leader of the Future* and the Drucker Foundation Future Series.

I do not use the term *parent* lightly. Marshall originated the idea of *The Leader of the Future*, and in his enthusiastic, thorough, and effective manner, provided his ongoing effort to ensure that it succeeded. Throughout his work on this book, Marshall exemplified the best of today's and tomorrow's leaders. He had the vision of a project important to the Foundation's work and to leaders in all sectors.

He built a small team, and communicated his ideas to them. He and the team energetically approached their clients, associates, and friends to attract significant contributors. And he led through example and enthusiastic hard work.

Like a good parent, Marshall not only originated this book, but he nourished, nurtured, and guided it through its development. Through this and the forthcoming books in the Drucker Foundation Future Series, Marshall is providing the Foundation with remarkable opportunities. Each book furthers the mission of the Foundation by serving as a model of effective volunteerism, demonstrating the value of management and leadership examples from all three sectors and providing useful insight and instruction for leaders. In addition, the series generates income for the Foundation so that it may continue to develop educational opportunities and resources for the leaders of voluntary organizations.

Peter Drucker speaks of volunteerism as a means for knowledge workers to move from "success to significance." We are deeply grateful for Marshall Goldmith's extraordinary example and the significance of his accomplishments.

October 1995

Frances Hesselbein
President
The Drucker Foundation

The Leader
of the Future

Part I

Leading the Organization of the Future

1

CHARLES HANDY

The New Language of Organizing and Its Implications for Leaders

Charles Handy was for many years a professor at the London Business School. He is now an independent writer and educator, working with a wide variety of organizations in business, government, health, and education. His book The Age of Paradox *is a sequel to* The Age of Unreason, *which was named by both* Fortune *and* Business Week *as one of the ten best business books of 1994.*

I recently met with a German senior manager. "In Germany," he said, "our organizations are largely run by engineers. Such people think of the organization as a machine, something that can be designed, measured, and controlled—managed, in other words. It worked well for us in the past, when our organizations typically produced efficient machines of one sort or another. In the future, however, we can see that organizations will be very different, much more like networks than machines. Our brains tell us this," he went on, "but our hearts are still with the machines. Unless we can change the way we think and talk about organizations, we will stumble and fall."

What he said was true not just of German organizations, but of those in many other countries. Our models of organizations, and the way we talk of them, has hardly changed for a century. They were thought of as pieces of engineering, flawed pieces, maybe, but capable of perfectibility, of precision, of full efficiency. The very word *management*, with its origins in the running of the household or, some say, of army mule trains, implies control backed by power and authority, which is perhaps why it is a word that is much disliked by professional and volunteer groups that value autonomy highly.

The Language of Politics

The newly emerging language of organizations is very different. The talk today is of "adhocracy," of federalism, of alliances, teams, empowerment, and room for initiative. The key words are *options*, not *plans*; the *possible* rather than the *perfect*; *involvement* instead of *obedience*. This is the language of politics, not of engineering; of leadership, not of management. It is therefore interesting to observe how organizations are dropping the title of manager and replacing it with terms such as *team leader*, *project coordinator*, *lead partner*, *facilitator*, or *chair*. Soon we will see political theory take its rightful place as a core course in our business schools. It will be a recognition, at long last, that organizations are communities of individuals, not arrays of human resources.

Subsidiarity

When political theory does arrive in our schools, students will be faced with a range of concepts that are strange to the world of organizations they used to know. The first concept, and in some ways the most important, is *subsidiarity*. *Subsidiarity* is an old term in political theory, borrowed long ago by the Catholic church to make a moral point and resurrected recently in arguments over the balance of power in a federal Europe. The principle of subsidiarity holds that a higher-order body should not assume responsibilities that could and should be exercised by a lower-order body. The state, for instance, should not try to usurp the role of the family, because to do that is to demean the place of the family in society. More simply put, the principle means that stealing people's responsibilities is wrong because it ultimately deskills them. Yet under the old language of organizations, such stealing was quite normal and justified if the organization was to avoid mistakes.

In fact, organizations used to be designed to make sure that mistakes never happened. That turned out to be quite expensive in terms of controls, very inhibiting, and uncreative. No mistakes also meant no experiments. Under conditions of subsidiarity, control comes after the event. Individuals or groups have to be trusted to deliver until it is clear that they cannot do so. The task of the leader is to make sure that the individuals or groups are competent to exercise the responsibility that is given to them, understand the goals of the organization, and are committed to them.

Earned Authority

The second concept is that of *earned authority*. In machine organizations, power stems from one's position. In political organizations, power is granted by the people over whom it will be exercised. Political leaders are elected by their fellow citizens, except in dictatorships, where power derives from force. In the new organizations, titles and roles carry little weight until the leaders prove their competence. All authority has to be earned before it is exercised.

In practical organizational terms, this means that leaders must be given the time and the space to prove themselves. Leaders grow; they are not made. I like the Japanese idea of what I call the horizontal fast track. Asked whether there was not a fast track to responsibility for the best and the brightest in the midst of Japan's traditional "slow-burn" development, a Japanese manager replied that there was a fast track but it was, if anything, horizontal: "We move the better people around the organization as fast as we can in their early years, exposing them to different areas, different groups, and different responsibilities. That gives them a chance to discover themselves and to demonstrate their strengths."

As more and more organizations reengineer themselves into what are, in effect, collections of projects and task forces, more opportunities exist for leaders to emerge in the middle of the organization instead of just at the top. A career is now not so much a ladder of roles, but a growing reputation for making things happen. Influence, not authority, is what drives the political organization today in all organizations.

Virtuality

The third concept is *virtuality*. The new organizations are dispersed. Workers are employed in many different offices and locations, wear different hats, and do not necessarily owe all their loyalty to one organization. This has always been true in the political community; now it is also true of the work organization. No longer does everyone have to be in the same place at the same time to get the work done. They do not even need to be on the payroll. Today's organization is typically a 20/80 place, with only 20 percent of the people involved being employed full-time by the organization. The others are suppliers or contractors, part-timers, or self-employed professionals. More and more, the organization is a "box of contracts" rather than a home for life for all its people. A virtual organization is one that you do not necessarily see, certainly not all together in one place, but that nevertheless delivers the goods.

A Distributed Leadership

Virtuality means managing people you cannot see and cannot control in any detail. This kind of management by remote control can only work when trust goes in both directions. Trust, like authority, has to be earned, tested, and, if necessary, withdrawn. How many people can you know well enough and long enough to trust them and be trusted by them? Some say twenty, some fifty. Some note that throughout the ages, communities have settled into configurations of no more than 150 people. In response to the requirements of trust, organizations are beginning to regroup themselves into semi-permanent task forces in which the members know and understand each other well.

The leadership of these groups is not of the old-fashioned "follow me" type. You could call it a distributed leadership. I inadvertently got a glimpse of what this might look like when I facetiously compared an English team to a rowing crew on the river: "eight people going backward as fast as they can, without speaking to each other, steered by the one person who can't row." I thought it rather witty, but an oarsman in the audience corrected me: "How do you think," he said, "that we could go backward so fast, without communicating, if we were not completely confident in each other's competence, committed to the same goal, and determined to do our best to reach it? It's the perfect prescription for a team."

I had to agree that he was right. But then I asked, "Who is the leader of this team?" "Well," he said, "that depends. In the race, on the job, it is the little person at the back of the boat, the one who can't row, who is in charge. He, or often she, is the task leader. But there is also the stroke, who sets the pace and the standard we all must follow. Off the river, however, the leader is the captain of the boat. He or she is responsible for choosing the crew, for our discipline, and for the mood and motivation of the group, but on the river the captain is just another member of the crew. Finally, there is the coach, who is responsible for our training and development. There is no doubt who is the leader when the coach is around. We don't have any one leader," he concluded, "nor do we give anyone that title. The role shifts around, depending on the stage we are at."

So it is, increasingly, in all our organizations. The leadership in the middle of the organization is a distributed function, often going by other names. At the top of the organization, however, it has to be very different. Here the leadership has to be personalized, because the task at this level is to provide the soft glue that holds this virtual community together. The glue is made up of a sense of common identity, linked to a common purpose and fed by an infectious energy and urgency. Mere words cannot create this glue—it has to be lived. This infectious energy has to start with one individual or, very rarely, a tiny group at the center who live what they believe.

The words used by these top leaders are symptomatic: "I am a missionary," said one multinational CEO. "I endlessly circle the globe explaining to our people what we do and why we do it." "I am a teacher," said another. "My job is to inform and educate our key managers, so that they have the information and the perspective to do their job without instructions from above." "I have to live up to what I say we are," said another. "If I don't walk my talk I can't expect them to."

The Necessary Attributes

It is a tough task to run a community of individuals where authority has to be earned. Few people do it successfully, because it demands an unusual combination of attributes:

- A *belief in oneself* is the only thing that gives an individual the self-confidence to step into the unknown and to persuade others to go where no one has gone before, but this has to be combined with *a decent doubt,* the humility to accept that one can be wrong on occasion, that others also have ideas, that listening is as important as talking.

- A *passion for the job* provides the energy and focus that drive the organization and that act as an example to others, but this also has to be combined with its opposite, *an awareness of other worlds,* because focus can turn to blinkers, an inability to think beyond one's own box. Great leaders find time to read, to meet people beyond their own circle, to go to the theater or see films, to walk in other worlds.

- The leader must have *a love of people,* because in a community of individuals, those who find individuals a pain and a nuisance may be respected or feared, but they will not be willingly followed.

Yet this attribute, too, requires its opposite, *a capacity for aloneness*, because leaders have to be out front. It is not always possible to share one's worries with anyone else. Few will thank the leader when things go right, but many will blame the leader if things go wrong. Great leaders have to walk alone from time to time. They also have to live vicariously, deriving their satisfaction from the successes of others and giving those others the recognition that they themselves are often denied.

Living with these paradoxes requires great strength of character. It also requires a belief in what one is doing. Money alone will not be enough to provide the motive to live with these contradictions. Even a love of power is insufficient, because power irons out the contradictions rather than holding them in balance. Great leaders are bred from great causes, but leaders, at their best, also breed great causes. Sadly, for want of a cause, we too often create a crisis, which is not the same thing at all. Until and unless business creates a cause bigger and more embracing than enrichment of the shareholders, it will have few great leaders. We are more likely to find them in the nonprofit arena. If that is so, then that sector may yet become the training ground for business and perhaps even for politics.

2 WILLIAM BRIDGES

Leading the De-Jobbed Organization

*William Bridges is a speaker, author, and trainer
in the field of organization development. He is the
author of* JobShift: How to Prosper in a Workplace
Without Jobs, Transitions: Making Sense of Life's
Changes, Surviving Corporate Transition, *and*
Managing Transition. *He is also past president of
the Association for Humanistic Psychology. The*
Wall Street Journal *listed him as one of the top ten
independent executive development presenters in the
country.*

What people believe about leadership reflects the more general values and concerns of their time. Every generation rebels, not only against particular leaders but against the very style of leadership that they espoused. In our day, we are reacting to the "patriarchal" style of leadership that enabled people—not coincidentally *male* people—to lead the great military organizations of the Second World War and, thereafter, to run the great industrial organizations that came to dominate the Cold War period.

The military-style executive not only dominated that era, but was appropriate to it. It is clear that such a leader is not as appropriate today, though why that is so is not as obvious as one might imagine. Does it have to do with the "feminization" of the workplace as the percentage of working women has constantly and remarkably risen? Does it come, rather, from the rise to power of the generation whose outlook was influenced by the human potential movement, the antiwar movement, and the ethnic liberation movements of the 1960s and early 1970s? Or does it come, instead, from the populism that feeds consumer action lawsuits and a tendency to believe that whoever holds power in Washington—or at company headquarters—is likely to lie to us?

There was a time when leadership metaphors favored the physiological, with the leader as the head and the organization as the body. Today we read that such things cut across the grain of nature. Nature, that argument runs, is not hierarchical. Wisdom is distributed throughout the system: all the cells repel the invader, all the fish in the school swerve as one, all the geese in the V take turns at the point and then drop back to recuperate in the airstream of other wings. In fact, some people imply that until our day organizational dynamics were mechanistic and artificial and are only now coming back to the organic, integrated, holistic, and natural.

When an age changes its leadership metaphors, that is a major event. But it is a result, not a cause. The cause lies elsewhere, with (I blush to use such an old-fashioned phrase) "the means of production." For old (and, yes, patriarchal) Karl Marx was right, and we don't have to accept his political theory to recognize the power of his insight: that the manner in which a society gets its work done shapes most of the other things the society believes and does.

I want to suggest that three things characterize the way we are getting more and more of our work done today, and that together they shape the kind of leadership we require. The first is that we work in organizations, industries, and societies that change quickly and often. The second is that whatever business or profession we are in, most of us spend much more time manipulating information about things than manipulating the things themselves. And the third is that the production and support activities that used to be integrated within a single organization are now more and more frequently "unbundled" and parceled out among different organizations. Let's consider these things one at a time.

The Speed of Change

Everyone exclaims about the speed of change and we constantly repeat statistics about the percentage of the world's total knowledge that has been discovered since last Tuesday. All of that is true, but the relevant "changes" are those that force us to reconfigure the organization in order to profit from them or even to survive them. These changes are usually related to technological developments, and technology is central to them in three different ways:

1. It forces people to learn whole new ways of making things or of communicating with one another.
2. Those changes make possible, and even force other organizations to keep up with, rapid modifications in products and services.
3. Improved communication means that changes that once were visible only locally are now experienced everywhere at the same time.

The first two factors increase change absolutely, while the third increases it relative to particular people or organizations by exposing them to a much higher proportion of the changes that are going on at any particular time.

Change that is so frequent forces us to develop new organizational forms and practices. Every book on quality and customer service reminds us how important responsiveness and flexibility are, and most organizations are genuinely trying to increase these qualities. But we have not thought through the implications of what

Peter Drucker has recently noted, that "every organization has to build the management of change into its very structure" (*Harvard Business Review*, Sept.–Oct. 1992, p. 97). Too many organizations are trying to become flexible and responsive in behavioral terms without recognizing how much inflexibility and unresponsiveness is built into their structure and systems.

Take jobs. Jobs are not very flexible. Because of that, they are part of the problem, not part of the solution. As the vice president of operations at a large computer company said recently, "I just can't move the boxes around the organizational chart fast enough any-more to keep up with our new products and new strategies!" A Condé Nast executive made a similar point, in different words, when she said, "Employees who try to keep a tight hold on their job miss the point and fail to comprehend the reason why they were hired in the first place: to contribute to the molecular activity at the magazine."

Jobs make it hard for an organization to respond to change effec-tively. The market changes, but people keep doing their job instead of shifting their attention to whatever most needs to be done. Why wouldn't they? They were hired to do a job. They are evaluated and promoted on the basis of how they do their job. They are paid to do their job. The job of their supervisor is to see that they do their job.

In a rapidly changing environment, however, a company can go bankrupt while all its employees are doing their job perfectly. In fact, the modern organizational game is not played effectively by people who do their job, but in the spirit caught by one CEO thus: "I think of [our] company as a volleyball team. It takes three hits to get the ball over the net and it doesn't matter who hits it."

Knowledge-Based Work

The second factor that makes jobs dysfunctional today is that more and more work is knowledge-based rather than industrial. (Even the new industrial work is knowledge-based: the latest model of car has more built-in computing power than some of the first generation of satellites.) When work was primarily physical, it was easy to divide it up into separate jobs, each with its different job description. The jobs, in turn, were clustered into separate departments, each with its different mission.

But knowledge work is harder to divide that way. Instead of being made up of repetitive actions, it consists of a dialogue between the individual and the data. Job descriptions, the basis of the industrial organization, become so general as to call job categories and pay grades into question. That is one reason why knowledge work is so often done by cross-functional teams. On such teams, cross-training is common, which further erodes the outlines of the job.

Further, such teams are, by their very nature, inconstant in their shapes. Leadership passes back and forth from person to person as the phases of the project succeed one another and different skills become critical. The resources needed to complete the project also change, so that people come and go with each new need. And with every change in personnel, responsibilities subtly reconfigure themselves.

Unbundling the Organization

The final factor that is breaking down the familiar outlines of the job is the discovery by these protean organizations that it is uneconomical to employ all the workers they would need to do all the work that needs to be done. Instead, they hire people for no more time than necessary, drawing some from temporary agencies and others from informal pools of consultants and individual professionals.

Still other workers are "hired" in blocks, by outsourcing whole tasks, functions, or undertakings to firms that specialize in that type of work. The organization "unbundles" its activities, depending on its own full-time workers for only part of its needs. It outsources or uses subcontractors for the rest. In some cases, it simply turns work over to the customers themselves—as banks do through automatic teller machines, as IKEA Inc. does with the final assembly of its furniture, or as Toronto's Shouldice Hospital does with the prepping of patients for their hernia surgery.

Leaders for the De-Jobbed Organization

Now, the big question is: what does this kind of de-jobbed organization require from its leaders? What does it take to lead a constantly shifting group of people, some of whom work for your organization in a traditional sense and some of whom don't? What does it take to lead an organization that is not arranged like a human pyramid at the circus? What does it take to lead an organization where people forget their job and do, instead, the work that needs doing? The answer is that it takes a new kind of leadership—not because such leadership is transformational or because patriarchal leadership doesn't work. It requires new leadership because the de-jobbed organization poses new leadership challenges.

We say "leadership," but the leadership required by this kind of protean organization really takes three different forms:

1. The formal leadership that is responsible for integrating, resourcing, and orchestrating the activities of the various project clusters

2. The ad hoc leadership required within each of those project clusters

3. Leadership in every member of every project team that incorporates the initiative, the self-management capacity, the readiness to make hard decisions, the embodiment of organizational values, and the sense of business responsibility that in the traditional organization were limited to the top people in the organization

The leadership needed by the de-jobbed organization has nothing to do with telling people to do things or pointing to the top of the hill and yelling, "Charge!" Or, rather, it is not the "job" of any particular leader or class of leader to issue commands in that military sense. An organization full of such leaders is like a current where the flow pattern is produced by an inner dynamic rather than by an external force.

A traditional organization is hung upon a skeletal system of position-based leaders. De-jobbed organizations, on the other hand, are patterned like an energy field, and leaders function as energy nodes around which activity clusters. These ad hoc leaders tend to be self-selected far more often than they would be in a traditional organization. They emerge in the natural course of business. Like everything else, leadership is the thing that people do wherever and whenever it is needed.

Wherever they exist, the de-jobbed organization's leaders are responsible for generating and delivering the resources needed by the working units in the organization. Robert Greenleaf's powerful metaphor of the leader-as-servant fits the de-jobbed organization well. It is important to understand that there is nothing inherently "better" or "higher" about this kind of leadership. Too often, the literature on the subject takes a moralistic tone and leaves people with the impression that participation is next to godliness, when in fact it is simply a different tool for a different task. If you have an organization full of job holders and a hierarchical framework to keep them in place, the traditional patriarchal leader works fine. Or it does as long as the organization isn't exposed to a constantly and radically changing environment.

Because the leadership required by the de-jobbed organization is "softer" and more diffused than that needed by the traditional organization, it sometimes seems as though such an organization is leaderless. But it is not. The de-jobbed organization is going to require more leaders and leaders with more sophisticated skills, not the opposite. A major task of training and development in the years ahead is going to be to strengthen the skills of those leaders.

I suspect that, given the degree of de-jobbing going on in today's organizations, most of that training is going to come from individual and organizational contractors. So I'd guess that the only thing the de-jobbed organization is going to need as much as it needs a whole roster full of such leaders is people who know how to develop them out of the more traditional raw material that already works for the organization.

The unfortunate fact is that young, entrepreneurial organizations have attracted a large share of the people whose temperaments and personal values make them this kind of leader by nature. From here on out, it will be nurture that creates most of the leaders that de-jobbed organizations will need. If I were putting together a personal plan for the future, I'd build into it a good dose of that kind of leadership development. If I had leadership responsibility for a current organization, I'd be sure that as it moved away from jobs, it was also building this kind of leadership into its core competencies as fast as possible. If I were a trainer, I'd develop services and products related to it.

Perhaps the simplest way to talk about the leaders needed by the de-jobbed organization is to say that leadership itself is being de-jobbed. In the traditional organization, we say that everything that needs to be done is somebody's job. (If it isn't, we'll create a new job and hire somebody to fill it.) Like everything else, leadership was boxed into jobs that were clustered near the top of the pyramid. The task now is to forget jobs and move toward the work that needs doing. Leadership needs doing. What are you waiting for?

3 SALLY HELGESEN

Leading from the Grass Roots

Sally Helgesen is the author, most recently, of The
Web of Inclusion: A New Architecture for Building Great Organizations, *in which she explores how
innovative organizations make use of the talents and
ideas of all their people, learning lessons in transformation in the process. She is also the author of* The
Female Advantage: Women's Ways of Leadership.
*She speaks nationally on topics related to organiza-
tions and the future.*

A great, almost urgent, renewal of interest in the subject of leadership has characterized the last two decades. Scholarly and
popular books that identify strong leaders and attempt to analyze
the nature of their success have found a wide and hungry audience.
Universities have initiated courses, or even whole departments, to
study, teach, and encourage leadership. Organizations seeking to
adapt to a level and pace of change that can seem frightening and
that *is* unpredictable have funded countless forums and workshops
to instill leadership skills. Those of us contributing to this book
have played a role in that renaissance: we have observed a variety
of leaders at work, attempted to define and categorize exactly what

it is they do, and exhorted our audiences and readers to develop their own capacity for leading.

This renaissance has brought much of value, yet its limitations are becoming obvious, especially given the evolving shape of our organizations. For most studies of leadership in recent years have proceeded from the unspoken presumption that *leaders are leaders by virtue of their position*. And so if we want to study leadership at General Electric, we look to Jack Welch; if we want to understand the role of leadership in the turnaround at IBM, we scrutinize Louis Gerstner. Scholars lay the groundwork, and the popular media abets and reinforces this approach. *Fortune* and *Business Week* run articles on America's most admired executives and "their" companies, virtually equating the quality of an organization's leadership with its CEO.

The equation is understandable, but I would argue that it is also both demoralizing and increasingly obsolete. It is demoralizing because the relentless aggrandizement of those at the top leads organizations to fall prey to a heroes-and-drones syndrome, exalting the value of those in powerful positions while implicitly demeaning the contributions of those who fail to achieve top rank. This attitude, although officially denied in often pious and condescending terms ("Our people are our most important asset"), is nevertheless evident in a variety of slogans that have enjoyed great popularity during the last decade, such as "Lead, follow, or get out of the way" or, even less appealing, "Unless you're the lead horse, the view never changes." The fact is, of course, that most people never *will* become the "lead horse" in their organization: the number of jobs at the top is simply too limited. Thus the equation of leadership skills with position must by its nature breed frustration and cynicism among those in the ranks, denying them a feeling of ownership in the enterprise in which they are engaged and discouraging their full-hearted participation.

The equation of leadership with positional power also reveals assumptions about the nature and shape of our organizations that are fast becoming obsolete. Certainly, such a linkage fails to reflect the decentralized and organic structure of what Peter Drucker has called the knowledge organization, which is *the* dominant form in our emerging postcapitalist era. Drucker notes that "the knowledges" that today's organizations exist to make productive are by definition widely distributed. They are to be found not only among those at the top, the "lead horses," but also among those who constitute what in the industrial era we called the rank and file. Indeed, people in the ranks are no longer interchangeable ciphers performing simple repetitive tasks; in the knowledge organization, they are all knowledge workers. Each possesses specific sets of skills and varieties of expertise, all of which are subject to continual upgrading.

In addition, those in the ranks have at their command powerful technologies that give them access to a depth and range of information that was formerly restricted to those at the top, as well as the means to apply that information directly in their work. Technology is the key here, for by quickly disseminating all kinds of specialized information throughout the organization, today's sophisticated networks erase old industrial-era distinctions between those who make decisions and those who carry them out, between those who conceive of tasks and those who execute them. In so doing, networked technology takes power from the *head* of an organization and distributes it among those who comprise the *hands*. Power is thus vested at every level in today's organizations; this is what makes them flexible and lean.

The shift in the distribution of power is clearly manifested in the growing emphasis on the role of teams. A team is not simply a task force, for task-force members are appointed by their superiors, who define their mission and set the criteria for judging its fulfillment. A true team, by contrast, both defines its objectives and finds ways to meet them, integrating the conception of tasks with their execution. Since teams in the knowledge organization set their own goals, they are also free to use any new information that comes their way to refine their methods and objectives as they do their work. Autonomous teams thus enable people at the grass roots to organize themselves in ways that permit real-time use of information technology.

The importance of those in the ranks is enhanced because they stand at the point of intersection between an organization and its customers and clients. So an organization cannot be truly responsive to the needs of those it is configured to serve unless its front-line people are given autonomy and support. This is the true reason that the top-down, hierarchical style of leadership is widely perceived as doomed to failure, even by those who aren't sure precisely why this should be so. Top-down leaders, by withholding power from those in the ranks, deprive them of the ability to use the expertise and information vested in them to respond directly and with speed to customer concerns.

Knowledge organizations exist and flourish *now*, not in some distant future. They mirror the shape of the technology that determines how we do our work. Yet despite this, most of us persist in regarding leadership as synonymous with—indeed solely derived from—high position. Perhaps the notion of grass-roots leadership strikes us as too much of an oxymoron; confronted with apparent paradox, our imaginations fail. Or perhaps grass-roots leaders are just too difficult to identify. After all, if leaders are to be found in the ranks, those of us who seek to study them can no longer simply look at titles on a chart in order to find our subjects. Whatever the reason, our continued habit of linking leadership with position signals our inability to grasp how organizations are changing.

I believe that in the future, our ideas about the nature of leadership will undergo a radical transformation. As the instrumental use of knowledge continues to redefine the nature and purpose of organizations, we will begin to look to those on the front lines for leadership. This has already begun to happen in the political arena, where citizens are finding ways to use power more directly. And as grass-roots leadership becomes more common, we will begin to recognize as well led the organizations that are most adept at nourishing leadership independent of official rank or status.

What will this kind of leadership look like? And what will characterize the organizations that permit it to flourish? I got some insight on this during a conversation with someone who exemplifies nonpositional leadership: Ted Jenkins, a senior engineer at the Intel Corporation. Although Jenkins prides himself on having been the sixth person hired by that company, he does not sit on its executive committee, nor would his title seem to qualify him as the subject of a study of Intel's leadership. Nevertheless, he is the kind of leader who I believe will come to play an increasingly important role in the years ahead. He has a deep knowledge of his company, his thinking about it has a philosophical cast, and he influences those around him to work in more powerful and innovative ways. Because he has had direct working experience with so many people in the company over the years, he knows their abilities, and he uses this knowledge to direct resources where they are needed. He is a facilitator of power who helps to determine how work actually gets done.

Jenkins is firmly convinced that one of his company's strengths lies in its willingness to recognize and value nonpositional power. He notes that in many organizations, people who assume leadership roles that are not commensurate with their rank are regarded as infringing upon turf that by rights belongs to others. In such organizations, resources can flow only to those in a position to commandeer them. As Jenkins observes, "The typical result is that a few powerful people have more resources than they actually need, while everybody else has to make do with less. It's static, irrational, and inefficient."

Position is a crude way of measuring power; it fails to reflect the subtleties of actual alignment. In order for an organization to operate with flexibility, power must derive from more than rank. Jenkins describes three possibilities: the power of expertise, of specialized knowledge or skills; the power of personal relationships and connections; and the power of that great intangible, personal authority or charisma. An organization that permits people to manifest and develop these kinds of power without regard to their official status will have a head start in nurturing leadership within the ranks.

We are presently engaged in what Margaret Wheatley, in *Leadership and the New Science* (1992, p. 17), describes as "nothing less than the search for new sources of order in our world." Such an order must accurately reflect our understanding of how the universe works. In recent years, our understanding has come to encompass a vision of life as one great interconnected web—a vision that has erased old hierarchical presumptions. As we come to recognize the dynamic connectedness of the various parts within a whole, top-down structures begin to seem less a reflection of any natural order and more a way of arranging our human world to reflect outmoded perceptions. The emphasis upon top-down power thus continues to be eroded; networked technology reflects and hastens the trend. As organizations adapt to new understandings, leadership will begin to flourish in places and ways we can hardly imagine.

4 GIFFORD PINCHOT

Creating Organizations with Many Leaders

Gifford Pinchot is an author, speaker, and consultant on innovation management. His best-selling book Intrapreneuring: Why You Don't Have to Leave the Corporation to Become an Entrepreneur *defined the ground rules for an emerging field of enterprise: the courageous pursuit of new ideas in established organizations.* His second book, with coauthor Elizabeth Pinchot, The End of Bureaucracy and the Rise of the Intelligent Organization, *broadens the vision to include a revolutionary way of organizing all work from the most innovative to the most mundane.*

The very highest leader is barely known by men.
Then comes the leader they know and love.
Then the leader they fear.
Then the leader they despise.
The leader who does not trust enough will not be trusted.
When actions are performed without unnecessary speech
The people say, "We did it ourselves."

Lao Tsu

L eaders move people from selfish concerns to serving the common good. This requires vision and the ability to guide people
toward it. Leaders can refocus people's energy with direct interventions or do so indirectly by adjusting the system so that people naturally gravitate toward what needs to be done.

The most direct methods of leadership include commands, decisions about resources and promotions, and personal guidance of
individuals and teams. As organizations become larger and more
complex, direct interventions by senior leaders can carry less of the
load. Less direct leadership focuses on communicating an inspiring
vision and inspiring values, on listening to and caring for followers,
on leading by personal example. The most indirect and potentially
invisible forms of leadership focus on creating conditions of freedom that, like the "invisible hand" of Adam Smith, automatically
guide people toward serving the common good.

When indirect leadership is at its best, the people say, "We did
it ourselves." The more indirect the method of leadership, the more
room there is for other leaders within the organization.

Three Approaches to Empowering Many Leaders

Different models of the organization lead to different approaches to
empowering people and bringing forth many leaders. Let us consider three systems of increasing opportunities for leadership: dele-
gating within a traditional hierarchy, creating a community with
common purpose and shared values, and establishing a free-market
system.

Delegating Within a Traditional Hierarchy

In a hierarchy, delegation is the primary tool for creating opportunity for more leaders. The subordinate leaders accept the scope of
their command and use leadership to accomplish the tasks given to
them. If delegation is the norm, each leader can create subordinate
leaders.

Given the rules of bureaucracy, subordinate leaders have limited scope for big-picture or cross-functional thinking. As a result, the people at the top have too much to do, and everyone else is "waiting for orders." Delegation is a good first step in creating space for leadership to emerge, but it does not fully meet the needs of information-age organizations.

Creating Community

Many great corporate leaders such as Max DePree of Herman Miller and Ben Cohen of Ben and Jerry's see their organizations as communities. They create space for more leaders with inspiring goals and trust that employees guided by community spirit will generally use their freedom to do good rather than harm. Under Frances Hesselbein, the Girl Scouts of the United States searched for and found a succinct mission: "To help each girl reach her own highest potential." Seeing the need to include minorities in this goal, the leaders set the target of tripling minority participation. But how could they impose this goal on the many local volunteer leaders over whom they had no control? They succeeded by creating a community in which local leaders chose to strive for this worthwhile goal.

If people feel part of the corporate community, if they feel safe and cared for, if they are passionate about the mission and values and believe that others are living by them, they will generally give good service to the whole. And if they are dedicated members of the community, it will be safer to trust them to create their own leadership roles across the organizational boundaries. As community members, they will worry less about defending their turf, trusting that if they take care of the organization, it will take care of them.

Effective leaders today use the tools of community building to create an environment in which many leaders can emerge. They contribute inspiring descriptions of a shared vision to align everyone's energies. They care for and protect their employees. They listen and do their best to accept the contributions and divergent ideas of employees as honest attempts to help. They give thanks for the gifts of ideas, courage, and self-appointed leadership that employees bring to the community. They discourage backbiting and politics. They do their best to treat each member of the organization as a spiritual equal worthy of respect. They share information so that everyone can see how the whole organization works and how it is doing. They publicly celebrate the community's successes. In tragedy they mourn its losses. I have watched Jack Ward Thomas, chief of the U.S. Forest Service, cry in public over the loss of fire fighters.

Community is a phenomenon that occurs most easily when free people with some sense of equal worth join together voluntarily for a common enterprise. Great leaders create a sense of freedom, voluntariness, and common worth. They do this most easily in smaller organizations that allow a lot of face-to-face contact. As organizations become larger, more complex, and more widely distributed geographically, it becomes harder to create enough common vision and enough community spirit to guide actions without increasing reliance on the chain of command. When people are separated by distance, vast differences in power and wealth, and conflict over resources and promotions, political struggle often replaces community.

The larger the role of the chain of command in the system, the more the equality and freedom necessary for community become undone. This produces a nasty feedback loop. As the power of community spirit is stretched thin, the chain of command fills the void and the sense of community declines further.

Liberating the Spirit of Enterprise

With machines increasingly taking over routine work and the percentage of knowledge workers growing, more leaders are needed in the organization. The work left for humans involves innovating, seeing things in new ways, and responding to customers by changing the way things are done. We are reaching a time when all employees will have to take turns leading, when they see that they must influence others in order to realize their vision. To create room for everyone to lead when their special knowledge provides the key to the right action, we must move beyond traditional concepts of hierarchy. Becoming lean and mean is not enough. In the times to come, leaders must find ways to replace hierarchy with indirect methods of leadership that allow greater freedom, lead to more accurate allocation of resources, and provide a stronger force for focusing on the common good. Where do we find the models for this new form of leadership?

The organizations that first hit the wall of complexity and thus first had to invent the institutions to distribute leadership and power were the largest organizations we know of—whole societies and whole nations. For this reason, the leaders of corporations, nonprofit organizations, and even government agencies have much to learn from the methods of leadership and control used by successful nations.

Centuries ago, many nations reached the limits of direct leadership. Even with the help of a brilliant set of ministers, the diversity of enterprises within a great nation was simply too great for any king or dictator to run effectively. Every Western European nation has long since given the free market a major role in its economy. The nations in the Warsaw Pact, which until recently persisted in running their economies with centrally controlled ministries, fell far behind in both wealth and human happiness. By freeing their nation's entrepreneurial spirit from the monopolistic power of the Communist party, China's leaders have achieved double-digit economic growth. After introducing freer markets, South Korea, Chile, Singapore, Peru, and Taiwan have all achieved astounding economic growth. Can the same level of explosive growth in productivity and innovation become available to leaders of corporations and nonprofit organizations who create institutions that liberate the entrepreneurial energies of their people?

In national economies, the free market seems to be an indispensable institution for creating productivity and prosperity.

According to Adam Smith, the free market acts with an "invisible hand" to guide entrepreneurs who are pursuing their own selfish aims into serving the needs of their customers and thus the common good. To the degree that this is true, this automatic action of the market parallels the job of leaders and thus makes it easier. When national leaders establish an effective market system, many entrepreneurial leaders arise to help them satisfy people's needs. The job of effective national leadership goes from impossible to merely very difficult.

Market institutions provide feedback and control that is more accurate, detailed, and locally appropriate than any leader could hope to provide directly. By using institutions that create a self-organizing system, the leader *indirectly* motivates and inspires followers to find the most efficient and effective ways to serve the larger community or group.

Internal Markets

Early in the era of AIDS, the New York Blood Bank asked DuPont's medical products department for help in tracking the history of every pint of blood it distributed. They needed a massive data base to be developed in ninety days. Normally, the medical products department supplied the blood bank with blood analyzers, not computer software. But the blood bank was a good customer and desperate to prevent needless HIV infections. So the Medical Products people sought help from their departmental and corporate information technology staffs. Neither could deliver within the ninety-day window.

According to the rules of bureaucracy, the Medical Products account executive had done all he could for his customer. But he had heard of a very special, small information technology group within DuPont's huge fibers business. The fibers department made fibers for textiles, carpets, and industrial uses like tire cords. Within it, Information Engineering Associates (IEA) had recently been formed to exploit computer-aided software engineering (CASE) tools, a new technology for writing software faster. They had previously solved a problem very similar to that of the New York Blood Bank by building a data base to track the history and quality of every bobbin of Kevlar fiber as it moved through their Richmond, Virginia, plant.

Again, according to the rules of bureaucracy, a staff group from one division is not supposed to do major jobs for other divisions. But this was an emergency, so IEA got the job. They delivered the blood-tracking data base within the ninety-day deadline and Medical Products delivered a service that far exceeded a major customer's expectations. Breaking the rules of bureaucracy saved lives! As shown in Figure 4.1, users in Medical Products got better service because they had more choices of internal vendors. As IEA's reputation spread throughout DuPont, they found themselves creating a ground-water data base to track radiation in the ground water in the test wells around DuPont's nuclear materials production site at Savannah River in South Carolina. When they again succeeded in ninety days, groups all over DuPont wanted their services.

Figure 4.1. IEA as a Third Choice for Information Technology.

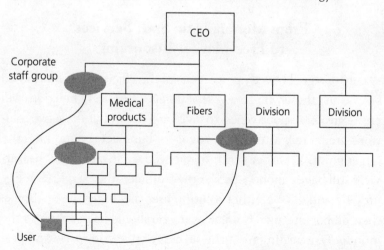

Soon IEA's success began to be a problem. The fibers department paid their salaries while other departments used their services, and the management of Fibers began to complain. A creative leader in the corporate finance department saw the chance for indirect leadership and created a system that made it easy for others to pay for the service they received. As he put it, "Corporate tradition won't let a staff group like you be a profit center, but I have arranged for you to be a 'negative cost center.'" IEA went from being a staff group supposedly serving only Fibers to being an *intraprise* (short for intracorporate enterprise), with clients throughout DuPont. As a result of one leader changing the rules, businesses all over DuPont began getting better information technology service.

While other information technology groups in DuPont were downsizing, IEA grew to 120 employees. The new technology spread rapidly across organizational boundaries. Lives were saved and the customers were amazed. Serious safety problems were brought under control. This was a result of leadership—the direct intrapreneurial leadership of the IEA team and the indirect leadership of the finance department, which created the conditions in which IEA could bring their talents wherever they were most valuable and be paid for doing so.

From Monopolistic Staff Services to Free-Market Insourcing

A debate rages between proponents of the efficiency of centralized service and those who believe that decentralization of functions will create greater responsiveness to divisional needs. But these two solutions are merely alternative flavors of bureaucracy and miss the larger point. Whether centralized or lodged in the divisions, services still have a monopoly over the customers they serve. (See Figures 4.2 and 4.3.) Neither solution uses the discipline of choice; their proponents merely argue over who should be in charge of the monopoly. Learning from the success of free enterprise and pioneering examples like IEA, information-age leaders will change the

Figure 4.2. Centralized Staff Service.

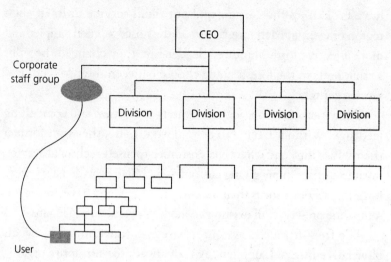

Figure 4.3. Decentralized Staff Service.

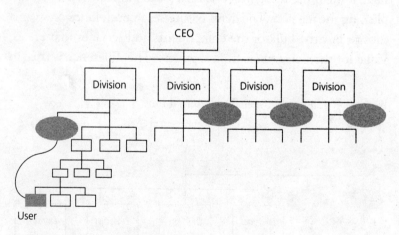

terms of the debate from centralization versus decentralization to monopoly versus user choice.

Consider the U.S. Forest Service's technical service function, which was available from two technical service centers, each with a monopoly in its own territory. Customers in the 127 national forests were complaining about the service. Senior leaders could have intervened directly by defining acceptable service standards or changing the leaders of the technical service centers. They could have broken up the centers and put small service units in each region or even in each forest. Instead they used a much simpler and more effective form of indirect leadership: they changed the rules so that users in the forests could choose between the two technical service centers.

Once users had a choice, the centers got honest and compelling feedback. Without having to be told what to do, they transformed themselves into cost-effective, customer-focused technical service organizations. Simply giving customers a choice provided a stronger force for customer focus than decentralization would have and at the same time preserved all existing economies of scale. (See Figure 4.4.)

The free-intraprise system is based on free choices between alternative internal suppliers. An advanced free-intraprise organization has a structure much like that of a virtual organization. Both have a small hierarchy responsible to the top leaders for accomplishing the mission. The main businesses in both kinds of organizations buy the bulk of the components and services that create value for their customers from suppliers. The difference is this: in

Figure 4.4. Choice Between Two Internal Providers.

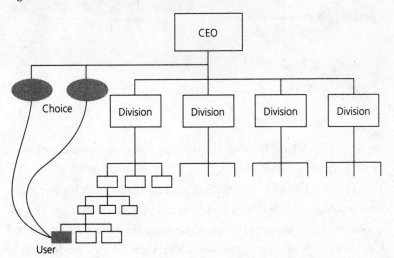

a virtual organization those suppliers are outside firms, and in a free-intraprise organization many are internal intraprises, controlled by the free internal market but still part of the firm.

James Brian Quinn points out that what almost everyone does at work is to provide a service. Whether the service is market research, maintenance, engineering design, or clerical work, it can be defined and bought and sold. Quinn suggests that this points to the value of outsourcing these services. The biggest advantage of outsourcing is that resources are dealt with through a market, using choice rather than the monopolistic structures of a chain of command. This same advantage can be obtained without firing employees or giving key skills and competencies to outside firms that also serve competitors.

In the organizations of the future, most employees will work in intraprises that provide services to the core businesses. The core businesses will be run by small groups of line managers who will buy much of the value they add from internal intraprises. Figure 4.5 shows the virtual organization. The rectangular line organizations buy from the enterprises represented by ovals, all of which are outside the boundary of the organization. In the free-intraprise

Figure 4.5. The Virtual Organization.

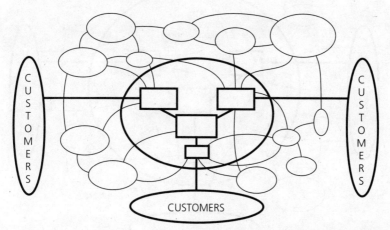

organization (Figure 4.6), the rectangular line organizations buy both from intraprises inside the firm (dark ovals) and from outside firms (white ovals).

Free intraprise provides the core discipline for the horizontally networked organizational form we are all seeking to build. It allows senior leaders to project strategic intent through a small hierarchy without creating much bureaucracy and to indirectly shape the direction of the intrapreneurial leaders, whose teams are hired by line managers reporting to them. Free intraprise creates opportunities for large numbers of intrapreneurial leaders in the network supporting the line managers.

If you had the task of trying to enliven a command economy like that of an old Communist nation, you would get nowhere by telling local party leaders to take more risks or by training the managers in the central ministries to be more empowering. To crack that bureaucracy, the leaders of those nations had to allow entrepreneurs to compete with the state-owned monopolies. Similarly, to cure corporate bureaucracy, training managers in empowerment is not sufficient. Let intrapreneurial teams offer services that compete with

Figure 4.6. The Intelligent Network Organization.

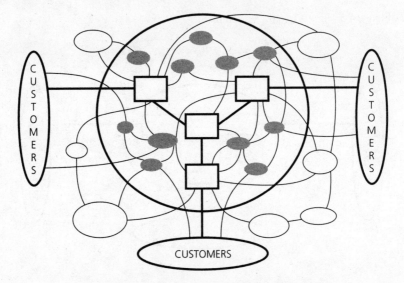

the functional and staff monopolies. Free choice between different providers will sort out what works to serve the mission and values of the organization.

Leaders can use free-market choice inside the organization to achieve many of the benefits nations received when they liberated the entrepreneurial spirit of their people by creating free-market institutions. They can develop a self-organizing network that spreads learning and capabilities across organizational divides without the need for detailed senior leadership intervention or even direct inspiration. They can create a feedback system that sorts out the most effective internal services without having to evaluate and decide themselves.

To establish a free-intraprise system, leaders will:

- Allow choice between several internal suppliers of services and components

- Establish the right of employees and teams to form intraprises

- Protect intraprises against the efforts of former bureaucrats to reestablish their monopolies by political means

- Establish accounting systems that support free intraprise

As organizations move toward indirect leadership, the key role of senior leaders is to increase their people's choices in ways that still focus the organization on its mission. Internal markets provide a way to be sure that everyone's contributions to that mission are cost-effective without relying on the accuracy of appraisals from above. Many leaders find it difficult to turn from direct intervention in the businesses of the corporation to creating conditions that empower others to address those issues. Indirect leadership takes a little getting used to. But what greater legacy is there than the liberation of an organization to a higher level of productivity, innovation, and service.

Creating space for more leaders follows three stages, each characterized by a different view of the organization:

- Phase I: Organization as *hierarchy*, where the key tool is delegation

- Phase II: Organization as *community*, where the key tools are worthwhile vision and values, a gift economy

- Phase III: Organization as *economy*, where the key tools are free intraprise, education, and effective leadership of core businesses

The organizations of the future will be communities of intrapreneurs. They will be structured from many smaller interacting enterprises, more like the market structure of a free nation than that of a totalitarian system. Each of these enterprises will require leadership. The new organizations will be pluralistic to the core, preferring conflict between competing points of view and the struggle of competing suppliers to the illusory security of bureaucratic command and internal monopolies of function. The power to make fundamental work decisions—such as what to do and with whom to do it—will continue to be divested by the hierarchy and gradually distributed to smaller, self-managing groups who make those decisions together.

There is so much emphasis today on the leader's role in creating vision and values that the leader's role in creating *systems* that support and guide liberty is often ignored. Once we have gotten good at defining and communicating vision and values, liberation of many potential leaders is the next critical step in creating an organization with many leaders.

As the complexity of any organization reaches beyond the grasp of direct leadership, the leader's central role becomes that of contributing to the corporate culture and corporate institutions that make freedom work and that create a freer society within the organization. This freer society will be based on values with which we are all quite familiar, values such as respect for all people and their opinions; freedom of choice, speech, and assembly; fairness; and justice. The role of senior leadership will then be akin to the role of the best kind of government of a free nation. By listening to their followers, these leaders will not be primarily players, or even coaches, but designers of the game who bring out the best in others. And when they do their job of indirect leadership well, the people will say, "We did it ourselves."

5

PETER M. SENGE

Leading Learning Organizations

The Bold, the Powerful, and the Invisible

*Peter M. Senge is a faculty member at the Massachu-
setts Institute of Technology and director of the Center
for Organizational Learning at MIT's Sloan School of
Management, a consortium of corporations, including
Ford Motor Company, Federal Express, Motorola,
AT&T, GS Technologies, Intel, Electronic Data
Systems, Harley-Davidson, and Shell Oil, that work
together to advance methods and knowledge for building
learning organizations. He is the author of the widely
acclaimed book* The Fifth Discipline: The Art and
Practice of the Learning Organization *and coauthor
of* The Fifth Discipline Fieldbook: Strategies and
Tools for Building a Learning Organization.

"No significant change will occur unless it is driven from the top." "There's no point in starting unless the CEO is on board." "Nothing will happen without top-management buy-in."

Note: This article is a shortened version of P. Senge, *Leading Learning Organizations* (MIT Center for Organizational Learning Research Monograph), (Cambridge, Mass.: MIT Center for Organizational Learning, 1995). Copyright © 1995 by Peter M. Senge.

How many times have we all heard these familiar refrains and simply accepted them as "the way things are"? Yet there are good reasons to challenge these hoary truisms. The evidence of top-management impotence is abundant. Everywhere one hears CEOs and other top executives talking about the need to "transform" their organizations, to overthrow stodgy bureaucratic cultures, to "become learning organizations." Nevertheless, the evidence for successful corporate transformations is meager. Moreover, the basic assumption that only top management can cause significant change is deeply disempowering. Why, then, in the "age of empowerment," do we accept it so unquestioningly? Isn't it odd that we should seek to bring about less hierarchical and authoritarian organizational cultures through recourse to hierarchical authority?

Two Views on Leadership

Why do we cling to the view that only the top can initiate significant change? Is it just our unwillingness to give up a familiar mental model? Is it the fear of stepping out of line without the imprimatur of the hierarchy? Perhaps, also, there is an element of self-protection—the comfort of being able to hold someone else, namely, top management, responsible for the lack of effective leadership. There is no doubt that a CEO opposed to fundamental change can make life difficult for internal innovators, but this hardly proves that only the CEO can bring about significant change. At the very least, shouldn't we be suspicious of the knee-jerk tendency of people in organizations to "look upward" and expect top management to fix things?

Consider a different view: "Little significant change can occur if it is driven from the top." "CEO proclamations and programs rolled out from corporate headquarters are a good way to undermine deeper changes." "Top-management 'buy-in' is a poor substitute for genuine commitment at many levels in an organization, and in fact, if management authority is used unwisely, it can make such commitment less rather than more likely."

"When I first came in as CEO," says Phil Carroll of Shell Oil, "everyone thought, 'Phil will tell us what he wants us to do.' But I didn't have a clue, and if I had, it would have been a disaster." "Anyone who thinks the CEO can drive this kind of change is wrong," says Harley-Davidson CEO Rich Teerlink. There are several reasons leaders like Carroll and Teerlink come to a more humble view of the power of top management. One is the cynicism that exists in most of our organizations following years of management fads. When the CEO preaches about "becoming a learning organization," people roll back their eyes and think to themselves, "Here we go again. I wonder what seminar he went to last weekend." Most corporations have had so many "flavor-of-the-month" initiatives from management that people immediately discount any new pronouncement as more "executive cheerleading" or, as they say at Harley-Davidson, "another fine program."

A second reason is the difference between compliance and commitment. When genuine commitment is needed, hierarchical authority becomes problematic. "It seemed that every year, someone pressured us to change our promotion review process to incorporate our values," reflects former Hanover Insurance CEO Bill O'Brien. "But we never caved in to this pressure. A value is only a value if it is voluntarily chosen. No reward system has ever been invented that the people in an organization haven't learned how to 'game.' We didn't just want new behaviors. We wanted new behaviors for the right reasons—because people genuinely believed that 'openness,' 'localness,' 'merit,' and our other guiding values would really lead to a healthier and more productive work environment" ("Moral Formation for Managers: Closing the Gap Between Intention and Practice," in *Character and the Corporation*, MIT Center for Organizational Learning Research Monograph, 1994.) Hierarchical authority, as it has been used traditionally in Western management, tends to evoke compliance, not foster commitment. The more strongly hierarchical power is wielded, the more compliance results. Yet there is no substitute for commitment in bringing about deep change. No one can force another person to learn if the learning involves deep changes in beliefs and attitudes and fundamental new ways of thinking and acting.

A third reason is that top-management initiatives often backfire and end up moving organizations backward, not forward. This can occur in obvious ways; for example, top-management downsizings and reorganizations that have the side effect of increasing fear, distrust, and internal competitiveness reduce cooperation and collaboration, thereby further undermining economic performance. But it can also occur more subtly, even in changes explicitly designed to improve learning. For example, the "360-degree feedback" process with which all managers must comply not only reinforces a compliance mentality; it also lessens the likelihood of people surfacing what Harvard's Chris Argyris, in "Good Communication That Blocks Real Learning" (*Harvard Business Review*, July/Aug. 1994), calls the "potentially embarrassing information" that might "produce real change." This kind of information will only come into the open when people have genuine trust, curiosity, and shared responsibility, conditions not usually fostered by mandated programs. "Corporate communication programs" rolled out from the top can "actually inhibit learning and communication," according to Argyris. Organizational surveys and focus groups, for example, by focusing attention on "telling" top management what is wrong, can block learning because they do nothing to encourage individual accountability and tend to reinforce the mindset that only top management has the power to fix problems.

The merit of these two alternative views regarding top management and change depends entirely on the nature of the change one is trying to bring about. By and large, reorganizations, downsizing, corporatewide cost reduction programs, or reengineering programs can only be implemented from top-management levels. But such changes do not change corporate cultures based on fear and defensiveness. They will not unleash the imagination and passions of people and enhance their ability to form genuinely shared visions. They do not change the quality of thinking in the organization and the ability of people to understand interdependency. They do not increase intelligence at the front lines as people confront increasingly complex and dynamic business environments. And they will do nothing to foster the trust and skills needed by teams at all levels if they are to reflect on hidden assumptions and to inquire into the flaws in reasoning lying behind their own actions.

For almost twenty years, I, and many colleagues, have been working with managers and teams in developing enhanced learning capabilities: systems thinking, improving mental models, fostering dialogue, nurturing personal vision, and building shared visions. For the last four years, a group of us at MIT have begun to develop a consortium of corporations to advance the theory and method underlying this work and to demonstrate what is possible when organizations "get serious" and when people work together over years to integrate new learning capabilities into important work settings. This consortium, the MIT Center for Organizational Learning, now involves about twenty corporations, mostly Fortune 100 firms.

Within the Learning Center companies, we regularly confront the dilemmas posed by the conflicting views described above. The more we appreciate the inherent limitations of executive leadership in bringing about deep change, the more frustrated we are likely to feel, given the immense need for change. While top management can move some changes quickly, it can also slow down or undermine other types of change. While people often want the support of top management, they also don't want it telling them what to do. Resolving these dilemmas requires fundamental shifts in our traditional thinking about leadership. In brief, we are coming to believe that leaders are those people who "walk ahead," people who are genuinely committed to deep change in themselves and in their organizations. They lead through developing new skills, capabilities, and understandings. And they come from many places within an organization.

In particular, we have come to think of three essential types of leaders in building learning organizations, roughly corresponding to three different organizational positions:

1. *Local line leaders*, who can undertake meaningful organizational experiments to test whether new learning capabilities lead to improved business results

2. *Executive leaders*, who provide support for line leaders, develop learning infrastructures, and lead by example in the gradual process of evolving the norms and behaviors of a learning culture

3. *Internal networkers, or community builders*, the "seed carriers" of the new culture, who can move freely about the organization to find those who are predisposed to bringing about change, help out in organizational experiments, and aid in the diffusion of new learnings

My purpose here is to briefly sketch what we are learning about these three types of leaders. Previously (in a 1990 *Sloan Management Review* article), I proposed thinking about "the leader's new work" in building learning organizations in terms of three generic roles played by leaders at all levels, those of *designer, teacher,* and *steward;* the skills and capabilities required for these roles; and the tools and methods that can help in developing these skills and capabilities. Here, I want to begin to explore how these generic roles are distributed among real people who lead from different organizational positions.

Local Line Leaders

Nothing can start without committed local line leaders. Local line leaders are individuals with significant business responsibility and "bottom-line" focus. They head organizational units that are large enough to be meaningful microcosms of the larger organization, and yet they have enough autonomy to be able to undertake meaningful change independent of the larger organization. In effect, they create organizational subcultures that may differ significantly from the mainstream organizational culture. To be useful in creating experimental laboratories, they must also confront issues and business challenges that are seen as both important and recurring within the larger organization. For example, a unique cross-functional task force may be important but less useful for a learning experiment than a team that manages a process that is ongoing, generic, and vital for future competitiveness, such as a product development team, a sales team, or a business division.

The key role played by local line leaders is to sanction significant practical experiments and to lead through their active participation in those experiments. Without serious practical experiments aimed at connecting new learning capabilities to business results, there is no way to assess whether enhancing learning capabilities is just an intellectually appealing idea or really makes a difference. Participating in serious experiments requires a significant commitment of time and energy. Typically, a Learning Center project will begin with a core team composed of line leaders who might work together for six to twelve months developing their own understanding and skills in systems thinking, collaborative inquiry into underlying mental models, and building a shared vision, and applying those skills to their own issues. Only then will they be able to begin to *design* learning processes that might spread such skills throughout their organization and eventually become embedded in how work is done.

For example, a team of sales managers and sales representatives at Federal Express worked together for over a year before they began to develop what eventually became the Global Customer Learning Laboratory. "We felt that we needed new tools for working with our key corporate customers as learning partners," says Cathy Stopcynski of Federal Express. "That's why the Global Customer Learning Laboratory is important. It gives us a whole new way to work together with customers to improve our collective thinking and come up with completely new solutions to complex logistics problems." At Electronic Data Systems (EDS), a growing network of local line leaders is bringing learning organization principles and methods into work with customers, through the EDS Leading Learning Communities program.

In addition to playing a key role in the design and implementation of new learning processes, local line leaders often become *teachers* once these learning processes become established. We often find that the most effective facilitators in learning processes such as the FedEx Learning Laboratory are not professional trainers but the line managers themselves. Their substantive knowledge and practical experience give them unique credibility. They are role models with whom other front-line people can identify. Last, as the old saw goes, "There is no better way to learn than to teach." Facilitating others' learning becomes a uniquely powerful way for line leaders to continually deepen their own understanding and capabilities.

However, engaging local line leaders may be difficult. As pragmatists, they often find ideas like systems thinking, mental models, and dialogue intangible and "hard to get my hands around." "When I was first exposed to the MIT work," says Fred Simon, former head of the Lincoln Continental program at Ford Motor Company, "I was highly skeptical. I had heard so many 'academic' theories that made sense but never produced for us. But I also was not happy with our team's ability to work together. I knew there must be a better way, and my business planning manager was convinced this could make a difference." Simon's view is very typical of line leaders at the outset: he is skeptical, but he recognizes that he has problems that he cannot solve, and he has a trusted colleague who will engage with him. Again and again, we have found that healthy, open-minded skeptics can become the most effective leaders and, eventually, champions of this work. They keep the horse in front of the cart by focusing first and foremost on business results. If they can find new approaches to enhance results, they will commit time and energy to them. Such people invariably have more staying power than the "fans" who get excited about new ideas but whose excitement wanes once the newness wears off.

The limitations of local line leaders are natural counterparts to their strengths. Because their focus is primarily on their business unit, they may not think much about learning within the larger organization, and typically they have little time to devote to diffusion of their efforts. They may also be unaware of and relatively inept at dealing with antilearning forces in the larger organization. They can become impatient when the larger organization does not change to match their new ideas of what works and may start to feel misunderstood and unappreciated. They can easily develop an "us against the world" siege mentality, which will then make them especially ineffective in communicating their ideas to the "unwashed."

Innovative local line managers are often more at risk than they realize. They typically share a mental model that says, "My bosses will leave me alone as long as I produce results, regardless of the methods I use." But the better-mousetrap theory may not apply in large institutions. Improved results are often threatening to others, and the more dramatic the improvement, the greater the threat. Complex organizations have complex forces that maintain the status quo and inhibit the spread of new ideas. Often, even the most effective local line leaders fail to understand these forces or know how to work with them.

Despite these limitations, committed local line leadership is essential. At least half of the Learning Center companies that have made significant strides in improving business results and developing internal learning capabilities and infrastructures have had little or no executive leadership. In some instances, hundreds and literally thousands of people are now involved in growing networks of internal practitioners with no active top-management leadership. On the other hand, we have seen *no* examples where significant progress has been made without leadership from local line managers, and many examples where sincerely committed CEOs have failed to generate any significant momentum.

Executive Leaders

Our fervor at the Learning Center with practical experiments led by local line managers has frequently made us blind to the necessary complementary roles played by executive leaders. We have gradually come to appreciate that local line leaders can benefit significantly from "executive champions" who can be protectors, mentors, and thinking partners. When dramatic improvements achieved in one line organization threaten others, executive partners can help in managing the threat. Alternatively, new innovative practices are often simply ignored because people are too busy to take the time to really understand what the innovators are doing. Working in concert with internal networkers, executives can help in connecting innovative local line leaders with other like-minded people. They also play a mentoring role in helping the local line leaders to mature, to understand complex political crosscurrents, and to communicate their ideas and accomplishments to those who have not been involved.

For example, in one organization where a local line organization had achieved what it regarded as dramatic improvements in the product development process, its process improvement efforts lacked credibility outside the team when judged by more traditional metrics. For instance, at critical checkpoints the team had record numbers of engineering change orders. The team interpreted this as evidence that people were more open, trusting, and willing to surface and fix problems early in the development process. But outside the team, these same orders were seen as evidence of "being out of control." Eventually, executives in the company commissioned an independent audit, which showed that the team was indeed highly effective. The executives also supported a "learning history" to help others understand how the team had accomplished its results.

Part of the problem in appreciating effective executive leadership in learning is that all of us are so used to the "captain of the ship" image of traditional hierarchical leaders. We are used to thinking of top managers as *the* key decision makers, the most visible and powerful people in the organization. Although undoubtedly some key decisions will always have to be made at the top, cultures are not changed through singular decisions, and decision-making power does not produce new learning capabilities. When executives lead as teachers, stewards, and designers, they fill roles that are much more subtle, contextual, and long term than the traditional model of the power-wielding hierarchical leader suggests.

"We in top management are responsible for the operating environment that can allow continual learning," says Harley-Davidson's Teerlink. Although executive leadership has traditionally focused on structure and strategy, Teerlink and other executives with whom we at the Learning Center work are increasingly thinking about the operating environment in less tangible ways. For example, over the past three years, Teerlink and his colleagues have redesigned Harley-Davidson's traditional organizational structure into three core "circles of activity," each led by a leadership team. But according to Teerlink, "implementing the new organization was the easy part. Now we have to make it work, and that requires people learning from each other."

Effective executive leaders build an operating environment for learning in several ways. The first is through articulating *guiding ideas*. "I have always believed that good ideas will drive out bad ideas," said Hanover's Bill O'Brien in a speech. "One of the basic problems with business today is that our organizations are guided by too many mediocre ideas, ideas which do not foster aspirations worthy of people's commitment." Guiding ideas are different from slogans or the latest management buzzwords. They are arrived at gradually, often over many years, through reflection on an organization's history and traditions and on its long-term growth and opportunities.

The power of guiding ideas derives from the energy released when imagination and aspiration come together. Understanding this power has always been a hallmark of great leaders. The promise of learning organizations is, at least in part, the promise that this power will become deeply and widely embedded in a way that rarely, if ever, happens in traditional authoritarian organizations. "There are two fundamentally differing views of human nature and work," said O'Brien. "The 'objective view' sees work as a source of economic means. The 'subjective' view is concerned with the effects of work on the person. By the early twenty-first century, quality will become a commodity and companies will be distinguished by the wholeness of their people."

A second way to build operating environments for learning is through conscious attention to *learning infrastructure*. I believe that executives will increasingly come to realize that, in a world of rapid change and increasing interdependence, learning is too important to be left to chance. "We have plenty of infrastructure for decision making within AT&T," says Chairman Bob Allen. "What we lack is infrastructure for learning" (Peter M. Senge, et al., *The Fifth Discipline Handbook*, 1994, p. 34).

I have met many CEOs in recent years who have lamented that "we can't learn from ourselves," that significant innovations simply don't spread, or that "we are better at learning from competitors than from our own people." Yet those very same executives rarely recognize that they may be describing their own future job description. When we stop to think, certain questions arise: Why *should* successful new practices spread in organizations? Who studies these innovations to document why they worked? Where are the learning processes whereby others might follow in the footsteps of successful innovators? Who is responsible for these learning processes?

There can be little doubt of the long-term business impact of executive leadership in developing learning infrastructure. When the Royal Dutch/Shell Group's central "group planning" leaders became convinced that "scenario thinking" was a vital survival skill in the turbulent, unpredictable world oil markets, they didn't initiate a set of scenario-planning courses for Shell's management. They redesigned the planning infrastructure so that management teams regularly were asked not just for their budget and their "plan" but for multiple plans describing how they would manage under multiple possible futures. "Planning as learning" has gradually become a way of life within Shell, a change to which many attribute Shell's ascent to preeminence in the world oil business.

A third way to build operating environments for business is the executive's own "domain for taking action"—namely, the *executive team* itself. What is important, first, is that executives see that they, too, must change, and that many of the skills that have made them successful in the past can actively inhibit learning. They are forceful, articulate advocates, but they usually are not very good at inquiring into their own thinking or exposing the areas where their thinking is weak. Reflecting on a two-year process both to "rethink the corporate strategy and to develop new capacities to think strategically together," Herman Miller CEO Kerm Campbell said, "We started off as a collection of individuals with strong views, which we often kept under wraps lest we get into destructive battles with one another, and a set of assumptions we rarely questioned about the keys to success in our industry. As we have progressed, I think we have come to see that having an effective strategy and having the capacity to think together strategically are inseparable."

How radical are ideas like these about executive leadership? I think they will eventually lead to a very different mind-set and, ultimately, skill-set among executives. "Gradually, I have come to see a whole new model for my role as a CEO," says Shell Oil's Phil Carroll. "Perhaps my real job is to be the *ecologist for the organization*. We must learn how to see the company as a living system and to see it as a system within the context of the larger systems of which it is a part. Only then will our vision reliably include return for our shareholders, a productive environment for our employees, and a social vision for the company as a whole."

Achieving such shifts in thinking, values, and behavior among executives is not easy. "The name of the game is giving up power," says Carroll. Even among "enlightened" executives, giving up power is difficult. "It's not that I don't miss the old system sometimes," reflects Carroll. "Being the commander in chief was kind of fun."

Internal Networkers

The most unappreciated leadership role is that of the internal net-workers, or what we often call internal community builders. Internal networkers are effective for the very reasons that top-management efforts to initiate change can backfire. One of the most interesting paradoxes in fostering deep change may be that "no power *is* power." Precisely because they have no positional authority, internal net-workers are free to move about a large organization relatively un-noticed. When the CEO visits someone, everyone knows. When the CEO says, "We need to become a learning organization," every-one nods. But when someone with little or no positional authority begins inquiring to see which people are genuinely interested in changing the way they and their teams work, the only ones likely to respond are those who are genuinely interested. And if the inter-nal networker finds one person who is interested and asks, "Who else do you think really cares about these things," he or she is likely to receive an honest response. The only authority possessed by internal networkers comes from the strength of their convictions and the clarity of their ideas. This, we find time and again, is the only legitimate authority when deep changes are required, regard-less of one's organizational position. The internal networkers have the paradoxical advantage that this is their *only* source of authority.

It is very difficult to identify the internal networkers because they can be people from many different organizational positions. They might be internal consultants, trainers, or personnel staff in organi-zation development or human resources. They might be front-line workers like engineers, sales representatives, or shop stewards. They might, under some circumstances, be in senior staff positions. What is important is that they are able to move around the organization freely, with high accessibility to many parts of the organization. They understand the informal networks, what researchers call the informal "communities of practice," whereby information and stories flow and innovative practices naturally diffuse within organizations (J. Seely Brown and P. Duguid, *Organization Science*, Feb. 1991, pp. 40–57).

Internal community builders work on different levels, commensurate with their different levels in the organization. Front-line workers are typically the most effective community builders within line organizations. Corporate staff people are often the most effective networkers within larger corporations because they usually have a broad perspective and extensive contacts. What matters is that effective internal networkers are seen as credible, knowledgeable, committed individuals who are not a particular threat to anyone. "The most effective community organizer is he who is invisible," says Saul Alinsky in *Reveille for Radicals* (1969), and the same can be said of the best internal networkers.

The first vital function played by internal networkers is to identify local line managers who have the power to take action and who are predisposed to developing new learning capabilities. Much time and energy can be wasted working with the wrong people, especially in the early stages of a change process. Convincing people that they should be interested in systems thinking or learning is inherently a low-leverage strategy. Even if they are persuaded initially, they are unlikely to persevere. When the Liaison Officers from the Learning Center companies, a group that includes many of our most effective internal networkers, asked, "How did each of us get started in this work?" they responded, virtually unanimously, that they were "predisposed." All of them had something in their background—perhaps an especially influential college course, a particular work experience, or just a lifelong interest—that predisposed them to the systems perspective, to a deep curiosity about learning or mental models or the mystery of profound teamwork. In turn, they felt attuned to others they met who shared this predisposition.

In ongoing experiments within line organizations, internal networkers can help in many ways. In our own Learning Center projects, they serve as project managers, as cofacilitators, or as "learning historians," people trained to track a major change process and to help those who are involved to better reflect on what they are learning. As practical knowledge is built, internal networkers continue to serve as organizational "seed carriers," connecting people of like mind in diverse settings to each other's learning efforts. Gradually they may help in developing the more formal coordination and steering mechanisms needed to leverage from local experiments to broader, organizationwide learning. At Ford, for example, an informal Leaders of Learning group was formed of multiple local line leaders to share learnings and to serve as a strategic leadership body, supporting continuing experiments, connecting to the interests of top management, and wrestling with the challenges of broader, organizationwide capacity building and learning. Such groups, which gather together innovative line leaders, may eventually evolve into an important element of the learning infrastructure. The initiative to form this group came from Ford's internal networkers.

The limitations of internal networkers likewise are not difficult to identify. Because they do not have a great deal of formal authority, they can do little to directly counter hierarchical authority. If a local line leader becomes a threat to peers or superiors, they may be powerless to help her or him. Internal networkers have no authority to institute changes in organizational structures or processes. So, even though they are essential, they will be most effective in concert with local line leaders and executive leaders.

Conclusion

The leadership challenges in building learning organizations represent a microcosm of *the* leadership issue of our times: how human communities, be they multinational corporations or societies, productively confront complex, systemic issues where hierarchical authority is inadequate for change. None of today's most pressing societal issues—deterioration of our natural environment, the international arms race, erosion of the public education system, or the breakdown of the family and increasing social anomie and fragmentation—will be resolved through hierarchical authority. In all these issues, there are no simple causes, no simple "fixes." There is no one villain to blame. There will be no magic pill. Significant change will require imagination, perseverance, dialogue, deep caring, and a willingness to change on the part of millions of people. I believe it is also the challenge posed in building learning organizations.

Recently a group of CEOs from the Learning Center companies spent a half-day with Karl Henrik Robèrt, the founder of Sweden's path-breaking Natural Step process for helping societies become ecologically sustainable. The next day, Rich Teerlink of Harley-Davidson came in and said, "I don't know why I stay awake at night trying to figure out how to transform a six-thousand-person company. Yesterday, we talked with someone transforming a country of four million."

The challenges of systemic change where hierarchy is inadequate will, I believe, push us to new views of leadership based on new principles. These challenges cannot be met by isolated heroic leaders. They will require a unique mix of different people, in different positions, who lead in different ways. Although the picture sketched above is tentative and will undoubtedly evolve, I doubt that it understates the changes that will be required in our traditional leadership models.

6 EDGAR H. SCHEIN

Leadership and Organizational Culture

Edgar H. Schein is professor of management at the Sloan School of Management at the Massachusetts Institute of Technology. He is the author of Organizational Culture and Leadership, The Clinical Perspective in Field Work, Organizational Psychology, *and* Career Anchors. *He is considered one of the founders of the field of organizational psychology.*

In approaching this topic it is always tempting to start fresh with new insights and to forget history. Yet the question of what the leader of the future should be like is not new. It is, in fact, one of the oldest questions in the field of leadership. Because of this, we ought to reflect a bit on what will be genuinely different in the future before answering the question. The first task is to talk about the aspects of leadership that will *not* change.

Note: This essay is based in part on material drawn from *Organizational Culture and Leadership* (2nd ed.), by Edgar H. Schein (San Francisco: Jossey-Bass, 1992).

What Is Not New

Leaders have been studied throughout history, and social psychology has, from the outset, made leadership a main focus of research. One of the most consistent findings by historians, sociologists, and empirically oriented social psychologists is that what leadership should be depends on the particular situation, the task to be performed, and the characteristics of the leader's subordinates. One reason so many different theories of leadership exist is that different researchers focus on different elements. At one level all of these theories are correct, because they all identify one central component of the complex human situation that is leadership, analyze that component in detail, and ignore others. At another level, all of these theories lack a concern with organizational dynamics, particularly the fact that organizations have different needs and problems at different stages in their evolution. We tend to treat the topic of leadership in a vacuum instead of specifying what the leader's relationship to the organization is at any given time. As we look ahead, I suspect that the relationship between the leader and the organization will become more and more complex, so a beginning model for analysis should be useful.

Given the above issues, I would like to focus on the unique characteristics of the challenges that face people who create organizations (entrepreneurs) and those who run organizations (CEOs) at various stages in the organization's life cycle. In thinking about organizations as dynamic systems with a life cycle of their own, we can identify such unique challenges and consider their implications for leadership behavior. Although the nature of organizations will undoubtedly change in the future, the challenges of creating, building, maintaining, and changing (evolving) organizations to new forms will remain the same.

Creating: The Leader as Animator

At the early stages of organizational creation, a unique leadership function is to supply the energy needed to get the organization off the ground. Much is said about the *vision* of entrepreneurs, but not enough is said about the incredible *energy* they display as they try one approach after another, facing repeated failures, in their efforts to start an enterprise. I have watched this process in a number of young companies and am always struck by the fact that the leaders have so much energy and manage to transmit that energy to their subordinates. It is an energy born out of strong personal convictions, which motivates the entrepreneur and builds excitement in others. Such people often literally breathe life into the organization; hence we should use a term like *animator* to describe this kind of leader.

Building: The Leader as a Creator of Culture

Once an organization has the potential to live and survive, the entrepreneur's beliefs, values, and basic assumptions are transferred to the mental models of the subordinates. This process of building culture occurs in three ways: (1) the entrepreneurs only hire and keep subordinates who think and feel the way they do, (2) they indoctrinate and socialize subordinates to their way of thinking and feeling, and (3) their own behavior is a role model that encourages subordinates to identify with them and thereby internalize their beliefs, values, and assumptions.

It is crucial to recognize at this stage that if the organization is successful and the success is attributed to the leader, the leader's entire personality becomes embedded in the culture of the organization. If the leader has conflicts, such as wanting a team-based consensus process for decision making and, at the same time, wanting to maintain complete control and reward subordinates for individual prowess in solving problems, we will see inconsistent policies regarding decision making, incentives, and rewards. Leaders, then, can actually create "neurotic" organizations, which live with various degrees of conflict and exhibit uneven patterns of strengths and weaknesses. The point in highlighting this stage is that once the conflicts become embedded in the culture of the organization, they cannot easily be changed, because they have also become associated with the organization's prior history of success and are therefore taken for granted as the best way to do things.

Maintaining: The Leader as a Sustainer of Culture

As history has shown over and over again, successful organizations attract imitators, who may become successful competitors. Products and markets mature and what made an organization successful in its youth is often insufficient to maintain it. The "neuroses" of youth that may have provided some of the energy needed to build the organization can become liabilities as the organization attempts to adapt to maturing markets, more severe competition, its own increasing size and complexity, and the aging of its leaders and work force.

The creators and builders of organizations often falter at this stage. What was good for the young organization—the high energy level and compulsive vision of its founders—becomes a liability as the organization finds that it needs to stabilize itself, become more efficient, deal with the fact that its products have become commodities, and most important, evolve new generations of leaders for a different kind of future. The problem in making this transition has two components: (1) the founder-builder does not want to let go of the leadership role or is emotionally incapable of doing so or (2) the founder-builder creates (often unconsciously) a variety of organizational processes that prevent the growth of the next generation of leadership.

Management development is typically a very weak function in young organizations and succession is often based on criteria that are not relevant; for example, the organization may promote the people who are most like the entrepreneur or who are technically the most competent in the area of the organization's work, rather than seeking out people who have managerial talent. Founder-builders often glorify the "technical" functions such as research and development, manufacturing, and sales and demean "managerial" functions such as finance, planning, marketing, and human resources. At the personality level, leaders often prevent potential successors from having the kind of learning experiences that would enable them to take over or, worse, they undermine any successors who display the strength and competence to take over.

The successful leaders at this stage are the ones who either have enough personal insight to grow with the organization and change their own outlook or recognize their own limitations and permit other forms of leadership to emerge. If neither of these processes occurs, the organization often finds itself having to develop other power centers, such as boards of directors or political cabals, who force the founder out of the CEO role into other roles or out of the organization altogether. A new CEO then comes in with a mandate to help the organization grow and remain successful.

Such growth requires the CEO to understand the organization's culture, with all of its strengths and weaknesses, and to consolidate the elements that are needed to maintain the organization's ability to function and grow. This is a period that we often think of as "institutionalization"; it consists of identifying the successful elements and giving them permanence and stability. If the organization continues to be successful, it grows in size and age, forcing leaders to consider how to evolve processes that worked on a small scale and with young people into processes that work on a global scale with maturing employees—a totally different leadership task. The elusive qualities of judgment and wisdom are probably the most critical for leaders to possess at this stage of organizational evolution.

Changing: The Leader as Change Agent

Unfortunately, as the rate of change in the technological, economic, political, and sociocultural environments increases, the very strengths that were institutionalized can become liabilities. Leaders now have to begin to think like change agents, because the problem is not only how to acquire new concepts and skills, but also how to *unlearn* things that are no longer serving the organization well. Unlearning is an entirely different process, involving anxiety, defensiveness, and resistance to change.

Leaders who find themselves in a mature organization that has developed dysfunctional processes, and who therefore must think of themselves as agents of change, need two particular characteristics. First, they have to have the emotional strength to be supportive of the organization while it deals with the anxieties attendant upon unlearning processes that were previously successful, that is, the ability to create for the organization a sense of "psychological safety." And second, they need a true understanding of cultural dynamics and the properties of their own organizational culture.

The critical thing to understand about cultural dynamics is that leaders cannot arbitrarily *change* culture in the sense of eliminating dysfunctional elements, but they can *evolve* culture by building on its strengths while letting its weaknesses atrophy over time. Culture cannot be manipulated by announcing changes or instituting "programs." If the organization has been successful doing things in a certain way and has evolved mental models based on those methods, it will not give them up. However, mental models can be broadened and enlarged. (I am indebted to Geoff Ainscow for the insight that one does not necessarily give up cultural elements when one learns something new, but adds those elements to what is already there. When a native of England becomes American, he or she does not necessarily give up being English but adds what it means to be an American to his or her total personality.)

An organization built on individual incentives cannot become a set of teams simply because the CEO announces that teamwork is now necessary and launches a team-building program. However, if the CEO understands cultural dynamics, he or she will begin to reward individuals for helping others and for contributing to other projects, thereby acknowledging the deep individualism of the organization but broadening the concept of individual competence to increasingly include "working with others," "building trusting relationships," "opening up communication across boundaries," and so on.

The essential learning mechanism here, what I have called "cognitive redefinition," involves (1) new semantics, that is, redefining in a formal sense what individualism means; (2) broadening perceptions to enlarge one's mental model of individualism to include collaborative behaviors as well as competitive behaviors, while still seeing oneself as individualistic; and (3) developing new standards of judgment and evaluation so that competitive behavior may now be viewed as more negative while collaborative behavior is viewed as more positive. Culture is "changed"—in reality, enlarged— through changes in various key concepts in the mental models of people who are the main carriers of the culture.

Note, however, that such transformations do not occur through announcements or formal programs. They occur through a genuine change in the leader's behavior and through embedding new definitions in organizational processes and routines. It is here that the leader must "walk the talk," and that, of course, implies that the leader has also undergone a personal transformation as part of the total change process. If the leader's behavior and organizational routines both change, the organization will remain culturally individualistic but the ability of its members to function as team members will increase. Whereas previously, individualism might have meant personal competition to get ahead by playing political games, the concept is now broadened and redefined to include whatever teamwork is necessary to get the job done, and individuals are rewarded on this basis.

If the organization is in deeper trouble, and its culture is genuinely inhibiting the kind of growth and change that are needed, the leader, as a change agent, sometimes has to bite the bullet and destroy some more central elements in the organization itself that are the culture carriers. For example, some managers may be so indoctrinated with the idea that individualism means competing with others in the organization to get ahead that they are unable or unwilling to open themselves up to any other alternatives. To become more collaborative would be tantamount to "not being themselves." Sometimes such individuals leave when leaders bring in new concepts, but if not, the organization faces what we colloquially call "turn-arounds."

It is no accident that when the "turn-around manager" comes in, the top layers of management are usually replaced and massive reorganizations occur. The function of these drastic measures is to destroy elements of the old culture and to initiate a new culture-building process by removing the people who carry and represent the old culture. It is incorrect to think of this stage as "creating a new culture," because that is not possible. The leader can create a new organization with new procedures, but the formation of culture requires collective learning and repeated experiences of success or failure.

It is more correct to think of this point in the organization's history as a time when the organization-building cycle starts afresh. Turn-around managers can then be thought of as needing many of the same qualities as entrepreneurs, particularly the ability to animate a new organization. In addition, however, the turn-around manager must deal with the anxiety and depression of the employees who remain and who feel guilty that they survived while many of their colleagues and friends did not. Rebuilding their motivation and commitment often requires higher levels of animation than building an organization in the first place.

What cannot be ignored by leaders is that the destruction of culture is extremely costly on a human level. Large numbers of people have to face the fact that the way they have been thinking and feeling is no longer functional. Personal change at this level is typically difficult, so people who represent the old way tend to be forced out of the organization. The new people who come in have to start a building process all over again, and it is not even clear whether this is always possible. A mature dysfunctional organization may disappear altogether and be replaced by young organizations that start from scratch, with new generations of entrepreneurs whose initial mental models were different and better adapted to current realities.

The organizations that have survived and made important transitions over many decades seem to have always had a cultural core that was fundamentally functional—a commitment to learning and change; a commitment to people and to all of the stakeholders in the organization, including customers, employees, suppliers, and stockholders; and a commitment to building a healthy, flexible organization in the first place. If such a cultural core does not exist from the beginning, the organization may not survive in the long run, especially as environmental turbulence increases.

A Look Toward the Future

What, if anything, do or should these leadership roles have in common? As we look back in history, it should be evident that the builders are fundamentally different from the maintainers and changers. It takes strong vision, conviction, and energy to create and animate an organization; it takes great judgment, wisdom, and skill in pulling large groups of people together to institutionalize processes on a global scale with a population that varies widely geographically and in age. And it takes learning ability and personal flexibility to evolve and change organizations. It is around this last point that we connect with the future and what it will bring.

The one thing that is becoming clearer and clearer is that the institutions of the past may be obsolete and that new forms of governance and leadership will have to be learned. Furthermore, as the rate of change itself increases, learning ability will not consist of the one-time learning of a new system; *perpetual* learning and change will be the only constant. Leaders of the future will therefore have to have more of the following characteristics:

- Extraordinary levels of perception and insight into the realities of the world and into themselves

- Extraordinary levels of motivation to enable them to go through the inevitable pain of learning and change, especially in a world with looser boundaries, in which loyalties become more difficult to define

- The emotional strength to manage their own and others' anxiety as learning and change become more and more a way of life

- New skills in analyzing cultural assumptions, identifying functional and dysfunctional assumptions, and evolving processes that enlarge the culture by building on its strengths and functional elements

- The willingness and ability to involve others and elicit their participation, because tasks will be too complex and information too widely distributed for leaders to solve problems on their own

- The willingness and ability to share power and control according to people's knowledge and skills, that is, to permit and encourage leadership to flourish throughout the organization

Perhaps the most salient aspect of future leadership will be that these characteristics will not be present in a few people all the time but will be present in many people some of the time, as circumstances change and as different people develop the insight to move into leadership roles. Leadership will then increasingly be an emergent function rather than a property of people appointed to formal roles. Whereas today the process of appointing leaders is a critical function of boards of directors, electorates, government agencies, and so on, we can imagine that, in the future, appointed leaders will not play the key leadership roles but will be perpetual diagnosticians who will be able to empower different people at different times and to let emergent leadership flourish. They will *not* assume that all groups need leadership, they will *not* assume that leadership means hierarchy and control of others, and they will *not* assume that accountability must always be individual. Instead, the leader of the future will be a person with the characteristics mentioned above who can lead and follow, be central and marginal, be hierarchically above and below, be individualistic and a team player, and, above all, be a perpetual learner. If the world is to learn to manage itself better, many more people in organizations will have to be leaders and the leadership functions described above will have to be much more widely shared.

7 JOHN W. WORK

Leading a Diverse Work Force

John W. Work is the senior principal in Work Associates, Inc., a New York City–based management consulting firm founded in 1978. The firm provides human resource and organizational services to corporate and other organizations with respect to problem identification, program design and implementation, and program and activity evaluation. Work is the author of Race, Economics, and Corporate America, Towards Affirmative Action and Racial/ Ethnic Pluralism: How to Train in Organizations, The Diversity Task Force Exercise, *and* What Every CEO Already Knows About Managing Diversity. *He serves on the board of trustees of Tougaloo College, the board of directors of the Josephson Institute for the Advancement of Ethics, and the board of directors of the Professional Examination Service.*

Real and fictional, our heroes have been shoved into near oblivion by a society determined to break the ties of class regimentation, rend asunder the castelike character of race and gender relations, declare God dead, and be the beneficiaries of the "good life" portrayed on television, in the movies, and in the creative madness of Madison Avenue. More and more Americans have become obsessed with "doing their own thing" and with an independence unencumbered by standards and values perceived to be imposed by heroes and the larger society.

Notwithstanding changing attitudes and behaviors, heroes are the embodiment of a society's most fundamental and enduring values. They and their values may serve as anchors in a society caught up in Alvin Toffler's notion of "accelerative thrust." However, when heroes are relegated to lesser roles, or are absent, substitutes must be created. It is my contention that one such creation is an updated version of the leader and notions of leadership.

It is important to note, however, that no societally accepted heroes in the past, nor any today, have had value matrices that were dispositive with respect to eliminating racism, bigotry, and discrimination; gender inequities; poverty; religious intolerance; or disabling forms of intergroup conflict. On the contrary, their values have tended to reinforce the status quo.

Although leaders may be described in broad terms, those of the future will have to have value systems sufficiently expansive and flexible to accommodate socioeconomic dynamics and rates of change greater than those of today. Unlike the hero, the true leader must be able to embrace change and utilize it in socially beneficial ways. Critically, the leader has come to replace the hero, and leadership, heroism.

The accompanying and unending social tasks that characterize the ongoing development of the leader and leadership concepts consist of analyzing, defining, describing, and, ultimately, assigning social values and crafting usages. Thus, as I contemplate leadership in the future, I will anticipate the "unending social tasks" as they may affect organizations and corporate leadership within the nation's workplaces.

Leadership and the "Great Social Problem"

What is leadership? Are leaders born or made? How do we know when we are in the presence of a leader? What are the differences, if any, between so-called great leaders and not-so-great leaders? A review of the literature will reveal almost as many different responses to these and other questions as there are respondents. Nonetheless, although we may have some difficulty in laying bare precisely and definitively the components of leadership and the working relationships among those components, we do seem to think that we know leaders when we see them: they are those individuals who, in their inimitable ways, inspire confidence, undermine despair, fight fear, initiate positive and productive actions, light the candles, define the goals, and paint brighter tomorrows.

It may be fairly said that the character of a society's leadership may substantially determine how that society fares in an environment of change. With respect to the United States today, a number of the important changes are related to the nation's changing demographics, in particular, changes in the distributive characteristics of the population and labor force relative to race, ethnicity, culture, gender, age, religion, and so on. Moreover, these demographic changes appear to correlate highly with other important socioeconomic developments, such as changes in some social values and in modes of production. It would be disingenuous not to observe that these changes are occurring against a historical backdrop of prejudice and discrimination brought about by the differences between us. Clearly, these differences become not only magnified by immigration, disparate birth rates, and labor demands but also distended with the potential for bitter social eructations.

Prejudices and patterns of discrimination flow from social and individual values that inform our actions and decisions; they tell us what's "right" and what's "wrong," what's "good" and what's "bad." Not so parenthetically, value systems also are likely to tell us *who* is good and bad and *who* is right and wrong. In particular, social value systems tell us how to think of people of other races, cultures, and nationalities; people of opposite gender and different religious and ethnic backgrounds; young people, old people, and middle-aged people; people who are so-called professionals and those who are not. In the workplace, value systems do even more: they train the eye to separate those who are naturally "lazy" from those who are culturally "hard-working," those who are "bright and talented" from those who are "dull and uninspired," those who possess "top-management potential" from those who have "severe limitations," and so on.

People who write and talk about the leadership phenomenon inevitably bring their values and biases to bear, thereby inadvertently delimiting cogent and reasonable definitions and descriptions. The result, all too often, is that we are left with an ineffable mysticism regarding leadership and with the idea that leaders, like Athena, issue from the head of Zeus. In fact, leaders are people with value systems not unlike those of their followers; leadership, as we know it, is straightforwardly born of intelligence, perhaps power and personal charisma, desire and commitment, and a willingness to do things that others are less willing to do.

Two general types of causes give rise to leadership. The first type may be called the *perceived-inequity cause*. This cause typically grows out of perceived inequities across diverse groups in corporate and organizational workplaces, communities, and other societal arenas. The second type of cause may be called the *search-for-excellence cause*. Here, corporate managers, organizational heads, and community and government officials with positions of responsibility and authority may perceive a need and be motivated to raise and improve an organization's level of efficiency, production and delivery of goods and/or services, and profitability.

Another scenario based on the search-for-excellence cause depicts a manager-leader who has a vision of the organization's *mission* in the future. The clear goal is to manage better in order to fulfill that mission. In doing so, improved levels of efficiency, higher levels of employee morale and productivity, and other such results are presumed to be good and natural consequences for customers and clients and the larger community. It should be noted that in this scenario, the manager-leader's motivation is not contoured by the ultimate desire for more profits as much as by a broader view of the organization's role in the society.

True Leadership and Social Benefit

Today, as we approach the beginning of the twenty-first century, the use of the term *leader* has been broadened to include almost anyone with organizational power and authority. Nearly every CEO and executive director is spoken of as a leader, every union and association head is a leader, every president of a neighborhood block association is a leader, and ministers, rabbis, and priests are all leaders. What has given rise to so common a use of the term? Is true and effective leadership really expected from all of these people, or has the term simply undergone a social metamorphosis as institutions have changed dramatically in response to society's changing values and expectations?

I believe that true leadership can only be meaningfully defined within a social context; that is, socially meaningful visions and other leadership values must be built on standards that benefit society. In this context, and current relativism notwithstanding, not all leadership visions are equally valuable. Some are more important and socially significant than others. True leadership must lead to *change* that translates into social betterment. Indeed, true leaders should not and must not support visions and processes that perpetuate or give countenance to social injustices. Far too many executives in both the for-profit and not-for-profit sectors who are praised for their "leadership" are not true leaders in this context. Although they may pay lip service to eliminating workplace discrimination, for example, they often do not give significant leadership in this area or even serve as positive role models.

True leadership is not without trials—it is a tough business! It requires individuals to take considerable risks and to do things that others are not willing to do. Leadership must be viewed in relation to the image of the hero. This requires the leader to commit to the essence of life and its noble values, to rise to a higher calling on behalf of human beings, to say no to the serpent, to accept the challenges of ever-changing demands on an organization's mission, and to lift those in the workplace to rewarding, fulfilling, and productive careers. Ultimately, true leadership makes a difference in the lives of people.

Leadership requires the collective unconsciousness to be transformed or, at the very least, transcended. We cannot expect that all true leaders will become great leaders. It's a bit like playing the piano. While there was only one Horowitz, millions of people play the piano at various levels of competency. And so it is with true leadership.

Unlike other activities and efforts that may immediately have a single and realizable result or outcome, leadership is a dynamic and ongoing process that produces a stream of both intangible effects and tangible results that are consistent with a socially meaningful vision. Less bounded by finite time constraints and one-time outcomes, the stream of leadership effects and results redounds not only to the benefit of those who are followers, but also of those who are not. In other words, the beneficial effects of true leadership cannot be limited, so to speak, to "the movement," whether it's civil rights, feminism, or another movement; rather, they must be felt by others and manifested in many of society's communities and institutions.

The Workplace of the Future Is Here

The world as we have known it is changing at a dizzying pace, fueled by advances in technology and innovation. People are crisscrossing the planet in numbers not imagined even fifty years ago, demands for consumer goods and services and capital goods are soaring world-

wide, and corporations, not-for-profit organizations, and other institutions are finding and developing new and significantly profitable
markets beyond regional and national borders. At the core of this
emerging global economy is a computer-driven information and
communications technology that serves to undergird and link the
world's production and consumption capacities and needs.

Notably, both the multicultural and technological aspects of
these powerful changes in American institutions and workplaces
are much in evidence. For example, numerous racial and ethnic
groups; differing languages, communication patterns, and cultural
values; an altered workplace structure and dynamics; and new patterns of educational and training demands are becoming common-
place and go well beyond the scope of traditional corporate cultures.

The ethnic, cultural, and gender characteristics of America's
population and labor force are rapidly changing. Largely because of
the emigration of nonwhite ethnics from Asia and Southeast Asia,
the Pacific Islands, Central and South America, the Caribbean, and
West and East Africa, the representation of these groups in the
American "melting pot" is rising relative to that of Americans of
European descent. When these immigrants are added to the African
Americans, Mexican Americans, Puerto Ricans, Asian Americans,
Native Americans, and others whose time here ranges from a few
decades to centuries, it is estimated that nonwhite ethnic and cultural groups will exceed one-third of all new entrants to the labor
force between now and the turn of the century. One clear and over-
riding implication of this fact is that the United States will have a
new face. Moreover, dramatically increasing numbers of women are
entering the work force in roles they would have been precluded
from playing just a few decades ago.

It is clear that as the characteristics of people in the workplace
change and the differences between them increase, for-profit and
not-for-profit corporations and organizations will face different
challenges than they did in the past. Primarily, these new challenges will incorporate a broad expanse of pluralism and diversity.

In addition to diversity in race, ethnicity, and gender, workplaces can expect increasing diversity of religious beliefs and practices, ages, and lifestyles and greater numbers of people with physical disabilities. These elements of diversity are bound together thematically in the changing matrix of social values by their common intrinsic elements.

In addition to changes in the human dimensions of the workplace, the concept and the reality of a global marketplace continue to develop, with its implicit requirements for intercultural and interpersonal communication; productivity becomes a function more of the cerebral processes of knowledge workers than of physical capacities, and diverse work teams become more universal.

What all this leads to is a critical need for managers and executives who can bring true leadership to workplace situations that, left leaderless, may well devolve into more complex patterns of discrimination, lowered levels of employee morale and productivity, a poor public and international image, and a failure to identify and develop new markets. True leaders will recognize the opportunities and potential benefits inherent in diversity, such as the creation of new markets, broadened customer bases, higher levels of productivity, more creativity and new ideas, and increased corporate capacity to effectively participate in different competitive and global configurations.

Within this context of true leadership, true leaders for the future must be willing to accept five fundamental challenges:

1. They must be willing to become more sensitive and understanding with respect to the ethnic, cultural, and gender differences within the workplace and to demonstrate that sensitivity and understanding.

2. They must have a vision for the workplace that ultimately results in a significant broadening of the corporate culture and the workplace environment.

3. They must be willing to craft and implement new and different employment and communication processes to enhance and promote perceptions of fairness and equity.

4. They must be willing to bring full and unquestioned commitment to the effective utilization of a diverse work force.

5. They must be the linchpin between their organization and the larger community, to establish the organization as a place where people want to work and be productive and to develop new markets and maintain existing ones.

In the final analysis, true leadership brings people of diverse backgrounds and interests together in ways that provide fair and equitable opportunities to contribute their best, achieve personal goals, and realize their full potential.

Conclusion

The seeming decline of heroes in our society as images possessed of enduring visions and values, capable of transforming the wretched into nobility, and serving as repositories for historic tales of victory over the implacable forces of evil is being offset today by the rise of the notion of leaders and leadership. But who are the leaders of today, and what is leadership? With respect to organizations and workplaces, true leaders are individuals with organizational visions and commitments and an embrace beyond traditional management concerns. They fashion higher standards of social concern than are required by fundamental management skills. Given this reengineered leadership, America's institutions and workplaces now can meaningfully adopt the values inherent in a diverse society.

8 KEN BLANCHARD

Turning the Organizational Pyramid Upside Down

*Ken Blanchard is chairman of Blanchard Training
and Development, Inc., a full-service management
consulting and training company, and is a prominent
author in the field of management. His One Minute
Manager Library, which includes* The One Minute
Manager, Putting the One Minute Manager to
Work, Leadership and the One Minute Manager,
and The One Minute Manager Builds High Performing Teams, *has collectively sold more than nine
million copies and has been translated into more than
twenty languages.*

For a long time, we have said that two different roles exist in
organizations. One has been called the leadership role—*doing
the right thing*. This has to do with vision and direction. The other
is the management role, which is *doing things right,* or implementation. I have never been a big fan of arguing about the difference
between leadership and management. Today I am even less interested in that argument, because I think that one of the problems we
have had in organizations is that the people who have created the
vision and the direction of the organization—the top managers—

don't roll up their sleeves and get involved in implementation. It always seems to be left to others in the organization. As a result, a lot of organizations are running with their brakes on. If you have ever driven a car with the brakes on, you know what happens when you finally release them. The car surges forward with tremendous energy. I think that will happen in organizations when we get the behavior or implementation of a vision lined up with that vision.

When people talk about *effectiveness*, they are basically talking about vision and direction. Effectiveness has to do with focusing the organization's energy in a particular direction. When people talk about *efficiency*, they are talking about systems and procedures—the way things are done. Efficiency is all about implementation. One of my colleagues, Dick Ruhe, has taken these two factors and put them into a two-dimensional model, going from low to high in each dimension (Figure 8.1). By putting efficiency on the horizontal axis and effectiveness on the vertical axis, Ruhe creates four combinations of effectiveness and efficiency. Companies that are neither efficient nor effective not only do not know where they are going, they are not organized to get there if they did. They are in the lower left-hand quadrant and are considered "lost." If you're lost, what do you start with—a vision or systems implementation? Obviously, you start with a vision.

What if your company is well organized? If you're high in efficiency but you're not clear about where you're going, you are in the lower right-hand quadrant and are considered a "questing" organization. You are looking for visionary leadership.

What if you're clear about where you're going but your systems aren't set up to implement the vision? Then you are in the upper left-hand quadrant and are considered what Ruhe calls "astray." Now you need to align your systems with your vision.

Only when your vision and implementation strategies are aligned can you get to the upper right-hand corner and be considered an "ultimate" organization, in which people can be empowered. The leader of the future has to manage the journey to effectiveness and efficiency to create an ultimate organization that knows where

Figure 8.1. The Quality LEAP Model.

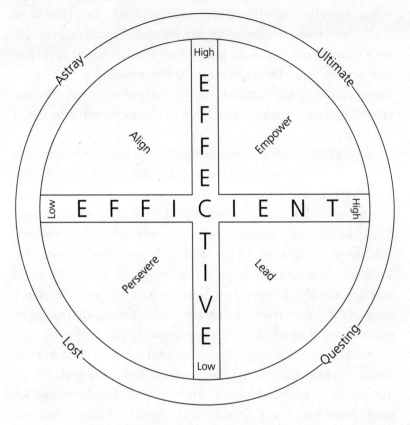

The Four Stages
with Interventions

it is going and in which everyone is committed, organized, and ready to implement an agreed-upon vision.

We can't have one group coming up with the vision, the values, and the direction and another group implementing them. Although the vision has to start at the top of the organization, everyone must be able to provide input and at least buy into that vision and direction. And once people know where they are going, top managers cannot divorce themselves from the implementation process. They have to get in and roll up their sleeves and be facilitators, cheerleaders, and supporters of getting the systems, the strategies, and the behaviors in line with that vision. In other words, they have to be both effective and efficient in future leadership. Even though people have talked about this in the past, I don't think it has been as clear as it is today that the leadership of the future must involve both vision and implementation. One is not a leadership role and the other a management role—both are in the arena of the leader of the future.

Saying that vision and implementation are both leadership roles makes some top managers nervous. Why? Because they know that something is going to have to change. Most organizations are typically pyramidal in nature. Who are at the top of the organization? The chief executive officer, the chairperson, the board of directors. Who are at the bottom? All the employees—the people who do the work, who make the products, sell the products, service the products, and the like. Now nothing is wrong with having a traditional pyramid for certain tasks. The paradox is that the pyramid has to be right side up or upside down depending on the task.

It is absolutely essential for the pyramid to stay upright when it comes to setting the vision, values, mission, and major goals. Moses did not go up to the mountain with a committee. If he had, he would never have come down. Nobody objects to vision, direction, and values coming from the top of the organization. But if the pyramid remains right side up when visions and goals are being implemented, all the energy and attention continues to flow back up the pyramid, away from the customers. As a result, we find people who have customer contact responding to requests by saying, "I'm sorry. We can't do that. It's against our policy." And the customer says, "What do you mean, it's against your policy? It's a stupid policy." And the reply? "I'm sorry. I just work here. They don't pay me to think. I leave my brains at the door and pick them up at the end of the day."

Why does this occur? Because the energy of the organization is going away from the customers. People are defending policies rather than serving customers. When the pyramid is right side up, who do you think you work for? The person above you. The minute you think you work for the person above you, you are assuming that this person—your boss—is *responsible* and that what your job consists of is being responsive to the boss and to his or her whims and wishes. When it comes to a choice between responding to a customer need or pleasing your boss, who wins? Your boss. That's because in the typical hierarchical organization, your future depends on your political skills up the hierarchy.

The leader of the future, realizing that vision and implementation are both leadership roles, will learn to care little about defending the traditional hierarchy. As a result, she or he will be willing to turn the pyramid upside down to implement a vision.

Who are at the top of the upside-down organization? The customer-contact people. Who are *really* at the top? The customers. Who is at the bottom? Top management. When you turn a pyramid upside down philosophically, you work for your people in implementing visions and goals. Although it seems minor, this one change makes a major difference. The difference is between who is *responsible* and who is *responsive*. In a traditional pyramid, the boss is always responsible and the subordinates are supposed to be responsive to the boss. When you turn the pyramid upside down, those roles are reversed. The people become responsible, and the job of management is to be responsive to them. This creates a very different environment for implementation. If you work for your people, your purpose as a leader is to help them accomplish their goals. The implementation job of leaders is to help people win by supporting them and removing barriers so that they can accomplish the goals that will make the vision become a reality.

To help people win, the leader of the future must be able to manage energy and change people's physical state of being. Setting the vision will focus people's attention and provide direction. Once that vision is set and people are committed to it, the role of the leader is to turn his or her attention to physiology—how people are acting and performing within the organization—and to align their performance with the vision. Here is where the leader of the future will excel as a cheerleader, supporter, and encourager rather than as a judge, critic, or evaluator. Helping people align their behavior with the organization's vision will solidify the attaining of desired goals and move energy in the desired direction. This results in an ultimate organization where people not only know where they are headed but are empowered to get there.

Part II

Future Leaders in Action

---

9 ROSABETH MOSS KANTER

World-Class Leaders

The Power of Partnering

*Rosabeth Moss Kanter holds the MBA Class of 1960
Chair as professor of management at Harvard Business School. Her latest book is* World Class: Thriv-
ing Locally in the Global Economy. *Among her
other best-selling, award-winning books are* When
Giants Learn to Dance, The Change Masters, *and*
Men and Women of the Corporation. *An adviser
and consultant to leading organizations worldwide
about the management of change, she was a cofounder of the Boston-based consulting firm Good-
measure, and serves on many public interest boards
and government commissions.*

Leadership is one of the most enduring, universal human responsibilities. The practice of leadership is sufficiently similar across
historical eras and civilizations that lessons are often drawn from

such disparate figures as Jesus Christ, Mahatma Gandhi, Attila the Hun, and Niccolò Machiavelli. Mary Parker Follett's perspectives on the relationship between leaders and followers, written seven decades ago, ring true today, as the recent rediscovery of her writings makes clear. Thus, in most important ways, leaders of the future will need the traits and capabilities of leaders throughout history: an eye for change and a steadying hand to provide both vision and reassurance that change can be mastered, a voice that articulates the will of the group and shapes it to constructive ends, and an ability to inspire by force of personality while making others feel empowered to increase and use their own abilities.

But there is one important difference today, one factor that will be even more critical to leaders of the future than to those of the past, one issue that must be added to the agenda for leadership development.

Many leaders of historical renown and many contemporary leaders of traditional institutions succeeded by focusing on the needs of their own organization and by being the best advocate for the interests of their own group. They could attract resources to their institution and then defend its borders, drawing sharp distinctions between insiders and outsiders, "us" and "them," and keeping outsiders at arm's length. Large bureaucratic corporations once made customers a remote abstraction, and only the sales force had regular contact. Nonprofit organizations once courted their donors for funds but did not include them in program activities, and sometimes their managers and professionals actively discussed how to keep the board or the clients from "interfering" with professional decisions. And each organization seemed to feel that it could best meet its goals by protecting its own base, thereby engendering suspicion about its relationships with other organizations.

Leaders of the future can no longer afford to maintain insularity. It is simply not an option in an increasingly borderless world of boundaryless organizations driven by "customer power": the fact is that people can increasingly bypass local monopolies or protected local suppliers and shop the world for the best goods and services. In short, leaders of the past often erected walls. Now they must destroy those walls and replace them with bridges.

The Need for Cosmopolitan Leaders

Leaders must become *cosmopolitans* who are comfortable operating across boundaries and who can forge links between organizations. Leaders must take their ability to craft visions, inspire action, and empower others and use it to encourage people from diverse functions, disciplines, and organizations to find common cause in goals that improve the entire industry, community, country, or world and expand the pie for everyone, rather than pushing in narrow parochial interests that pit group against group, wasting resources in a scramble for shrinking slices of the pie. They must become cosmopolitans who have the vision, skills, and resources to form networks that extend beyond their home base and to bring benefits to their own group by partnering with others.

Cosmopolitans are not simply well-traveled global citizens; some people who travel remain hopelessly parochial, and many broad-thinking cosmopolitans are highly committed to their local communities. Cosmopolitans are leaders with open minds and outreach to partners. They are receptive to information from outside their current framework and take pleasure in new experiences and ideas. They are a step ahead of others in envisioning new possibilities that break the mold.

These abstractions about leadership in the emerging global economy and information age come to life when I think about exemplary leaders who have already changed their role in organizational construction to wall destroyers and bridge builders, paving the way (to extend the construction metaphor) in industries of the future.

The New Cosmopolitans in Action:
From Software to City Year

Consider Mitchell Kertzman, founder and chairman of Powersoft, a fast-growth company that is a respected world standard setter in networking software tools and, since early 1995, part of Sybase. Software is one of the most rapidly growing fields for employment, a driver of the information age, and an inherently boundaryless industry that thrives on networks, alliances, and partnerships. Powersoft's culture, as shaped by Kertzman and his colleagues, is highly cosmopolitan. "Born global," Powersoft recognized from the start the importance of international sales and standards, even to sell products at home, because its customers more easily cross borders and must be supported wherever they are.

To accommodate intense competition, Powersoft must be entrepreneurial, innovating constantly. Therefore, the company's culture must be open in two directions: open to customers, whose voices and views are the best guide to product development, and open to all of Powersoft's people, whose ideas must be heard. As reflected in focus group discussions, Kertzman and other top executives are lauded by associates for their friendliness, accessibility, and interest in the associates' ideas, which encourages initiative.

Perhaps Kertzman's most significant bridge-building effort involves Powersoft's large set of partners, some casual but many very close. With under eight hundred people in early 1995, Powersoft is far from a giant, but its reach is vast. Its partnership network mushrooms to include tens of thousands of people working in its interests. For example, thirteen thousand software developers received training in Powersoft tools in 1993 and serve as an extended family. In an industry characterized by dense ties, Powersoft's emphasis on relationships stand out; it even has a department to manage relationships, guided by an executive for alliances. Multiple advantages come from a major relationship with Lotus, headquartered a short drive away: sharing manufacturing space; taking advantage of

Lotus's packaging technology, which dropped the cost for Powersoft packages from about eleven dollars to about one dollar per box; and contributing Powersoft ideas to Lotus through shared development projects. Joint projects with other companies help to integrate Powersoft tools with their programs. Marketing allies and resellers are affectionately known as "power channels" and are treated as partners to be included in planning discussions.

In many sectors, entrepreneurial leaders who are building new models for their industries are thinking across boundaries and leading through partnering, forming networks, and managing collaborations. Ruth Owades founded Calyx & Corolla to sell fresh flowers by catalog, thereby bypassing an entire established distribution chain of growers, wholesalers, regional produce markets, local florists, and their national network, FTD, which permitted local shops to fulfill orders for one another throughout the country. Owades's vision of an attractive alternative (flowers arriving at the consumer's doorstep as fresh as or fresher than flowers from a local shop) was built around an alternative network: a partnership with a score of leading growers and Federal Express.

Some networks not only build bridges across industries; they also bridge the for-profit and not-for-profit sectors. Rina Spence opened her first Spence Center for Women's Health in 1995 in Boston and was influenced by my ideas about partnering. Rather than duplicating services that established institutions were already providing (and might provide better), she focused on the customer service interface and formed alliances between her for-profit, investor-owned company and a range of other institutions: for example, she asked Brigham and Women's Hospital to run a radiology lab. She explored partnering with a retailer and with a publisher of medical books to offer their health-oriented wares in her facilities. And she focused her own staff on integrating both external and internal resources for the benefit of her customers.

One of the things that makes these new (or newly popular) kinds of relationships effective is that they follow the traditional guidelines for leadership: clarity of vision and creation of a strong culture that includes and empowers people. But in addition, the vision has room for partners who will also benefit from it, and the culture produces strong people who feel stronger when they connect than when they protect.

This kind of leadership is alive and well among the members of the next generation. Alan Khazei and Michael Brown, cofounders and codirectors of City Year, are stunning examples. Created in 1988 in Boston by these Harvard Law School graduates as a private sector domestic Peace Corps, City Year has since expanded to Providence, Rhode Island; Chicago; Columbus, Ohio; San Jose, California; and Columbia, South Carolina. A model for America's national youth service program, its impact resonates not only in improvements to the communities its corps members serve but also through the lives of corps members, the involvement of employees of corporate sponsors, and the growth of civic collaborations.

City Year's six hundred diverse corps members, aged seventeen through twenty-three, earn $125 per week during their year of service and receive a $4,725 grant for college or a $4,000 savings bond on graduation. Corps members begin each day with calisthenics in a high-profile downtown location, then disperse with their team to work in areas where they might assist public school or day care teachers, serve meals to elders, run recycling programs, or create a health immunization tracking system. Privileged suburbanites serve on teams alongside inner-city youth, enabling friendships to form across class and race lines. To graduate, corps members must learn first aid and CPR, learn to write a résumé and file taxes, get a library card, and register to vote, and corps members without high school diplomas must participate in City Year's GED program. Graduate Stephen Noltemy declared, "City Year saved my life."

City Year's activities are performed in partnership with social service agencies, neighborhood groups, public schools, and other community institutions that define projects for corps members as well as for the adult volunteers who turn out for Serve-a-Thons (periodic days of service). In Boston, the 1994 Serve-a-Thon included ten thousand volunteers washing 5,839 windows, painting fifteen miles of walls and fifty-three schools, cleaning 465 elders' apartments, beautifying thirty-five parks, and salvaging eleven tons of food at 296 sites.

Corporate partners contribute service as well as money. Bank of Boston was the first company to sponsor a City Year team with $25,000 and eventually donated nearly $600,000, sponsoring teams whose City Year uniforms bear the bank's logo; in addition, five hundred bank employees regularly participate in Serve-a-Thons. "What could we lose?" senior vice president Ira Jackson recalled. "It had all the right elements: urban Peace Corps, kids, help the city." City Year also attracts cosmopolitan companies located far outside the city that have come back downtown to serve it, including Digital Equipment, Reebok, and Timberland, which is just across the New Hampshire line from Boston and provides the outfits for corps members.

The Timberland partnership is especially strong and represents a pioneering model. Jeff Swartz, Timberland's chief operating officer and City Year's board chair, feels that Timberland's partnership with City Year has transformed his company's culture. Timberland's personnel policies guarantee associates at least four service days a year on company time. Performing community service together through City Year is an important way Timberland develops its internal working teams; City Year staff have also run their team-building sessions for Timberland employees. In April 1995, City Year and Timberland introduced a unique joint venture between a nonprofit and a for-profit firm: City Year Gear, a line of T-shirts and accessories that tout community service, fund City Year programs and Timberland's community service, and allow people to sign up for service.

City Year draws companies into the service fold that have not traditionally contributed to local communities and encourages them to cooperate with one another, including consulting firms and law

firms, which might jointly sponsor a City Year team. By encouraging active employee participation rather than approaching companies only for fund-raising, City Year offers a model for treating
donors as partners and involving them in service.

Any number can sponsor teams, which allows many companies
to put their brand on an activity or take pride in what their people
do at Serve-a-Thons. Breadth of sponsorship is a City Year value,
because it increases civic engagement. City Year applauds the model
of a decentralized organization that matches public funds with local
contributions, and it operates a national program that is really
"multilocal": communities concentrating on their own needs but
learning from one another.

City Year's core concept is innovative, and staff are encouraged
to be entrepreneurial in seeking new concepts; its organizational
competence is built around constant learning, and its connections
become the basis for three-way partnerships among the public, private, and nonprofit sectors. The City Year model is successful
because it concentrates the resources of many organizations on
high-priority problems and engages many organizations and many
people in the work of the community.

That's how the organization works as a model of the new partnering. Behind this model are Khazei and Brown, the leaders who
set it in motion and who reflect the new leadership style:

• Like Hewlett and Packard, they began as a team and have
concentrated on sharing and spreading leadership rather than
encouraging a cult of personality (perhaps one reason Hewlett-
Packard has leaped ahead of single-founder-driven rivals such as
Digital Equipment).

• They are extremely learning-oriented. They keep track of
lessons drawn from experience in "what's worked" lists that are
shared with everyone, and they try to articulate principles that will
transfer experience from one activity to another. They include
many members of the staff in brainstorming. They encourage open-

ness to new ideas and do not assume that they already have the answers within their own minds or within the organization.

• They respect their partners. They embrace them literally as well as figuratively. They are not afraid of affection, nor do they close the circle to outsiders. Sponsors, funders, angels, and champions are welcomed by City Year members. Indeed, several executives from companies sponsoring City Year teams have joined City Year full-time.

• They see across boundaries. They look at the whole system in a community and see how to connect with it, to add value to already-established activities. They think beyond the category into which they are placed—just a "youth corps"—and see how to leverage their skills and get more people involved in more activities. They connect with companies in other sectors and see even more opportunities to enlarge their network.

From Force of Personality to Quality of Mind

Cosmopolitan leaders of the future must be *integrators* who can look beyond obvious differences among organizations, sectors, disciplines, functions, or cultures. They must be *diplomats* who can resolve conflicts between the different ways that organizations or communities or countries operate and who can influence people to work together, to find common cause. They must be *cross-fertilizers* who can bring the best from one place to another. And they must be *deep thinkers* who are smart enough to see new possibilities and to conceptualize them.

The intellectual functions of leaders have often been neglected in discussions of leadership. Charisma, force of personality, or interpersonal skills have often been stressed more than the brainpower required for leaders to think through problems and find new solutions. Mental agility is especially essential in times of social transformation. In the global economy of the information age, ideas and events are reshaping—or threatening to reshape—every social and economic institution. In every area, received wisdom about categories, distinctions, and groupings is being challenged. Trying to lead while the system itself is being reshaped puts a premium on brains: to imagine possibilities outside of conventional categories, to envision actions that cross traditional boundaries, to anticipate repercussions and take advantage of interdependencies, to make new connections or invent new combinations. Those who lack the mental flexibility to think across boundaries will find it harder and harder to hold their own, let alone prosper.

Generating new ideas challenges boundaries. Innovations grow out of unexpected, surprising, and even irreverent mental connections. Developing them requires collaborations and adjustments by many parts of organizations and the networks surrounding them. Entrepreneurial opportunities do not respect territories; they do not present themselves in the boxes established on organizational charts. The more rigid the walls between functions or between companies, the less likely it is that people will venture out of their boxes to try something new. It is up to cosmopolitan leaders to encourage others to open their minds and tap the power of partnering within organizations as well as across them.

10 JAMES M. KOUZES
BARRY Z. POSNER

Seven Lessons for Leading the Voyage to the Future

*James M. Kouzes is chairman and chief executive
officer of TPG/Learning Systems, a company in the
Tom Peters Group, based in Palo Alto, California.
Barry Z. Posner is professor of organizational behavior
and managing partner of the Executive Development
Center, Leavey School of Business and Administra-
tion, Santa Clara University. In addition to the best-
selling and award-winning book* The Leadership
Challenge, *Kouzes and Posner have coauthored*
Credibility: How Leaders Gain and Lose It, Why
People Demand It, *selected by* Industry Week *as
one of the five best management books of 1993.*

The cynics are winning. People are fed up, angry, disgusted, and
pessimistic about their future. Alienation is higher than it has
been in a quarter-century. Loyalty to institutions—and institutions'

Note: Portions of this article are adapted from *The Leadership Challenge: How to
Keep Getting Extraordinary Things Done in Organizations,* by James M. Kouzes and
Barry Z. Posner (San Francisco: Jossey-Bass, 1995). Copyright © 1995 by James M.
Kouzes and Barry Z. Posner. All rights reserved.

loyalty to people—is sinking like a stone. No longer would we
rather fight than switch; we just switch. Nearly half the population
is cynical, and cynics don't participate in improving things. In such
a climate, how can a leader possibly mobilize a seemingly unwilling
constituency toward some unknown and even more uncertain
future? Who would want to?

Perhaps it would be Charlie Mae Knight. When Knight was
appointed the new superintendent for the Ravenswood School District in East Palo Alto, California, she was the twelfth superintendent in ten years. She encountered a district in which 50 percent
of the schools were closed and 98 percent of the children were performing in the lowest percentile for academic achievement in California. The district had the state's lowest revenue rate. There were
buckets in classrooms to catch the rain leaking through decrepit
roofs, the stench from the restrooms was overwhelming, homeless
organizations were operating out of the school sites, and pilfering
was rampant. Gophers and rats had begun to take over the facilities. As if this weren't challenging enough, Knight had to wrestle
with a lawsuit that had gone on for ten years, whose intent was to
dissolve the district for its poor educational quality and force the
children to transfer to schools outside of their community.

These challenges would discourage almost anyone. But not
Knight. After assuming the post, she immediately enlisted support
from Bay Area companies and community foundations to obtain
the badly needed resources. The first project she undertook was
refurbishing the Garden Oaks School. Volunteer engineers from
nearby Raychem Corporation repaired the electrical wiring and
phone systems. A volunteer rat patrol used pellet guns to eliminate
the pesky rodents from the site. The community helped paint the
building inside and out, and hardware stores donated supplies.

Before too long, local residents began calling to find out what
color paint was used for the school so they could paint their houses
in a matching shade. They went out and bought trees and sod and
planted them in front of their homes. New leadership came forth

from parents who began to demand more of a say. In response, an "Effort Hours" program for parents was set up so that they could volunteer time at the school. Teachers began to notice that something was happening, and they wanted to be part of it too. The district was on a roll.

Within two years of Knight's arrival, the children exceeded the goal of performing in the fifty-first percentile on academic achievement scores. (Today one of the district's schools has climbed to the sixty-eighth percentile, miles above the first percentile, where it started.) The district has one of the first schools in the state to use technology in every discipline, outdistancing every school in California technologically, and it has the first elementary school to join the Internet. The lawsuit has been dropped. Revenues are up from $1,900 per student to $3,500. And for the first time ever, East Palo Alto received the state's Distinguished School Award, based on its improved test scores and innovative programs.

If we are going to *have* a future—let alone thrive in one—we can learn a few things from the Charlie Mae Knights of the world. Here are seven lessons we've gained from her and thousands of other venturers about what it takes to clean up today's spirit-polluting cynicism and transform it into hope.

Lesson 1: Leaders Don't Wait

Like other leaders who achieve extraordinary results, Knight knew she had to produce some early victories. "It's hard to get anybody excited just about a vision. You must show something happening," she told us. "Winning at the beginning was so important because winning provided some indication of movement. I had to show some visible signs that change was taking place in order to keep up the momentum, and in order to restore confidence in the people that we *could* provide quality education."

This proactive leadership spirit is vividly illustrated in an early recruiting poster for Operation Raleigh, now called Youth Service

International, with U.S. offices in Raleigh, North Carolina. At the top of the poster, printed in big, bold letters, are the words: "Venturers Wanted!" Below the headline is a photograph of a group of people neck deep in a swamp with broad smiles on their faces. The recruiting copy reads in part:

> **Join the Voyage of Discovery**
>
> For 1500 young Americans between the ages of 17 and 24, it will be the adventure of a lifetime. Underwater archaeology on sunken ships, aerial walkways in tropical rainforests, medical relief for remote tribal villages—innovative, exciting, worthwhile projects. . . .
>
> Science and service are the themes and leadership development is a primary goal. It is the pioneer spirit of Sir Walter Raleigh's day rekindled, and you are invited to apply.

Leadership opportunities are indeed adventures of a lifetime and require a pioneering spirit. Starting a new organization, turning around a losing operation, greatly improving the social condition, enhancing the quality of people's lives—these are all uplifting human endeavors. Waiting for permission to begin them is *not* characteristic of leaders. Acting with a sense of urgency *is*. If you're going to lead now or in the future, the first thing you've got to do is launch a voyage of discovery.

Lesson 2: Character Counts

For the last two decades we have asked people to tell us what they "look for and admire in a leader, in a person whose direction they would willingly follow." The qualities that were the consistent winners were "honest," "forward-looking," "inspiring," and "competent."

These characteristics comprise what communication experts refer to as "source credibility." In assessing the believability of sources of information—whether they are newscasters, salespeople, managers, physicians, politicians, or priests—those who rate more highly on these dimensions are considered to be more credible sources of information.

What we found in our investigation of admired leadership qualities is that, more than anything, we want leaders who are credible. We must be able to believe in them. We must believe that their word can be trusted, that they are personally excited and enthusiastic about the direction in which we are headed, and that they have the knowledge and skill to lead. We call it the *first law of leadership:* "If you don't believe in the messenger, you won't believe the message."

At the core of personal credibility are one's beliefs. (Credibility derives from the Latin word *credo,* meaning "I believe.") People expect their leaders to stand for something and to have the courage of their convictions. If leaders are not clear about what they believe in, they are much more likely to change their position with every fad or opinion poll. Therefore, the first milestone on the journey to leadership credibility is *clarity of personal values*.

Lesson 3: Leaders Have Their Head in the Clouds and Their Feet on the Ground

Not only do we demand that leaders be credible; we also demand that they be forward-looking: that they have a sense of direction and a vision for the future. This capacity to paint an uplifting and ennobling picture of the future is, in fact, what differentiates leaders from other credible sources.

Visions are about possibilities, about desired futures, and it is images of great potential that Nolan Dishongh most definitely wants to spark in his at-risk students. Many of the fourteen- to sixteen-year-olds in Dishongh's construction trades class at Alice Johnson Junior High School, twenty-five miles east of Houston, have well-earned reputations as troublemakers, as the students with short attention spans, low grades, and little interest in learning. Many are from broken or abusive homes; some are known gang members.

Dishongh sets the tone at the start of each school year by asking his students to lay their heads on their desks. Then, in a deep, soothing tone, he instructs them to think about their mother, to feel her loving them even before they were born, to think about her holding them closely as infants, feeding them, and singing to them. He asks them to try to remember how that felt, and he encourages them to think about how proud she was when they said their first word and took their first step. "See her smiling," he implores. "See her eyes shining as she claps her hands with joy and hugs you." Dishongh asks them to think about what they have done to repay their mother for all that she has done to raise them: cooking their food, washing their clothes. He says, "She *loves* you, no matter what, but what makes her happy is being proud of you."

Next, Dishongh tells the students to be very still and breathe deeply, saying, "Imagine now that you are dying. The next four or five breaths will be your last. As you call out her name with your last breath, are you calling out to a mother you have made proud by the things you did in your life, or to a mother who will always feel sorrow for the life you led? I believe that each and every one of you *wants* your mother to be proud of you. I know I do. And that's what we're doing here. It's not about grades. It's about your mother being proud."

At this point it is not unusual to see a few boys wipe tears from their eyes. Dishongh promises to start them on a journey of self-discovery, to help them find a sense of their own self-worth and their ability to change, a journey that will permanently affect their lives, not just a year at school. The youths quickly realize that this is not a normal classroom and Dishongh is not a "normal" teacher. He cares. He believes that they can be someone to be proud of—not at risk but full of possibilities.

Lesson 4: Shared Values Make a Difference

As important as it is for leaders to forthrightly articulate their vision and values, what they say must be consistent with the aspirations of their constituents. Constituents also have needs and interests, dreams and beliefs, of their own. If leaders advocate values that are not representative of the collective will, they will not be able to mobilize people to act as one. Leaders must be able to gain consensus on a common cause and a common set of principles. They must be able to build a community of shared values.

In our own research we have carefully examined the relationship between personal and organizational values. Our studies show that shared values

- Foster strong feelings of personal effectiveness

- Promote high levels of loyalty to the organization

- Facilitate consensus about key organizational goals and the organization's stakeholders

- Encourage ethical behavior

- Promote strong norms about working hard and caring

- Reduce levels of job stress and tension

- Foster pride in the organization

- Facilitate understanding about job expectations

- Foster teamwork and esprit de corps

People tend to drift when they are unsure or confused about how they ought to be operating. The energy that goes into coping with, and repeatedly debating, incompatible values takes its toll on both personal effectiveness and organizational productivity. Consensus about long- and short-term values creates commitment to where the organization is going and how it's going to get there. Although leaders do not wait for anyone, if they don't build consensus on vision and values, they will be all alone!

Lesson 5: You Can't Do It Alone

Early in our research we asked Bill Flanagan, vice president of operations for Amdahl Corporation, to describe his personal best. After a few moments, Flanagan said that he couldn't do it. Startled, we asked him why. Flanagan replied, "Because it wasn't *my* personal best. It was *our* personal best. It wasn't *me*. It was *us*." Leadership is not a solo act. In the thousands of personal-best leadership cases we have studied, we have yet to encounter a single example of extraordinary achievement that occurred without the active involvement and support of many people. We don't expect to find any in the future, either.

Creating competition between group members is not the route to high performance; fostering collaboration is, particularly if the conditions are extremely challenging and urgent. Author and university lecturer Alfie Kohn, in *No Contest: The Case Against Competition* (1986), explains it this way: "The simplest way to understand why competition generally does not promote excellence is to realize that *trying to do well and trying to beat others are two different things*" (p. 55). One is about accomplishing the superior, the other about making another inferior. One is about achievement, the other about subordination. Rather than focusing on stomping the competition into the ground, true leaders focus on creating value for their customers, intelligence and skill in their students, wellness in their patients, and pride in their citizens. In a more complex, wired world, the winning strategies will always be based upon the "we," not "I," philosophy.

Lesson 6: The Legacy You Leave Is the Life You Lead

The first thing Les Cochran did after becoming president at Ohio's Youngstown State University (YSU) in July 1992 was to purchase an abandoned building on the edge of campus and spend his free weekends working with construction crews to transform it into a residence for his family. While it is not unusual for college presidents to live near their campus, Cochran's determination to do so attracted a great deal of attention and set the tone for his presidency.

To many, Cochran was literally putting his life on the line, for the once lovely neighborhoods surrounding YSU had surrendered to increasingly aggressive gangs and escalating drug-related crime following the collapse of Youngstown's steel-mill-dependent economy in the early 1980s. Cochran believed that the only way to reclaim YSU from the fear, hopelessness, apathy, and mistrust that paralyzed the campus and the surrounding community was to start the process by claiming as his home one of these decaying neighborhoods. His message was clear: "We are responsible, both individually and collectively, for the fate of this community." Thus, when he declared "Together we can make a difference" to be his philosophy of individual contribution to community involvement, people knew that he believed deeply in what he was saying. By buying and refurbishing a home in an area he was determined to reclaim for YSU, Cochran "walked the talk."

When asking others to change, as Cochran did, it is not enough for leaders to deliver a rousing speech. Even though compelling words are essential to uplift people's spirits, Cochran and other leaders know that constituents are moved by deeds. They expect leaders to show up, to pay attention, and to participate directly in the process of getting extraordinary things done. Leaders take every opportunity to show others by their own example that they are deeply committed to the aspirations they espouse. Leading by example is how leaders make visions and values tangible. It is how they provide the *evidence* that they are personally committed. That evidence is what people look for and admire in leaders, people whose direction they would willingly follow.

In our extensive research on credibility in leaders, we asked people to tell us how they know if someone is credible. The most frequent response was, "They do what they say they will do." Setting an example is essential to earning credibility. When it comes to deciding whether a leader is believable, people first listen to the words and then watch the actions. A judgment of "credible" is handed down when the two are consonant.

How you lead *your* life determines whether people want to put *their* life in your hands. If you dream of leaving a legacy, you'd better heed the golden rule of leadership: *Do what you say you will do*.

Lesson 7: Leadership Is Everyone's Business

Myth associates leadership with superior position. It assumes that leadership starts with a capital "L," and that when you are on top you are automatically a leader. But leadership is not a place; it is a process. It involves skills and abilities that are useful whether one is in the executive suite or on the front line, on Wall Street or Main Street.

The most pernicious myth of all is that leadership is reserved for only a very few of us. The myth is perpetuated daily whenever anyone asks, "Are leaders born or made?" Leadership is certainly not a gene, and it is most definitely not something mystical and ethereal that cannot be understood by ordinary people. It is not true that only a lucky few can ever decipher the leadership code. Our research has shown us that leadership is an observable, learnable set of practices. In over fifteen years of research we have been fortunate to hear and read the stories of over 2,500 ordinary people who have led others to get extraordinary things done. There are millions more. If we have learned one singular lesson about leadership from all of these cases, it is that leadership is everyone's business.

Just ask Melissa Poe of St. Henry's School in Nashville, Tennessee. On August 4, 1989, as a fourth-grader fearful of the continued destruction of the Earth's resources, Poe wrote a letter to President George Bush, asking for his assistance in her campaign to save the environment for the enjoyment of future generations.

After sending the letter, Poe worried that it would never be brought to the president's attention. After all, she was only a child. So, with the urgency of the issue pressing on her mind, she decided to get the president's attention by having her letter placed on a billboard. Through sheer diligence and hard work, the nine-year-old got her letter placed on one billboard free of charge in September 1989 and founded Kids for a Clean Environment (Kids F.A.C.E.), an organization whose goal is to develop programs to clean up the environment.

Almost immediately, Poe began receiving letters from children who were as concerned as she was about the environment and who wanted to help. When Poe finally received the disappointing form letter from the president, it didn't crush her dream. She no longer needed the help of someone famous to get her message across. Poe had found in herself the person she needed—that powerful someone who could inspire others to get involved and make her dream a reality.

Within nine months, more than 250 billboards across the country were displaying her letter free of charge, and membership in Kids F.A.C.E. had swelled. As the organization grew, Poe's first Kids F.A.C.E. project, a recycling program at her school, led to a manual full of ideas on how to clean up the environment. Poe's impatience and zest motivated her to do something—and her work has paid off. Today there are more than two hundred thousand members and two thousand chapters of Kids F.A.C.E. Poe is proof that you don't have to wait for someone else to lead, and you can lead without a title, a position, or a budget.

When leadership is viewed as a nonlearnable set of character traits or as equivalent to an exalted position, a self-fulfilling prophecy is created that dooms societies to having only a few good leaders. It is far healthier and more productive for us to start with the assumption that it is possible for everyone to lead. If we assume that leadership is learnable, we can discover how many good leaders there really are. Leadership may be exhibited on behalf of the school, the church, the community, the Boy Scouts or Girl Scouts, the union, or the family. Somewhere, sometime, the leader within each of us may get the call to step forward.

We should not mislead people into believing that they can attain unrealistic goals. Neither should we assume that only a few will ever attain excellence in leadership or any other human endeavor. Those who are most successful at bringing out the best in others are the people who set achievable goals that stretch them, and who believe that they have the ability to develop the talents of others.

From what we observed in our research, as more and more people answer the call, we will rejoice in the outcome. For we discovered, and rediscovered, that leadership is not the private reserve of a few charismatic men and women. It is a process that ordinary people use when they are bringing forth the best from themselves and others. We believe that whether you are in the private sector or the public sector, whether you are an employee or a volunteer, whether you are on the front line or in the senior echelon, whether you are a student or a parent, you are capable of developing yourself as a leader far more than tradition has ever assumed possible. When we liberate the leader in everyone, extraordinary things happen.

11 JAMES L. HESKETT
LEONARD A. SCHLESINGER

Leaders Who Shape and Keep Performance-Oriented Culture

*James L. Heskett is UPS Foundation Professor of
Business Logistics at the Graduate School of Business
Administration, Harvard University. He is the
author of* Managing in the Service Economy *and
coauthor of* Corporate Culture and Performance,
Service Breakthroughs: Changing the Rules of
the Game, *and* The Service Management Course.
*Leonard A. Schlesinger is the George Fisher Baker,
Jr., Professor of Business Administration, senior
associate dean, and director of external relations at
the Harvard Business School. He is the author of
more than forty articles and eight books, including*
The Real Heroes of Business . . . and Not a CEO
Among Them, *with Bill Fromm, and* Out in Front:
Building High-Capability Service Organizations,
with James L. Heskett.

Over the last several years, we have sought in various ways to discover the linkages between leadership behavior and organizational performance. We weren't so naive as to assume that the popular perception of the successful leader as commander, controller, decision maker, assimilator of power, and teller of truths, most often ensconced in a top-floor office and purposely isolated from the day-to-day fire fighting of the organization, would prove to characterize our leaders. But neither were we prepared for what we did find.

What we found were leaders of the best-performing organizations in their respective profit-making and social sector "industries" who defined their jobs in terms of identifying and constantly communicating commonly held values, shaping such values to enhance performance, ensuring the capability of people around them, living the commonly held values, listening a great deal of the time, and literally speaking a different language than their traditional counterparts. In short, they saw themselves as *shapers* and *keepers* of performance-oriented cultures.

The leaders in our sample do not march in lockstep to a different drummer. Nor do they necessarily represent a leadership style for all seasons and all national cultures. But the parallels in their behavior form a powerful collective picture that must give any observer of effective leadership in today's society pause for thought. To illustrate these parallels, we cite just six out of a much larger sample of possibilities: a special use of language, listening skills, values propagation, enhancement of employee capability, clarification of core values, and insurance of dignity.

Speaking a Different Language

The first thing one notices about our group of leaders is the surprising language they use. Although language is only a symptom, it's not a bad place to start in an exploration of leadership styles.

The CEO of Banc One, by several measures the best-performing large bank in the United States, has defined his job as managing an "uncommon partnership" that fosters maximum local autonomy for carefully selected managers combined with effective centrally provided services and common performance measures. The chairman of the board of ServiceMaster, the most successful support services organization in the United States, looked for a "servant's heart" as the primary criterion in selecting his successor to serve as CEO. The former head of what many regard as the best-led and best-managed social sector organization, the Girl Scouts, described her job as ensuring that the organization remained "mission-focused, values-based, and demographics-driven," with the latter term directed at the need for greater diversity in the organization. The CEO of the most successful major U.S. airline, Southwest Airlines, talked to us about hiring as a "near-religious experience."

This is not the language one expects from tough-minded, tough-talking leaders. But tough talk by others apparently has not produced the kind of results that these leaders have delivered.

Listening Versus Telling

Front-line managers are often trained to listen to the needs of customers. Those who perform well are generally rewarded with promotion away from customers. With each succeeding promotion, they are increasingly looked to for "the word," and are venerated to greater degrees. They also tend to acquire the habit of telling more and listening less. This behavior runs counter to the leadership behavior we have encountered in our small sample of performance-oriented organizations.

The head of Banc One is known for disclaiming any knowledge of how to run the many banks he leads. Instead, he regards his role as watching the performance numbers, listening to requests for assistance from associates, and making sure that those in need are put in touch with colleagues in the organization who can help them. In order to encourage everyone in his organization to listen, the chairman and former CEO of ServiceMaster required all managers to do a day of work in the field cleaning floors, walls, and toilets or serving food to customers and customers of customers. What they found out was useful. The signals they sent to employees and customers were invaluable.

Most of our sample leaders and their organizations practice the "open-door" policy that is often associated with paternal organizations of the past. For example, the CEO of Southwest Airlines goes to Employees (always capitalized at Southwest) if they will not come to him. It enables them to listen better. The break with the past comes in what they do with the information. Instead of using it to take action against someone, more often, they use it to launch new initiatives or put people in touch with each other who can provide mutual assistance and support. As long as information is used in this manner, the organization responds and performs.

Living the Values

In our research, we have found that organizations with strong cultures do not have any special claims to success and longevity. Those that embrace values that honor and support adaptability do. These values reward sensitivity to the needs of customers, employees, suppliers, and other important constituencies. They are stated in terms such as the erstwhile corporate slogan, "People who care," at Banc One; an "ends" goal, "to help people develop" (in addition to a "means" goal, "to grow profitably"), at ServiceMaster; a goal of "helping every girl achieve her full potential" for the Girl Scouts; and an emphasis on "family" at Southwest Airlines, with family including customers as well as employees.

Adaptability requires a different set of leadership behaviors. Banc One executives travel constantly to provide face-to-face opportunities to listen. At ServiceMaster, senior executives work alongside employees of customers' organizations and engage in extensive outside charity work. At the Girl Scouts, the former executive director consistently used the same language to convey the mission and values of the organization, indicating to us that "the power of language is so important in this job." At Southwest Airlines, the CEO leads the work at the "family's" adopted charity,

Ronald McDonald houses, and over 90 percent of the company's Employees engage in similar activities in their communities.

Ensuring Employee Capability

Our research on a broad array of organizations with strong performance has led us to one of the best-kept secrets of competitive success. It is that the most important determinants of profit and growth are customer loyalty and satisfaction, factors that directly relate to employee satisfaction and the loyalty and productivity that go with it. Repeatedly, we have been told by employees that the capability to do their respective jobs is the most important determinant of their satisfaction. Capability is developed in many ways, not the least of which are effective selection and job assignment, training, the appropriate technological support, and efforts to put employees in touch with others who can help them. The outstanding leaders we have observed know this and spend their time accordingly.

The central notion of the Uncommon Partnership at Banc One is the provision of outstanding products and support technology and processes to the people in local banking outlets who are responsible for relations with retail customers. ServiceMaster spends several times more than its competitors to develop cleaning materials, equipment, and processes that ensure maximum productivity and quality in the work of the people it supervises and to train the people who apply them. For years, the Girl Scouts has sponsored what, by any measure, has to be one of the world's largest training programs in leadership outside the military. With more than 750,000 volunteers, many of whom are leading for the first time, it considers leadership training the key to organizational and individual capability. At Southwest Airlines, the guideline is: "Do whatever you feel comfortable doing for the customer." This requires not only that Employees have the necessary latitude to act but also that they have the information and other support with which to do so intelligently and the loyalty to do so in the best interests of the company as well as its customers. The leaders of these organizations take a personal interest in ensuring the capability of their associates. As the CEO of Banc One put it, "My role is chief personnel officer. If I get the right people in the right job, that's all I have to do."

Defining, Shaping, and Using Core Values

At the heart of the new leadership is a rediscovery of the need to define, shape, and use the commonly held core values of the organization. Notice that we said "rediscovery." This is not new. It is something that the founders of some of the largest companies intuitively recognized as important in the early days of American business. An IBM CEO characterized that company's core values as recently as 1960, when he reminded everyone in the company of the importance of respect for the individual, customer service, and excellence, the values on which his father had built the company. It is all too rare today for values to be defined, shaped, communicated, and used, but this is always done in the organizations whose performance has caught our attention.

The process of definition and communication requires leadership. It's the CEO at Banc One who periodically validates the importance and communicates the elements of the Uncommon Partnership. The values underlying the Partnership are applied whenever each of Banc One's many acquisition prospects are evaluated; they must have integrity and the capability to manage themselves. At ServiceMaster, values are reviewed as part of a longer-range planning process every five years under the leadership of the CEO. Here, too, the values are used as a template against which to appraise the management of potential acquisitions. Just as important, they are being codified to help ServiceMaster in selecting managers into the organization. Girl Scouts abide by The Promise and The Law, much of which anyone who has been a Girl Scout can recite years later. They are reviewed, although rarely altered, as part of a three-year planning cycle. At Southwest Airlines, an Employee team entrusted with designing initiatives to help maintain the company's culture takes its cues from a charismatic CEO who spends much of his time communicating commonly held values in a rapidly growing organization.

Power Through Dignity

None of the leaders of the top-performing organizations we have observed qualify as stereotypes of the "take-charge" philosophy of leadership. They are powerful, but they derive their power in ways that suggest a redefinition of the term. In fact, one important source of their power is the dignity they nurture in those around them and at all levels in their respective organizations.

Those who have studied power characterize its sources in terms of positional (or bestowed) power, expert power (knowledge of the job), personal attraction (affective appeal), and effort (personal commitment). Our leaders are experts in many areas and certainly derive some portion of their power from that fact. But their expertise lies not in their knowledge of others' jobs or their ability to appear as experts. (In response to a question about how he accounts for his organization's performance, the CEO of Southwest Airlines says, "I'd like to attribute it to brilliant leadership, but I can't. It's the people of the airline and their feelings for customers and one another.") These leaders place little reliance on traditional conceptions of positional authority and show little evidence that they cement their positions by herculean work efforts. Rather, their power lies in the areas of expertise we have outlined here: use of language, listening skills, propagation of values, enhancement of employee capability, clarification of core values, and assurance of dignity. Further, their power lies in their ability to foster relationships, both between themselves and others and among others. *Relational power* thus is a term that might be added to the lexicon.

Keeping the Culture

CEOs in the organizations we have studied understand the competitive advantage that the right kind of culture bestows, and they work to preserve it. At no time is this more important than in the search for, and preparation of, a successor. This process raises a number of as yet unanswered questions in the organizations in our sample. Nevertheless, our observations suggest several patterns that need to be tested by more extensive study over a longer period of time, including the following:

1.   There is little motivation or reason to look outside of the organization for successors. For example, at ServiceMaster and the Girl Scouts, the two organizations described here that have had a transition in leadership, insiders were chosen.

2.   Strong, adaptive cultures are led by people who try to make themselves appear dispensable to the organization; members of the organization, however, too often view them as indispensable, creating a tension that is difficult to relieve. For example, at Southwest Airlines, there is a strong feeling within the organization that the current CEO is irreplaceable, no matter how diligently he tries to dispel the notion and to put in place mechanisms for ensuring preservation of the culture.

3.   Successors in such organizations are not developed overnight. They have to have been part of the culture for some time.

4.   A close association with the core activity of the organization may result in successors who are too accepting of the culture and too opposed to the adaptation that strong cultures require. Hence, the "outsider-insider" often demonstrates the greatest success in providing the continuity of leadership that our exceptionally performing organizations require. At ServiceMaster, where the most recent transition has occurred, the new CEO formerly headed up the company's consumer businesses, the newer of the firm's two important lines of business, after having joined the company sev-

eral years ago through an acquisition that was made, in part, because of the values of his former organization. He is the quintessential outsider-insider.

Leadership, Culture, and Performance

We do not believe that we have described airy concepts of leadership. The leaders we have profiled have helped to produce some of the best performance ever seen in the industries represented by their organizations. They have not stumbled onto a secret formula for competitive success. They understand what they are doing and make a conscious effort to carry out their role, and they play it so well that it often becomes second nature, ruling out any possibility of management by manipulation. From time to time, the leadership in competing organizations has seized on one or more observed behaviors and tried to emulate the leaders of these organizations in ways that might well be regarded as manipulative. The results have been predictably disastrous; this provides further confirmation of the possibility that there is a strong linkage between leadership, culture, and performance—in short, that state-of-the-art leadership delivers outstanding organizational results.

12 FRANCES HESSELBEIN

The "How to Be" Leader

*Frances Hesselbein is president of the Peter F.
Drucker Foundation for Nonprofit Management and
chairman of the Board of Governors of the Josephson
Institute for the Advancement of Ethics. She was chief
executive officer of the Girl Scouts of the U.S.A.
from July 1976 to February 1990. President Bush
appointed her to the board of directors of the Commis-
sion on National and Community Service in August
1991 and to his Advisory Committee on the Points of
Light Initiative Foundation in 1989. Hesselbein has
received numerous awards, including nine honorary
doctorates and the Excellence in Leadership Award
from the National Women's Economic Alliance.*

A business periodical asked a number of corporate chief executives "to look over the horizon of today's headlines," "size up
the future," and describe the most pressing tasks that lie beyond the
millennium for chief executives. I was invited to do so as well. In
my response I wrote, "The three major challenges CEOs will face
have little to do with managing the enterprise's tangible assets and
everything to do with monitoring the quality of: leadership, the

work force, and relationships." After the magazine came out, a corporate leader wrote to me and said, "Your comments make great sense to me. I believe that the three challenges you describe are like legs on a stool. Yet I see leaders attending to just one, or perhaps two, of the legs!"

In the tenuous years that lie ahead, the familiar benchmarks, guideposts, and milestones will change as rapidly and explosively as the times, but the one constant at the center of the vortex will be the leader. The leader beyond the millennium will not be the leader who has learned the lessons of *how to do it,* with ledgers of "hows" balanced with "its" that dissolve in the crashing changes ahead. The leader for today and the future will be focused on *how to be*—how to develop quality, character, mind-set, values, principles, and courage.

The "how to be" leader knows that people are the organization's greatest asset and in word, behavior, and relationships she or he demonstrates this powerful philosophy. This leader long ago banned the hierarchy and, involving many heads and hands, built a new kind of structure. The new design took people out of the boxes of the old hierarchy and moved them into a more circular, flexible, and fluid management system that spelled liberation of human spirit and endeavor.

The "how to be" leader builds dispersed and diverse leadership—distributing leadership to the outermost edges of the circle to unleash the power of shared responsibility. The leader builds a work force, board, and staff that reflect the many faces of the community and environment, so that customers and constituents find themselves when they view this richly diverse organization of the future.

This "how to be" leader holds forth the vision of the organization's future in compelling ways that ignite the spark needed to build the inclusive enterprise. The leader mobilizes people around the mission of the organization, making it a powerful force in the uncertain times ahead. Coordination around the mission generates a force that transforms the workplace into one in which workers and teams can express themselves in their work and find significance beyond the task, as they manage for the mission. Through a consistent focus on mission, the "how to be" leader gives the dispersed and diverse leaders of the enterprise a clear sense of direction and the opportunity to find meaning in their work.

The "how to be" leader knows that listening to the customer and learning what he or she values—"digging in the field"—will be a critical component, even more so in the future than today. Global and local competition will only accelerate, and the need to focus on what the customer values will grow stronger.

Everyone will watch tomorrow's leader, as we watch today's, to see if the business practices of the organization are consistent with the principles espoused by the leader. In all interactions, from the smallest to the largest, the behavior of the "how to be" leader will demonstrate a belief in the worth and dignity of the men and women who make up the enterprise.

Key to the societal significance of tomorrow's leaders is the way they embrace the totality of leadership, not just including "my organization" but reaching beyond the walls as well. The "how to be" leader, whether she or he is working in the private, public, or social sector, recognizes the significance of the lives of the men and women who make up the enterprise, the value of a workplace that nurtures the people whose performance is essential to furthering the mission, and the necessity of a healthy community to the success of an organization. The wise leader embraces all those concerned in a circle that surrounds the corporation, the organization, the people, the leadership, and the community.

The challenges presented from outside the walls will require as much attention, commitment, and energy as the most pressing tasks within. Leaders of the future will say, "This is intolerable," as they look at the schools, at the health of children who will make up the future work force, at inadequate preparation for life and work in too many families, at people losing trust in their institutions. The new leaders will build the healthy community as energetically as they build the healthy, productive enterprise, knowing that the high-performance organization cannot exist if it fails its people in an ailing community.

Today's concerns about a lack of workers' loyalty to the corporation and a corresponding lack of corporations' loyalty to the work force are sending a clear message to the leaders of tomorrow. The pit bulls of the marketplace may find that their slash-and-crunch and hang-on-till-death philosophies are as dead as the spirits of their troops. In the end, as organizations reduce their work forces, will it be the leader of a dispirited, demoralized work force who leads the pack or will it be the new leader, guiding from vision, principle, and values, who builds trust and releases the energy and creativity of the work force?

The great observers are not forecasting good times, but in the very hazards that lie ahead for leaders, remarkable opportunities exist for those who would lead their enterprises and this country into a new kind of community—a cohesive community of healthy children, strong families, and work that dignifies the individual. It is in this arena that leaders with new mind-sets and visions will forge new relationships, crossing all three sectors to build partnerships and community. This will take a different breed (or the old breed sloughing off the tired, go-it-alone approach), made up of leaders who dare to see life and community whole, who view work as an amazing opportunity to express everything within that gives passion and light to living, and who have the courage to lead from the front on the issues, principles, vision, and mission that become the star to steer by. Leaders of the future can only speculate on the tangibles that will define the challenges beyond the millennium. But the intangibles, the leadership qualities required, are as constant as the North Star. They are expressed in the character, the power within, and the "how to be" of leaders beyond the millennium.

13 RICHARD BECKHARD

On Future Leaders

Richard Beckhard is an organizational consultant who specializes in working with leaders in the area of organizational and institutional development and management of change and complexity. He is the author of The Fact-Finding Conference, Core Content, Organization Development, *and* Explorations on the Teaching and Learning of Managing Large System Change. *He is coauthor of* Changing the Essence: The Art of Making and Managing Fundamental Change *and* Organizational Transitions. *Beckhard was a professor of organizational behavior and management at the Sloan School of Management at the Massachusetts Institute of Technology, where he served on the faculty for twenty-one years. The Sloan School honored him by creating the Richard Beckhard Prize, awarded annually for the best article on this subject in the* Sloan Management Review.

A first principle of leadership is that it is a relationship between a leader and followers. Without followers there is no one to lead. A second principle is that effective leaders both are aware of and consciously manage the dynamics of this relationship.

The leader is the center of a number of forces, each with its own agenda. These forces "demand" that the leader behave in ways that further their goals. This combination of forces makes up a *demand system*. Each force, or *domain*, as they are often called, has its own demands. All of them must be managed together by the leader, since they all converge in her or him. The leader's behavioral responses to these forces make up the *response system*. The leader must decide how to respond to both individual demands and the interactions between various demands.

Domains that are likely to make demands on a leader include the board of directors, staff and employees, volunteers in the organization, suppliers, customers, the media, many levels of government, trade associations, competitors, special-interest groups and "the public" (that amorphous term), family and friends, and key figures such as pastors or mentors.

Other domains are inside the person. They include the choice of values to be articulated, the role of beliefs in determining behavior, the degree of conviction and commitment needed, learning challenges, and personal preferred management style.

In response to these many demands, the leader must balance two additional forces—how much energy to expend on getting results, and how much to expend on relationships.

Challenges of the New Century

Leaders in the twenty-first century will face greater and more complex demands than they did in most of the century just ending. Until recently, leaders had the power to shape their organizations in ways that supported their personal values, assumptions, and style.

The explosion of technology, the increasing awareness that people are the key factor in organizational effectiveness, and the realization that organizations must have both an economic and a social agenda, whatever the sector in which they operate, have all eroded the autonomy of the organization leader. The CEO of a business in today's society rarely has the freedom that was given to his or her predecessors. Boards of directors, historically passive, have become active participants in the governance of organizations and in the evaluation of the leader's performance.

In government, the power of the *official* leader has been drastically reduced. The president of the United States can only control fourteen of the hundreds of committees in government. The president's cabinet members must be responsive to the congressional committees that oversee their departments. The agricultural committees, for example, wield as much influence on the behavior of the Secretary of Agriculture as the president does. There is no longer a clear line of authority.

Leaders of nonprofit organizations tend to be more experienced and competent in managing their multiple constituencies. They also tend to be less comfortable and competent in managerial skills compared to their counterparts in the private sector.

In reflecting on the great twentieth-century leaders, we quickly recall Franklin Delano Roosevelt, Harry S Truman, and John F. Kennedy as the giant presidents. Martin Luther King, Jr., stands alone as a leader of social change. Sigmund Freud and Kurt Lewin provided significant leadership in the understanding of human nature. Applied social scientists Peter Drucker and Douglas McGregor are powerful leaders of thought. Alfred P. Sloan and George Eastman, and more recently Jack Welch of General Electric and Robert Galvin of Motorola, stand out as giants in the leadership of business organizations. In the voluntary, or third, sector, Frances Hesselbein is the outstanding leader.

These giants have several traits in common, among them high ego strength, the ability to think strategically, an orientation toward the future, and a belief in certain fundamental principles of human behavior. They have strong convictions and do not hesitate to display them. They are politically astute. They know how to use power both for efficiency and for the larger good as they see it. They are also empathic, in that they have the ability to "get into the heads" of others with whom they relate.

These leaders vary in their values, their managerial styles, and their priorities. Some are primarily concerned with making a difference in society, others are concerned with being the best in their industry or area. Their management styles range from highly autocratic to paternalistic to consultative to team-oriented. They also vary in their attitudes toward humankind and toward individual people. They vary in their convictions about the autonomy or interdependence of the organizations they head.

Future leaders will probably fit the above profiles. Any differences are likely to come from the increased complexity of the world in which they will function and the exponential increase in the rate of change that will come from explosions in technology and communications. It will be an increasing challenge to manage the tensions between these developments and the needs of individuals. Leaders will need to pay attention to the social issues of protecting the environment and the planet, of creating a more just society, and of attending to the increasing interest of significant numbers of people in finding meaning in their lives. Spirituality will not be a word reserved for the clergy.

Leaders will also have to adapt to the changing roles and relationships of different sectors of society. What will be the role of business and industry—the private sector—in the twenty-first century? Traditionally, they have been the producers of the nation's wealth, and we have argued over the distribution of that wealth. What direction will that argument take? What will be the role of government? What will be the effect of regulations on the freedom of leaders to control their own destiny? If the present trend of cutting government support for the social sector continues, leaders in that sector will have to reexamine their mission, their funding, and their relationships to other sectors.

A major challenge will be to effectively lead and manage the relationships among the organization's mission or purpose, its interaction and partnerships with other institutions and other sectors, and its overt statements of its values. A related challenge will be to effectively use the organization's role as culture setter to define the norms, rewards, and values that make up the culture and to underscore them through personal behavior.

Truly effective leaders in the years ahead will have personas determined by strong values and belief in the capacity of individuals to grow. They will have an image of the society in which they would like their organizations and themselves to live. They will be visionary, they will believe strongly that they can and should be shaping the future, and they will act on those beliefs through their personal behavior.

14 JUDITH M. BARDWICK

Peacetime Management and Wartime Leadership

Judith M. Bardwick is president and founder of Bardwick and Associates, an influential management consulting firm. Since 1978, she has concentrated on issues relating to improving organizational effectiveness and management structure. She is a leading expert on these subjects and has combined respected cutting-edge research with its practical application throughout her career. She is the author of Danger in the Comfort Zone, The Plateauing Trap, In Transition, *and* The Psychology of Women.

By definition, leaders lead change. When life is orderly, tasks are predictable, and most things are going well, people neither want nor need much leadership. When they are comfortable and secure, people want the status quo. Comfortable people are not in any psychological state of need that would lead them to embrace a leader and seek change. In those circumstances, they want peacetime leadership or, more accurately, peacetime *management*. "Peacetime" and "wartime" do not refer to conflict in this context, but rather to the difference between conditions in which events are reasonably predictable, with a sense of comfort and control, and conditions in which little can be anticipated accurately, with little comfort or sense of control. Many organizations, but especially those in business, have gone from peacetime conditions to those of warfare since the early 1980s.

Peacetime has neither crisis nor chaos, so no major change is needed. Instead, people are content with what already exists and change involves a gentle tweaking of an existing system in order to slowly improve it. Peacetime management consists of incremental modification of what already exists, without major disruption and, therefore, without any major emotional consequences. With no sense of emergency or urgency, leaders do not have to be special and they do not have to generate an emotional following. They are simply people who occupy positions that have power. Anyone in those positions is seen as a leader irrespective of what he or she does, because there is no need to do very much. And that's fine with the followers as long as life remains comfortable and orderly. (This explains the common conflict between those who want to lead others through major change as though it were wartime and those who refuse to become followers, insisting that it is still peacetime.)

We find fewer and fewer circumstances in which peacetime managers can be successful because, overall, peacetime conditions are over. In this era of globalization, "danger in the comfort zone" has been replaced by the need to find comfort in endless danger. Let me illustrate what is changing with a little anecdote. The importance of the story actually lies in its very ordinariness.

One day last year, I used one of my company's questionnaires to measure the organizational characteristics of an IBM unit in San Jose, California. At the end of the day, I made the mistake of promising to return in one week with the results. That didn't leave much time to get the data to Philadelphia, where they would be analyzed and the results sent back to me. The analysis was completed the night before I was to return to San Jose. During the night, the results were faxed to my hotel in Connecticut, and I got them when I checked out. I studied the data on the way to the airport and for another couple of hours on the plane. In the middle of the flight, I understood the meaning of the results.

I was in a DC-10 that was going about 550 miles an hour at an altitude of thirty-nine thousand feet. While we were streaking across the country, high in the sky, I called my office in La Jolla, California. "Diane," I said, "I need some charts made. Could you do that for me?" "Of course," Diane said. "Just tell me what you want." The charts that she created on the computer were faxed to my hotel in San Jose and arrived before I did.

This unexceptional incident is a perfect illustration of the ways in which technology has created a borderless world and, increasingly, a borderless economy. Quite simply, whether within one country or between different nations, distance and time are becoming less and less important. The result is that everyone has lost or will lose the protection distance and time afforded. More and more, it really doesn't matter where work is done anymore. This results in increased opportunities *and* increased competition. In a borderless economy, you can reach new customers, but just as easily, your competitors will have easy access to your customers.

The world has changed and the change is permanent. The comfort zone is increasingly being replaced by endless danger. In turn, peacetime managers, people who are most comfortable in static conditions, will have to learn to become wartime leaders, people who embrace major change because they see far more opportunity than threat in turbulence. Alas, many peacetime managers won't make the cut and will need to be replaced. Peacetime conditions are not conducive to generating wartime leaders. In peacetime, people do not have the opportunity to hone themselves on a hard stone that teaches them to be unafraid of change and of making the right, but difficult, choice.

Emotional neediness, or the desire for leaders, results from the conditions of change, crisis, and urgency that I call wartime. In the perturbation of wartime conditions, when the world is scary and the future is uncertain, when people are experiencing fear, dread, foreboding, and exhaustion, people have an emotional need for a leader, a person whom they can trust and to whom they want to make an emotional commitment. Leaders evoke emotional connections in followers only to the extent that the followers are emotionally needy.

What Wartime Leaders Do

When I look at organizations that are struggling with today's turbulent transitions, I find six things leaders must do that seem especially critical to creating a sense of strong leadership and achieving success. Leaders must (1) define the business of the business, (2) create a winning strategy, (3) communicate persuasively, (4) behave with integrity, (5) respect others, and (6) act.

Define the Business of the Business

The most important question in any organization has to be, "What is the business of our business?" The answer to this question determines what the organization should do—and what it shouldn't do. In swiftly changing, borderless economies, the question must be revisited often because the answer can change swiftly. Determining the business of the business is the first step in setting priorities. This is a major leadership responsibility because, without priorities, efforts are splintered and little is achieved. The best leaders get the organization to focus and to become involved only in what matters the most. In the competition of wartime, leaders must skillfully harness the natural sense of urgency that arises from external threats and use it to continuously reinforce an imperative focus on doing what counts. Achieving the mission against hard odds, hitting stretch targets in the business of the business—this is the glue that holds people together with a commitment to the good of all.

The best leadership frames the organization's mission and values in ways that members find transcendent: the goals of the business are transmuted from the dross of ordinary work into higher goals that are worthy of heroic efforts and even sacrifices. One example, related by Brian Dumaine in "Why Do We Work?" (*Fortune*, December 26, 1994, p. 196), tells of the difference between three stonemasons:

> In the days of misty towers, distressed maidens, and stalwart knights, a young man, walking down a road, came upon a laborer fiercely pounding away at a stone with hammer and chisel. The lad asked the worker, who looked frustrated and angry, "What are you doing?" The laborer answered in a pained voice: "I'm trying to shape this stone, and it is backbreaking work." The youth continued his journey and soon came upon another man chipping away at a similar stone, who looked neither particularly angry nor happy. "What are you doing?" the young man asked. "I'm shaping a stone for a building." The young man went on and before long came to a third worker chipping away at a stone, but this worker was singing happily as he worked. "What are you doing?" the young man asked. The worker smiled and replied, "I'm building a cathedral."

Create a Winning Strategy

It is leadership's responsibility to create a strategy that will cause the organization to succeed, to grow, to prosper, to beat the competition. In a borderless economy, the question "What is our strategy and what are our competitors' strategies?" must, like the question "What is our core business?" be raised and answered often because the strategy has to derive from the competitive reality of the business. Strategy is conceptual; a winning strategy must accurately designate what the organization will do better than anyone else in order to be the customer's choice.

For strategy to succeed it must anticipate, create, and guide change and create commitment in the organization's members. It should be so plausible, clever, bold, and achievable that in itself it generates a conviction that even if the journey is hard, it is worth taking because the strategy has created a major competitive advantage. Defining the business of the business shrewdly and wisely and creating a convincing strategy for winning are critical in terms of persuading people that they have real leaders and that success will be achieved.

Communicate Persuasively

Leaders know that trust is a competitive advantage in a world of adversarial competition. Basically, trust is a matter of predictability. People trust others when they are told that something will happen and it does. Major change, therefore, always threatens trust and thus, ultimately, confidence in leadership. Ineffective or nonexistent communication, especially in wartime, results in an enormous increase in mistrust, confusion, and cynicism and a huge decline in morale, belief in the organization, and confidence in the leadership. That's why the need for persuasive communication is especially critical in periods of major threat and change.

During periods of major change, most organizations send out too many communications because they want to avoid all the negative consequences that result when people don't know what's going to happen to them. But when too many messages are sent or the anxiety level is high, not much gets through. Therefore, organizations have to limit the number of their communications and simplify the messages they send. Leaders must decide what few pieces of information people really need to know, and those few foci must be amplified, stated far more simply and repetitiously than anyone would imagine to be necessary. And when the goals are to reduce anxiety and increase commitment to the leader and the mission, the most effective communication is in-person, personal, and in the form of a dialogue.

Behave with Integrity

Without integrity, trust is never achieved. The best leaders are transparent: they do what they say; they "walk the talk." People believe them because they act in line with the values they espouse. They do not play Machiavellian games of manipulation and duplicity. In that sense, they are simple.

Having integrity, I think, rests partly on personal courage. It requires truthfulness with oneself as well as with others in terms of what is genuinely valued and what is considered important. Behaving with integrity also means being consistent in one's choices and actions. In addition to courage, leaders must have some certainty about which direction to take and which path to choose. In turn, this requires leaders to have a clear conviction about values and a steadfastness of purpose in distinguishing between right and wrong, wisdom and foolishness.

Respect Others

The best leaders don't waste other people's brains. Leaders need a core sense of confidence that allows them to be comfortable receiving input, including disagreement, from others. Although the best leaders are often strikingly knowledgeable, especially about the larger picture, they're neither wimps nor Genghis Khans, neither humble nor arrogant. As a result, they don't think that needing other people's input is demeaning. Effective wartime leaders require input from everyone involved; they prefer spirited debate before decisions are made, although once a decision has been made, they require alignment. They require others to act enthusiastically, in line with the decision even if they had opposed it before.

Today, subordinates at all levels of an organization have experience, knowledge, and skill that they could bring to the table if their leaders were psychologically able to "hear." Hearing others, like empowering others, isn't a matter of process. It is, instead, a matter of respect.

Act

The peacetime manager is like a supply officer who is great at planning and logistics, tasks in which people work hard but no one gets hurt. In contrast, in wartime, leaders must be able to consider doing the unbearable. Wartime leadership is hard: it involves actions in which some will be injured and even die, in order for the group as a whole to live. ("Injury" and "dying" here refer to changes such as layoffs, downsizing, selling or closing unprofitable units, and merging and acquiring other organizations.) Wartime leadership, therefore, requires a strength of character, self-discipline, courage, and deviance from what's popular that peacetime managers don't need.

It is the job of leaders to inspire confidence in people who are racked by doubt. In wartime, when conditions are ambiguous and decisions are difficult, leaders must decide, choose, and *act*. They understand that when they don't act, they are perceived as being indecisive and weak, and this increases people's sense of anxiety, powerlessness, and insecurity. When others doubt a leader's ability, confidence, or effectiveness, the mission is sabotaged.

Thus, leaders have to be perceived as people with courage who will act and as people who believe that change creates more opportunities than threats. Even while leaders must stay in keen contact with reality, they must also be optimists.

Psychological Leadership

Psychologically, leaders lead because they convince others that they understand the issues better than anyone else. People follow them because they speak about solutions with persuasive conviction, project confidence when others are uncertain, and act decisively. Today and far into the future, leaders must convince people that dealing with unending change not only is necessary but also will result in something better.

People are leaders as long as they create followers. Leadership, ultimately, is an emotional bond, sometimes even a passionate commitment between followers and the leader and his or her goals. Leadership is different from other relationships in that *leaders generate hope and conviction in followers*. They are people whom others perceive as being able to make things better. At the emotional level, leaders create followers because they generate:

- Confidence in people who were frightened

- Certainty in people who were vacillating

- Action where there was hesitation

- Strength where there was weakness

- Expertise where there was floundering

- Courage where there was cowardice

- Optimism where there was cynicism

- Conviction that the future will be better

Ultimately, leaders lead because they create a passionate commitment in other people to pursue the leaders' strategy and succeed. In the end, leadership is not intellectual or cognitive. Leadership is emotional.

15 DAVID M. NOER

A Recipe for Glue

*David M. Noer is senior vice president for training
and education at the Center for Creative Leadership,
with worldwide responsibility for the center's training
and educational activities. He has written four books:*
Healing the Wounds, Multinational People Management, How to Beat the Employment Game,
and Jobkeeping.

As the traditional implicit employment contract between the
individual and the organization continues to unravel, many
of us are struggling with basic questions such as how to lead, motivate, and plan in this uncharted new environment where, like it or
not, we are all temporary employees. The increasingly voiced question is, "After all the layoffs, early retirements, downsizing, and
restructuring, what is the glue that holds this organization together?"

The quest for such glue is perhaps the most pressing search that
confronts today's organizations. A vivid contemporary example can

---

Note: Portions of this chapter originally appeared in *Issues and Observations*, a pub-
lication of the Center for Creative Leadership.

be found in the agony of an executive we will call Steve and his direct reports. Steve, the president of a medium-sized, high-technology manufacturing and sales organization, and his team were struggling with what they finally conceded to be a permanent shift to a situation they called *the new reality*. The magnitude of this new reality had seeped into the collective consciousness of Steve's group until, like fluid in their lungs, it nearly suffocated them. Theirs was not a happy team!

The framework of their new reality, which they phrased in very terse and personal terms, was displayed on two pieces of newsprint that were taped to the wall. There were six points:

1. "Layoffs will continue." This meant that they would continue "taking out" their friends and colleagues well into the future. In fact, they couldn't predict an end to it.

2. "Even *our* jobs aren't safe." There were two subcaptions under this main point: "He who lives by the sword dies by the sword," which summarized a spirited discussion about their cost-cutting culture, and "We are all temps."

3. "The old system is dead." The relationship of the person to the organization that most of them had internalized was that the obligation of the "good" employee was to fit in and behave in accordance with organizationally sanctioned rules and standards, and the obligation of the "good" employer was to take care of a "good" employee over a forty-year career.

4. "We are not happy campers." Each of the team members admitted feeling some combination of anger, anxiety, and frustration.

5. "We don't know how to manage anymore." The group concluded that they needed two very different sets of skills to help turn their organization around: competencies to help employees shake off the debilitating effects of "layoff-survivor sickness" and the skills needed to lead a liberated work force. These were very different from the skills required in the past.

6. "We're out of glue." No replacement was apparent to the group at that time for what they characterized as the "glue" that had held the old organization together.

It was this last point, the lack of glue, that caused one team member to come unglued himself. His lament is echoed in the hearts of many organizational leaders. "Everything we worked so hard to build here has come apart!" he blurted out. "Where's the loyalty in this new employment contract? How can we manage a bunch of mercenaries?"

The pain felt by Steve's team was real, and the frustration they experienced is increasingly shared by many organizational leaders who came up under the "old" contract, where individuals placed their self-esteem and sense of relevance in the organizational vault and the organization responded by taking care of them over a lifetime career. Their personal self-worth, ideas about what constituted loyalty and motivation, and concepts of leadership were forged under a very different paradigm from the one in which they now operate. What got them there won't keep them or their organizations there. Yet it is very difficult to let go. As a CEO said, "Old dawgs can learn new tricks, but it's damn hard! The old tricks is what let us get to be old dawgs in the first place!"

The primary task is cleaning away the old glue, which was external and applied from the top down, and replacing it with a new adhesive that is internal and self-administered. The old glue was made up of largesse, hierarchy, bureaucracy (in the positive sense of that misrepresented word), and upward mobility. Loyalty was equated with fitting in, and the major property of the adhesive was applied paternalism. In order to produce a new glue, we must understand five basic points:

1. Motivation and commitment are not irrevocably bound to lifetime employment, organizational loyalty, and fitting in.

2. It is possible—in fact, essential for survival—to do excellent work in the service of others without a lifetime guarantee of

employment and without placing all one's social, emotional, or financial eggs in the organizational basket.

3. Organizational commitment and productivity are not diminished by loyalty to oneself, the work team, and the profession.

4. Leadership is very different in a liberated work force that is unencumbered by fear, false expectations of promotions, or the distractions of politics and trying to impress the boss.

5. When people stay in a personal relationship because they choose to be there and know they have the no-fault option of leaving, when armies are made up of volunteers and not conscripts, and when people choose to stay in an organization because of the work and the customers, knowing that they may not be able to stay for an entire career, they tend to be much more productive and committed. This is perhaps the most profound learning, which I call *the paradox of freedom*. *The paradox of job security* is that when people choose to stay for the right reasons (the work and the customer), as opposed to the wrong reasons (false expectations of job security), their job security tends to increase!

At times, when I am working with organizational leaders in their search for this elusive new glue, I close my eyes and envision a large glue pot in the middle of the conference room floor. And I imagine what a recipe might look like:

Fill the glue pot with the fresh, pure, clear water of undiluted human spirit.

Take special care not to contaminate with preconceived ideas, or to pollute with excess control.

Fill slowly; notice that the pot only fills from the bottom up. It's impossible to fill it from the top down!

Stir in equal parts of customer focus and pride in good work.

Bring to a boil and blend in a liberal portion of diversity, one part self-esteem, and one part tolerance.

Fold in accountability.

Simmer until smooth and thick, stirring with shared leadership and clear goals.

Season with a dash of humor and a pinch of adventure.

Let cool, then garnish with a topping of core values.

Serve by coating all boxes in the organizational chart, paying particular attention to the white spaces. With proper application, the boxes disappear and all that can be seen is productivity, creativity, and customer service.

This is only one recipe. Each organization must come up with its own. And it must do its own cooking. The new glue cannot be bought off the shelf.

Part III

Learning to Lead for Tomorrow

16 STEPHEN R. COVEY

Three Roles of the Leader in the New Paradigm

Stephen R. Covey is founder and chairman of the Covey Leadership Center, which works with more than half of the Fortune 500 companies, as well as thousands of midsized and smaller organizations in the United States and throughout the world. Covey is the author of The Seven Habits of Highly Effective People, *which has sold well more than five million copies and is being published in more than thirty countries and in twenty-six languages. His other best-selling books include* Principle-Centered Leadership *and* First Things First.

The leader of the future, of the next millennium, will be one who creates a culture or a value system centered upon principles. Creating such a culture in a business, government, school, hospital, nonprofit organization, family, or other organization will be a tremendous and exciting challenge in this new era and will only be achieved by leaders, be they emerging or seasoned, who have the vision, courage, and humility to constantly learn and grow. Those people and organizations who have a passion for learning—learning through listening, seeing emerging trends, sensing and anticipating needs in the marketplace, evaluating past successes and mistakes, and absorbing the lessons that conscience and principles teach us, to mention just a few ways—will have enduring influence. Such learning leaders will not resist change; they will embrace it.

A White-Water World

The world has changed in a very profound way. This change continues to happen all around us, all the time. It is a white-water world. The consumer revolution has accelerated enormously. People are so much more enlightened and aware. So many more dynamic, competitive forces are operating. Quality standards have risen, particularly in the global marketplace, to the point where there is simply no way to fake it. It may be possible to survive in a local marketplace without meeting these standards, perhaps even in a regional marketplace, but certainly not in a global marketplace.

In all sectors—business, government, health care, social, or nonprofit—the marketplace is demanding that organizations transform themselves. They must be able to produce services and goods and deliver them in a fast, friendly, and flexible way and on a consistent basis that serves the needs of both internal and external customers. This requires a work force that is not only allowed to give of its full creativity and talent, but enabled, encouraged, and rewarded for doing so. Even though tens of thousands of organizations are deeply involved in quality initiatives designed to produce those very results, transformation is not being achieved. The fundamental reason most quality initiatives do not work is because of a lack of trust in the culture—in the relationships between people. Just as you cannot fake world-class quality, so also is it impossible to fake high trust. It has to come out of trustworthiness.

I put more faith in what the global economy is doing to drive quality than in any other factor. It is teaching us that principles such as empowerment, trust, and trustworthiness ultimately control the effective results we seek. The most effective leaders are, first, *models* of what I call principle-centered leadership. They have come to realize that we're all subject to natural laws or governing principles, which operate regardless of our awareness of them or our obedience to them. Our effectiveness is predicated upon alignment with these inviolable principles—natural laws in the human dimension that are just as real, just as unchanging, as laws such as gravity are in the physical dimension. These principles are woven into the fabric of every civilized society and constitute the roots of every organization that has endured.

To the degree that we recognize and live in harmony with such basic principles as fairness, service, equity, justice, integrity, honesty, and trust, we move toward either survival and stability on the one hand or disintegration and destruction on the other. Principles are self-evident, self-validating natural laws. In fact, the best way to realize that a principle is self-evident is by trying to imagine a world or, for that matter, *any* effective, enduring society, organization, or family based upon its opposite.

Correct principles are like compasses: they are always pointing the way. They don't change or shift, and if we know how to read them, we won't get lost, confused, or fooled by conflicting voices and values. They provide the true north direction to our lives as we navigate the "streams" of our environments. Thus we see that a changeless, principle-centered core is the key to having the confidence, security, power, guidance, and wisdom to change the way we address the changing needs and opportunities around us.

So the first role of the leader is to be a model of principle-centered leadership. Whenever a person or an organization is principle-centered, that person or organization becomes a model—an example—to other people and organizations. It is that kind of modeling, that kind of character, competence, and action, that produces trust among people, causing them to identify with this modeling and be influenced by it. Modeling, then, is a combination of character (who you are as a person) and competence (what you can do). These two qualities represent your potential. But when you actually *do* it—when you put action together with character— you've got modeling.

Three Roles of a Leader

What is it, then, that the principle-centered leader models? I suggest that you can break leadership into three basic functions or activities: pathfinding, aligning, and empowering. Let's explore each one in turn.

Pathfinding

The essence and power of *pathfinding* are found in a compelling vision and mission. Pathfinding deals with the larger sense of the future. It gets the culture imbued with and excited about a tremendous, transcendent purpose. But in relation to what? To meeting the needs of your customers and other stakeholders. Pathfinding, then, ties together your value system and vision with the needs of customers and other stakeholders through a strategic plan. I call this the strategic pathway.

Aligning

The second activity of a leader is *aligning*. It consists of ensuring that your organizational structure, systems, and operational processes all contribute to achieving your mission and vision of meeting the needs of customers and other stakeholders. They don't interfere with it, they don't compete with it, and they don't dominate it. They're only there for one purpose—to contribute to it. Far and away the greatest leverage of the principle of alignment comes when your people are in alignment with your mission, vision, and strategy. When people are filled with true understanding of the needs, when they share a powerful commitment to accomplishing the vision, when they are invited to create and continually improve the structures and systems that will meet the needs, then you have alignment. Without these human conditions, you cannot have world-class quality; all you have is brittle programs. Ultimately, we must learn that programs and systems are vital, but that *people* are the programmers.

Empowering

The third activity of a leader is *empowering*. What does that mean? People have enormous talent, ingenuity, intelligence, and creativity. Most of it lies dormant. When you have true alignment toward a common vision, a common mission, you begin to co-mission with those people. Individual purpose and mission are commingled with the mission of the organization. When these purposes overlap, great synergy is created. A fire is ignited within people that unleashes their latent talent, ingenuity, and creativity to do whatever is necessary and consistent with the principles agreed upon to accomplish their common values, vision, and mission in serving customers and other stakeholders. This is what we mean by empowerment.

But then you have to study what happens. What are the results? Are we really meeting the needs of the customers and the other stakeholders? Data and information that indicate whether these needs are truly being met must be fed back to the empowered people and teams inside the culture so that they can use it to make the necessary course corrections and improvements and continue to do whatever it takes to fulfill the mission and to serve the needs.

A New Paradigm of Leadership

These roles of modeling principle-centered leadership—pathfinding, aligning, and empowering—represent a paradigm that is different in kind from traditional management thinking. There is a very significant difference between management and leadership. Both are vital functions, and because they are, it's critical to understand how they are different so one isn't mistaken for the other.

Leadership focuses on doing the right things; management focuses on doing things right. Leadership makes sure the ladders we are climbing are leaning against the right wall; management makes sure we are climbing the ladders in the most efficient ways possible. Most managers and executives operate within existing paradigms or ways of thinking, but leaders have the courage to bring those paradigms to the surface, identify the underlying assumptions and motivations, and challenge them by asking, "Does this still hold water?" For example:

• In health care, new leaders might challenge the assumption that medicine should focus upon the diagnosis and treatment of disease. Some medical schools today don't even teach nutrition, even though one-third of all cancers are nutrition-related and two-thirds of all diseases are tied to life-style. Still, the medical community heads down the path of diagnosis and treatment of disease. They claim that they deal with the whole package—the health and welfare of people—but they have a treatment paradigm. Fortunately, new leaders are creating more preventive-medicine alternatives.

• In law, new leaders might challenge the assumption that law is best practiced in courtrooms using confrontational, win-lose litigation. They might move toward the use of synergy and win-win thinking to prevent and settle disputes. Alternative dispute resolution usually results in compromise. New leaders will seek "win-win or no deal" options that lead to synergy. Synergy is more than cooperation; it's creating better solutions. It requires empathic listening and courage in expressing one's views and opinions in ways that show respect for the other person's views. Out of genuine interaction come synergistic insights.

• In business, new leaders will challenge the assumption that "total customer satisfaction" represents the ultimate service ethic. They will move toward total stakeholder satisfaction, caring for everyone who has a stake in the success of the operation and making decisions that benefit all stakeholders. To bring about this new mind-set, leaders must develop a new skill-set of synergy. Synergy comes naturally from the quality of the relationship—the friend-ship, trust, and love that unites people.

If you can put the new skill-set of synergy together with the new mind-set of interdependence, you have the perfect one-two punch for achieving competitive advantage. When you have the mind-set and the skill-set, you create effective structures, systems, and processes that are aligned with your vision and mission. Every orga-nization is perfectly designed and aligned to get the results it gets. If you want different results, you need a new mind-set and a new skill-set to create synergistic solutions. It's only enlightened self-interest to keep all stakeholders in mind when making decisions, because we are so interdependent.

Who Is the Leader of the Future?

In many cases, the leader of the future will be the same as the leader of the present. There will be no change in personnel, but rather an internal change: the person becomes the leader of the future by an inside-out transformation. What drives leaders to change, to be-come more centered on principles?

I think the main source of *personal* change is pain; this pain may come from disappointment, failure, death, troubled or broken rela-tionships with family or friends, violated trust, personal weakness, discouragement, boredom, dissatisfaction, poor health, the conse-quences of poor decisions, loneliness, mediocrity, fear, financial stress, job insecurity, or life imbalance. If you aren't feeling pain, there is rarely enough motivation or humility to change. Most often there just isn't a felt need. Without personal pain, people tend to be too deeply invested in themselves and their world to rise above their own interests or the politics of running things, both at work and at home. When people are experiencing personal pain, they tend to be more open to a new model of living in which the common elements of humility and personal sacrifice lead to inside-out, principle-centered change.

The primary driving force of *organizational* change is the global economy. The standard of quality is now so high that unless you have an empowered work force and a spirit of partnership with all stakeholders, you can't compete, whether you work in the private sector, public sector, or social sector. When you're facing competitors who think more ecologically and interdependently, eventually the force of circumstances drives you to be humble. That's what is driving the quest for quality, learning, process reengineering, and other initiatives. But many of these initiatives don't go far enough. The mind shift is not great enough. The interests of all stakeholders must be dealt with in an orchestrated way.

We either are forced by circumstances to be humble or can choose to be humble out of a recognition that principles ultimately govern. To be humble is good, regardless of the reason. But it's better to be humbled by conscience rather than by circumstances.

The Leader of the Future—A Family Within

The leader of the future has the humility to accept principles and the courage to align with them, which takes great personal sacrifice. Out of this humility, courage, and sacrifice comes the person of integrity. In fact, I like to think of this kind of leader as having an entire family within him or her: humility and courage the parents, and integrity the child.

Humility and Courage the Parents

Humility says, "I am not in control; principles ultimately govern and control." It understands that the key to long-term success is learning to align with "true north" principles. That takes humility because the traditional mind-set is "I am in control; my destiny lies in my hands." This mind-set leads to arrogance—the sort of pride that comes before the fall.

Leaders of the future will have the courage to align with principles and go against the grain of old assumptions or paradigms. It
takes tremendous courage and stamina to say, "I'm going to align
my personal value system, my life-style, my direction, and my habits
with timeless principles." Courage is the quality of every principle
at its highest testing point. Every virtue is ultimately tested at the
highest level. That's where courage comes into play. When you confront an old approach directly, you experience the fear of ripping
out an old habit and replacing it with something new.

Integrity the Child

Out of the marriage of humility and courage is born the child of
integrity. We all want to be known and remembered as men and
women of integrity. Having integrity means integrating ourselves
with principles. The leaders of the future must be men and women
of integrity who internalize these principles. They grow in wisdom
and cultivate an abundance mind-set—a sense that there are opportunities for all. If you have integrity, you are not caught up in a constant state of comparison with others. Nor do you feel the need to
play political games, because your security comes from within. As
soon as you change the source of your security, everything else flows
from it. Your security, power, wisdom, and guidance increase,
because you constantly draw upon the strength of these principles
as you apply them.

A Final Note

We are becoming increasingly and painfully aware of the perilous
weakening of our social structure. Drugs, gangs, illiteracy, poverty,
crime, violence, breakdown of the family—these all continue in a
downward spiral. Leaders of the present are beginning to recognize
that such social problems put at risk *every* aspect of society. The
leaders of the future realize that the solutions to these problems are
far beyond the ability of the sectors that have traditionally been

expected to deal with them—namely, the government and social sectors. My intent is not to criticize these sectors. In fact, I believe that they would be the first to admit that they are bound to fail without a broader network of helping hands.

The problem is that, on the whole, there has been a marked weakening of the responsibility that neighborhoods, communities, churches, families, and individuals feel toward volunteering. It has become too easy to absolve ourselves from this responsibility to our communities. I believe that it is a family responsibility and that everyone should have a sense of stewardship about the community—every man, every woman, and every child. There should be some real sense of stewardship around service on the part of young people, particularly those who are at the most idealistic age, the late teens and early twenties.

The leader of the future will be a leader in every area of life, especially family life. The enormous needs and opportunities in society call for a great responsibility toward service. There is no place where this spirit of service can be cultivated like the home. The spirit of the home, and also of the school, is that they prepare young people to go forth and serve. People are supposed to serve. Life is a mission, not a career. The whole spirit of this philosophy should pervade our society. I also think that it is a source of happiness, because you don't get happiness directly. It only comes as a by-product of service. You can get pleasure directly, but it is fleeting.

How, then, do we influence our children toward the spirit of service and meaningful contribution? First, we must look inward and ask: Am I a *model* of this principle of service myself? Does my family see me dedicating my time and abilities to serving them and the community? Second, have I taken time to immerse myself and my family in the needs of others in the community in order to create a sense of vision about how our family and each of us as individuals can make unique and meaningful contributions to meet those needs (*pathfinding*)? Third, have I, as a leader in my home, *aligned* the priorities and structures of our life so that this desire to serve is supported, not undermined? Finally, have I created conditions and opportunities in the home that will *empower* my children to serve? Do I encourage and support the development of their minds and talents? Do I organize service opportunities for the entire family and do all I can to create a fun environment around those activities? Even if the answer to every one of these questions is no, we all still have the capacity to decide what our lives will be about from today on.

This inherent capacity to choose, to develop a new vision for ourselves, to rescript our life, to begin a new habit or let go of an old one, to forgive someone, to apologize, to make a promise and then keep it, in any area of life, is, always has been, and always will be a moment of truth for every true leader.

17 JAMES F. BOLT

Developing Three-Dimensional Leaders

James F. Bolt is chairman and founder of Executive Development Associates (EDA), a leading consulting firm specializing in the design of customized executive education and leadership development programs that directly support business strategy. Prior to founding EDA, Bolt was with Xerox Corporation for more than sixteen years, where he had companywide responsibility for executive education, management training, and executive succession planning. Bolt is the author of Executive Development: A Strategy for Corporate Competitiveness.

"*Wanted: Corporate executive to lead Fortune 500 company into twenty-first century. Must be visionary, authentic, courageous and a global citizen. Workaholics need not apply.*"

If such an ad were to run in the classified section of any major Sunday newspaper, the response of would-be CEOs would probably be overwhelming. But from the sea of résumés and curricula vitae replete with MBAs, few if any applicants would meet the requirements. Instead, American business leaders are "missing in action." At a time when leadership is more crucial than ever to our very survival, there is a severe shortage of qualified people to lead corporations into the next century.

This crisis is not limited to business; it touches all avenues of society. Disturbing and uncomfortable, it often is not articulated but lies at the surface of the subconscious. The most recent U.S. political elections provided a strong manifestation of this disenchantment.

America's Lagging Competitiveness

Although the shortage of leaders is a global issue, America's leadership gap is underscored by the dramatic reshaping of the world's economy, a world in which change, instability, and unpredictability are major constants. Once the world's economic giants, large American corporations today find themselves fighting for their very survival. The onslaught of foreign competition, the trend toward deregulation, environmental and social accountability, and even scandal are some of the factors that have propelled virtually every major company into a profoundly intense environment.

The forces of change, including competition, diversification, globalization, and technological development, have taken their toll on industry after industry in the United States. Consider that just twenty-five years ago, the United States controlled 35 percent of the world's economy. Today, our portion is barely 20 percent. A mere generation ago, Japan accounted for only 2 percent of the world's economy. Today it claims more than 10 percent, largely at the expense of the United States. Japan has emerged as the globe's richest creditor and we now enjoy the dubious distinction of being the world's largest debtor.

"For the rest of this century," writes John Kotter in *The Leadership Factor* (1988, p. 15), "we shall probably continue to see a world of business that looks fundamentally different from the 1950s and 1960s." He warns that within this unrecognizable and tumultuous landscape, a critical need for leadership exists: "It will be a world of intense competitive activity among very complex organizations. . . . It will be a world in which even the best 'professional managers' are ineffective unless they can also lead. In general, it will be a world in which the leadership factor in management will become increasingly important—for prosperity and even survival."

Is There a Leadership Crisis?

The dearth of leadership is apparent throughout society. No matter where we turn, we see a severe lack of faith in the leadership of our schools, religious organizations, and governments. To paraphrase a 1990 *Business Week* article, if Martians descended someplace in the United States and demanded that we take them to our leaders, we would have to think twice about where to take them.

Of course, this issue is not restricted to American organizations. Worldwide, corporations approach the twenty-first century with a severe deficit of business leaders equipped to deal with the complexities, volatility, and new rules of the global marketplace.

A Leadership Development Crisis

Based on my interviews with hundreds of Fortune 500 CEOs and other senior executives during the last thirteen years, as well as on the results of four quantitative surveys conducted by my firm during the same time period, I contend that this leadership crisis is in reality a *leadership development* crisis. It is this development crisis that leads me to agree that our leaders are "missing in action." I believe that two major training and development factors have incited this crisis. First, the traditional methods used to train and educate executives have not kept pace with the monumental changes taking place in the world, and second, on-the-job experiences and development do not produce the leadership our organizations need.

Outmoded Executive Education and Leadership Training

The fact that executive education and leadership training methods are outdated does not mean that attitudes toward executive education have remained static. Our surveys confirm that executive education, once relegated to the sidelines, has become a corporate priority. They also show that the single most powerful impetus behind this elevation is the influence of global competition. Faced with the need for new standards of productivity, cost-effectiveness, and quality and the need to revamp corporate cultures with new values, management styles, and business strategies, forward-thinking companies have increasingly turned to customized, internal executive education programs to help them achieve their strategic objectives and to act as a catalyst for organizational change.

In short, developmental efforts in leading corporations are now strategic: they are more often directly aimed toward building the capabilities that executives need to provide leadership in their turbulent, rapidly changing business environment. Furthermore, the survey respondents consistently rate leadership as their first priority in executive development.

Despite this increased attention, I contend that the training methods used by most corporations—and even more so, those used in universities and other institutions—have not and will not produce the leadership we need and want. For the most part, potential leaders receive the same education as their predecessors—education that was appropriate to the demands of a different era. Following are some of the major shortcomings of current executive and leadership development programs:

1. *Training is not comprehensive.* In his 1989 work, *The Managerial Mystique*, Harvard Business School professor Abraham Zaleznik writes that leadership is made up of "substance, humanity and morality. We are painfully short of all three qualities in our collective lives" (p. 124). Executive education has focused primarily on business skills. Also, most leadership seminars have presented

leadership as an isolated issue apart from the individual and business challenges executives face, suggesting that leadership can simply be added on top of other skills, much like picking up a foreign language before going overseas. Such narrow training produces leaders who are not fully developed. Executives seeking a complete development package must often acquire it piecemeal. To develop leadership skills, they may attend courses offered by management training companies. To improve their business skills, they might spend a summer in a university executive program. This ad hoc approach is ineffective.

2.   *Training offers a "quick fix."* The belief that leadership can be developed through an isolated day-long or week-long seminar is unrealistic. To be effective, training must be ongoing and long term.

3.   *Training is generic and outdated.* Until recently, university programs often ignored real-world problems. A recent *Business Week* article pointed out the lack of relevance in executive education programs offered by some of the world's most prestigious universities: "They [the participating managers] griped about having to debate dated case studies from the 1970s, which they deemed of little relevance in today's world. Some complained that cases they studied nearly 20 years earlier as MBA students are still being taught." Mini-MBA programs also tend to be too generic, lacking strategy-based, meaningful agendas. Few approaches give participants the opportunity to integrate a program's content with issues geared to their own organizations. Learning, then, tends to remain conceptual because executives never have the chance to put it into actual practice.

4.   *Training ignores leadership.* One of Zaleznik's primary complaints is that many so-called leadership training programs are actually management training programs, tending to be functionally and technically oriented. Our rigorous undergraduate- and professional-level MBA programs have produced legions of impeccably skilled managers with superb quantitative and management abilities. These executives later discover that they were taught how to manage but were never given the chance to learn how to lead.

On-the-Job Development

Many believe that nearly 80 percent of a typical executive's development is the result of on-the-job experience. Unfortunately, on-the-job experience has historically fostered management skills rather than leadership skills. For the most part, our managers develop leadership skills by chance, through the school of hard knocks. Also, they are products of a system that provides few on-the-job opportunities to develop leadership skills. These executives are part of a system that confuses management with leadership. Warren Bennis makes a clear distinction between the two. Managers, he purports, are more involved in the how-to, the short term, and the bottom line, while leaders must have vision, mission, strategic intent, and dreams.

The world has a wealth of exceptionally talented managers. Most on-the-job development produces one-dimensional executives with overly developed quantitative and analytic skills. They have a narrow functional-technical perspective as a result of spending their entire career in one area. They are often risk-averse—afraid to make decisions—because of the grave consequences of making mistakes, and they tend to mimic their bosses to ensure advancement. They often neglect family and friends in order to meet the demands of a system that too frequently encourages and rewards workaholism.

Few have any work experience outside of their country. With their narrow domestic focus, these executives reflect ethnocentricity. Many have learned that it is more desirable to be in their country of origin, where they won't risk being forgotten. International assignments, in fact, are frequently viewed as damaging to careers. Managers who do take international assignments may find it very difficult to return to an appropriate-level job or one that uses their international experience. "Some well known firms," writes John Kotter in *The Leadership Factor*, "have even used their international operations as a dumping ground for managers who have failed" (p. 128).

"Capable of managing but unfit to lead" is a fitting description of these executives. When they are placed in leadership positions, their style is often traditional and authoritarian, which is demonstrated by their need to overmanage, to be seen as the expert on everything, to solve all problems, make all decisions, and maintain control. They have learned from their experience that this is what works. That the training and job development system produces capable managers is undisputed. But we are now in the midst of a world in which even the best are ineffective unless they can also lead.

Three-Dimensional Leadership— The New Imperative

In place of a system that has tended to produce one-dimensional managers, I propose a holistic, three-dimensional leadership development framework, a comprehensive process that recognizes that executives need mind-sets, knowledge, and skills that are vastly different from those of the past. The three-dimensional framework calls for the development of an individual's *business*, *leadership*, and *personal effectiveness* skills. (See Figure 17.1.) Each is an equally

Figure 17.1. The Three-Dimensional Framework.

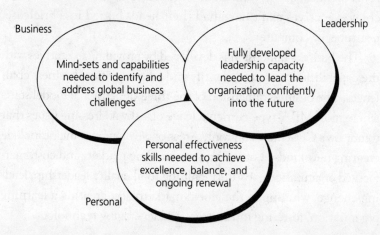

essential element of the leadership equation. It is not enough to be a consummate business expert; an executive must also be an excellent leader, while at the same time possessing exceptional personal effectiveness skills.

The *business* dimension has traditionally been the focus of most executive development. The three-dimensional framework does not diminish its importance; instead, it strengthens the leadership and personal dimensions to balance and integrate all three areas. The *leadership* dimension has traditionally been neglected in executive education because many people assume that it can't be taught—you're either born with it or you're not. It continues to be a controversial topic in executive training. The *personal* dimension has suffered because of the widespread view that business and personal matters must be separated. It has been ignored because of a corporate culture that rewards individuals who are consumed with business. It's based on the silly notion that we easily leave personal and family matters at the doorstep when we come to work and then leave work matters and stresses at the office when we leave. Nonsense! In the real world it all comes at us at once and that's how we have to deal with it.

True leaders must develop all facets of their potential in order to lead, not just the narrow few needed to manage. Jack Sparks, retired chairman of Whirlpool Corporation, has said that future chief executives can't have had their heads buried in a briefcase, test tube, or computer.

The business dimension is developed by providing executives with the capabilities needed to identify and address critical business challenges. The business dimension of the three-dimensional model starts where most MBA-type curricula leave off—by addressing issues that tomorrow's CEO must confront. Areas of development might include creating new kinds of organizations, building market- and customer-focused organizations, institutionalizing total quality leadership, leading change, winning in the global marketplace, creating a learning organization, fostering innovation, and leveraging technology.

The leadership dimension should differ from other approaches by concentrating on a study of a broad range of classical and contemporary theories and skills. From this foundation, executives can develop their own personal expression of leadership, based on integrity and authenticity. They must learn how to embody leadership. The leadership dimension recognizes that expertise alone is not enough. Instead, leadership is a combination of both competence and character.

The personal dimension is based on the belief that individuals cannot be effective leaders if they are ineffectual in their personal lives. Executives must learn the skills needed to achieve excellence and ongoing renewal. The personal dimension concentrates on helping to clarify and develop the individual's purpose, vision, values, and talents and to integrate work goals and priorities into his or her personal life. Other topics should include self-empowerment and personal responsibility; an appreciation of nature, science, the arts, and the humanities; emotional and physical well-being; and the development of a continuous-learning mind-set. An example of a curriculum that deals with all three dimensions is shown in Figure 17.2.

The three-dimensional framework is a powerful combination of mind-sets, knowledge, and skills whose total is far greater than the sum of its parts. One important ingredient is courage—the hallmark of a true leader. Courage is necessary to create a vision, to challenge the status quo, and to take risks. It is not the valor of heroic acts, say Joseph Badaracco and Richard Ellsworth, authors of *Leadership and the Quest for Integrity* (1989, p. 28), but rather "the courage to do and say what one believes to be right, rather than what is convenient, familiar, or popular; the courage to act on one's vision for [the] organization." Courage is also the ability to admit one's shortcomings and to recognize the need for ongoing learning and development. The courage to admit error is characteristic of a leader who recognizes that lessons generated by failure are as valuable as those that come from success. The three-dimensional framework is a practical approach to unlocking this courage.

Figure 17.2. The Development Focus in the
Three-Dimensional Framework.

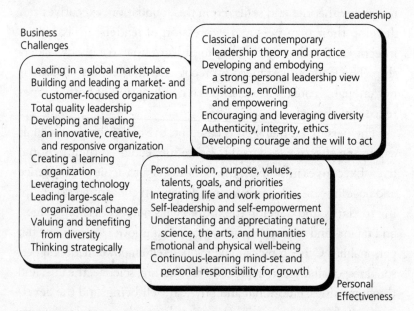

Leadership

Business
Challenges

Leading in a global marketplace
Building and leading a market- and
    customer-focused organization
Total quality leadership
Developing and leading
    an innovative, creative,
    and responsive organization
Creating a learning
    organization
Leveraging technology
Leading large-scale
    organizational change
Valuing and benefiting
    from diversity
Thinking strategically

Classical and contemporary
    leadership theory and practice
Developing and embodying
    a strong personal leadership view
Envisioning, enrolling
    and empowering
Encouraging and leveraging diversity
Authenticity, integrity, ethics
Developing courage and the will to act

Personal vision, purpose, values,
    talents, goals, and priorities
Integrating life and work priorities
Self-leadership and self-empowerment
Understanding and appreciating nature,
    science, the arts, and humanities
Emotional and physical well-being
Continuous-learning mind-set and
    personal responsibility for growth

Personal
Effectiveness

Note: Business challenges should be customized to your organization's specific
challenges.

Clearly, three-dimensional executive development is not common today; however, as Stanley M. Davis, author of *Future Perfect* (1990, p. 56) has said, "By 2001, when the new economy will have probably matured, we will observe our holistic approach to management and wonder how it could have ever been otherwise."

Implementing the Three-Dimensional Framework

How can companies use three-dimensional leadership development to their advantage? Here are five practical ways that organizations can apply the three-dimensional framework and some questions to ask to guide the development:

1. *Internal executive education.* A starting point might be an assessment of existing internal executive education programs or the development of new executive education programs. The framework can be viewed as a continuum (see Table 17.1) that allows organizations to identify the gaps between where they fall on the continuum and where they want to be. What are the shortcomings of their internal programs? For example, are leadership and personal effectiveness adequately addressed, or are efforts exclusively oriented to technical and business arenas?

2. *A guideline for external programs.* Companies can use the three-dimensional framework as a guideline in their selection of external education programs for their managers and executives. Do the programs being considered adequately address all three development dimensions?

3. *Succession planning.* The three-dimensional framework can be used as a key component of the process for selecting future leaders. How well developed are the executives in each of the three dimensions at this time? Where are the gaps? What assignments, experiences, or training are needed to fill the gaps? The framework can be used to systematically help prepare executives for future leadership roles.

4. *A template for the human resource system.* The three-dimensional model can serve as a template for an organization's entire human resource system. It can be used as the basis for recruitment, hiring, firing, succession planning, internal promotions, and incentives. If we want three-dimensional executives, why not hire, promote, and reward people who are as close to the model as possible?

5. *A self-assessment instrument.* Executives are urged to conduct self-assessments to see how they stack up as leaders. They can use the continuum in Table 17.1 to rate themselves on all three dimensions. They can also seek feedback from people who are knowledgeable and honest enough to provide candid input in order to identify the voids in their individual development. Following this

Table 17.1. The Three-Dimensional Executive: A Continuum.

Dimension	From	To
Business	Domestic	General perspective
	Quantitative and analytical	Global
	Technical and functional	Full complement of business skills and judgment
Leadership	Management mind-set	Student of leadership
	Focus on one leadership approach	Envisioning, enrolling, and empowering
	Unclear about personal leadership	Personal leadership view; integrity and authenticity
Personal Effectiveness	Little attention	Purpose, vision, values, and goals
	Addict	Self-empowered
	Other interests sacrificed	Integration of work and life; broad interests

initial self-analysis, a personal self-growth plan can be created that is aimed at filling the gaps in development that were identified in the three-dimensional framework self-assessment. The human resources department may be helpful in identifying specific developmental experiences to address those gaps.

Look to the Horizon

Organizational survival, it is clear, is directly linked to our willingness to cultivate leaders. Leadership is the factor that will ultimately determine our success or failure. No longer can organizations rely solely on technological superiority to achieve economic dominance; rapid changes in technology make obsolete what only yesterday was considered cutting-edge. The three-dimensional framework recognizes that our strength must derive from the strength of individuals. It recognizes that most people use only a fraction of their potential to lead and that the challenges faced by our organizations require the full development and expression of a wide range of leadership capabilities. It poses a tantalizing question: can leadership talent be a source of competitive advantage?

18 CAELA FARREN
BEVERLY L. KAYE

New Skills for
New Leadership Roles

*Caela Farren is the CEO of Farren Associates, in
Annandale, Virginia, and is a founding partner of
Career Systems, a leading publisher of career development products and services. Beverly L. Kaye is CEO
of Beverly Kaye and Associates and vice president of
Career Systems, of which she is also a cofounder. She
is the author of* Up Is Not the Only Way. *Farren
and Kaye are coauthors of* Designing Career Development Systems.

During the last quarter-century we have witnessed a period of
dramatic change on a global scale. The former Soviet bloc has
fallen into disarray. Our long-threatened nightmare of nuclear
Armageddon has apparently been averted. Information and communication technologies are merging into a worldwide electronic
nervous system. Lethal epidemics of viruses and violence spiral out
of control. Interdependence has increased a thousandfold: in the
1970s it required all the nations of OPEC to send the world's economy reeling; in 1995 a single unsupervised bank speculator with a

modem could plunge the international currency market into panic. We are all passengers in the same fragile craft, hurled by a cresting tide of uncertainty toward the half-glimpsed shores of the next millennium.

A New Workplace Contract

Amid all this upheaval, two trends have a particularly important bearing on our discussion of leadership. The first is *the changing nature of the workplace*. We are witnessing a transformation of the conditions of human labor so pervasive and basic that it can only be compared to the introduction of agriculture or the industrial revolution in its impact. Precision manufacturing that formerly required the efforts of hundreds of skilled workers can now be performed with greater speed and accuracy by automated systems with a few trained operators. The legions of administrators and midlevel functionaries who were once needed to oversee our bureaucracies are being replaced by networked terminals and a handful of floppy disks. We can sustain the highest levels of productivity in human history with fewer people than ever before.

Unfortunately, we are less adept at finding a productive use for all the people this process has displaced. Make no mistake: this is a permanent structural shift, not a temporary economic adjustment. Jobs are being rendered obsolete by the hundreds of thousands, and they won't be back. Organizations are eliminating layers of hierarchy and extraneous functions in a fierce competition to achieve speed and flexibility. Many functions such as recruitment, benefits administration, product distribution, and bookkeeping are outsourced to contractors using part-time or temporary employees. Dependable employment and employee loyalty, once the essential quid pro quo of the American workplace, are rapidly becoming archaic concepts. As traditional career expectations unravel, people find themselves cast in the role of independent artisans, seeking the highest bidder for their skills on a short-term basis. In this new workplace the key to a successful career is to choose a craft or profession, develop a portfolio of marketable abilities within it, and then search for opportunities to apply those abilities to specific organizational aims.

A second important trend is *an erosion of confidence* in traditional leadership, or, perhaps more to the point, an erosion of confidence in the management caste, which occupies structural positions that require leadership, but does not provide it. Beset by waves of economic and social change, people seek answers from their accustomed sources of leadership, and they aren't getting them, at least not in a satisfactory way. Unfortunately, it is difficult to name a major institution that has not been discredited by scandal and riven by dissent during the past twenty-five years. Presidents and generals, captains of industry and commissars, sports heroes and social reformers, have been exposed in deceptions both great and petty. Each fresh scandal is magnified and masticated ad nauseam by an insatiable media machine.

When we look to our designated leaders for direction, too often their responses are slick, shortsighted, or self-serving. We seem to want quick remedies and solutions from them, perhaps often unrealistically. Instead, what we may get are "spin doctors," who offer slogans and placebos intended to manipulate our perception of the problems rather than offering effective solutions to them. In the last two national elections in the United States, the public's disgust with its established leadership was expressed by voting overwhelmingly *against* incumbents who were identified with "business as usual." People are far less willing to trust the pronouncements or motives of those in authority because their most basic expectations have been so consistently dashed.

Outside the public arena we find this same widespread discontent. This dissatisfaction is being increasingly manifested by changes in the structure of the organizations in which leaders must practice their craft. Traditional organizational structures that were characterized by autocratic forms in which workers were directed or "told" what to do, how to do, and when to do (with little, if any, attention paid to *why* to do) are giving way to democratic forms of organizations that are characterized by a collaborative, participative style. Workers are demanding a voice in the decisions and decision processes that affect them. Being a true leader in such an environment requires a completely different approach and skillset. When leadership is distributed among a closely linked work force, coordination and control cease to be labor-intensive functions requiring a special mandarin class. As the workplace changes, so too does the nature of organizational leadership. This new workplace environment raises the important question: if the primary role of the leader is no longer to "tell" workers how to do their job, what is the role of the leader in this new, collaborative arrangement?

Building Careers for Leadership Leverage

If appeals to traditional authority are likely to be met with skepticism or resentment, what legitimizes the exercise of leadership in the new workplace? To put the question another way, how can one lead a group while standing within it rather than above it? We can no longer assume a coincidence of interests between the worker and the organization, but with a little ingenuity we can create a mutuality of interests. If we accept the premise that people are essentially contractors of their services in the workplace, then the key to enlisting their cooperation is to create collaborative projects that enhance their professional portfolio while advancing the strategic aims of the organization. People will work enthusiastically on a project that is clearly going to benefit their career. The focus of the art of leadership shifts from directing and instructing to facilitating and enabling.

There are many ways and many opportunities to help people develop their career. These actions can be divided into the five broad categories described below. Each category is a distinctive leadership role that corresponds to a different stage of the career development process. These roles are *facilitator*, *appraiser*, *forecaster*, *adviser*, and *enabler*. To engage people's career interests as a basis for leadership, it is necessary to be proficient at all five roles.

1. Facilitator

Helps people identify their career values, work interests, and marketable skills

Helps people recognize the importance of long-range career planning

Creates an open and accepting climate in which individuals can discuss their career concerns

Helps people understand and articulate what they want from their career

2. Appraiser

Provides candid feedback to team members regarding their performance and reputation

Makes clear the standards and expectations by which people's performance will be evaluated

Listens to people to learn what is important to them about their current job and their hopes for improving it

Points out the relationship between people's performance, reputation, and career goals

Suggests specific actions that individuals can take to improve their performance and reputation

3. Forecaster

Provides information about the organization, the profession, and the industry

Helps people locate and access additional sources of information

Points out emerging trends and new developments that may affect people's career prospects

Helps people understand the cultural and political realities of the organization

Communicates the organization's strategic direction to the team

4. Adviser

Helps people identify a variety of potentially desirable career goals

Assists individuals in their selection of realistic career goals

Relates potential career goals to the business requirements and strategic intent of the organization

Points out possible sources of support and obstacles to achieving career goals

5. Enabler

Helps individuals develop detailed action plans for achieving their career goals

Helps people achieve their goals by arranging useful contacts with people in other areas of the industry or the organization

Discusses team members' abilities and career goals with other people who could provide them with future opportunities

Connects people with the resources they need to implement their career action plans

Each of these leadership roles needs to be examined in detail. However, we will focus here on the forecaster role.

Leading from the Future

Most of our career decisions take into account only factors that have immediate and visible personal importance. As a result, people often fail to look beyond their present job or their organization as it currently exists to notice critical trends that are occurring in the larger systems of which they are also members. This perspective sufficed when people could realistically expect to work for a single employer for twenty or thirty years. Today, however, it is imperative that we study the broader range of systems that affect our career. Only a panoramic view of the present can encompass all the factors we need to consider to anticipate change and plan effectively for the future. The vital leadership contribution of the forecaster is to help others achieve this expanded awareness. This is accomplished by assiduously practicing two future-oriented skills: *trend watching* and *envisioning*.

Trend watching consists of paying close attention to new or unexpected developments in the work team's environment and speculating about how they might affect people's career options. Some of these developments may be sudden and sweeping, such as the virtual replacement of the typewriter by word-processing technology in the 1980s. Others are as gradual as the approaching retirement of a skilled senior colleague. Trend watching is a way of thinking about how the future is shaping itself and what that will mean for the organization and the members of the work team. To be an effective trend watcher you must be a perpetual learner, studying newspaper reports and industry or professional journals, and scanning the culture and the people around you for signs of the new and previously unrecognized. Five distinct levels of systems must be scrutinized by the aspiring trend watcher: *industries*, *professions*, *organizations*, *jobs*, and *individuals*.

Industries

Industries are clusters of organizations that provide products or services to meet a common human need. They exist because we require certain basic things in order to take care of ourselves and each other. For example, people need to travel from place to place (transportation industry), they need to eat (agricultural and food-processing industries), and they need to organize their communities for safety and order (government services). Although individual organizations come and go with the economic tides, industries are as enduring as the basic needs from which they arise. New knowledge and technology periodically change the way people take care of needs such as health care, but you can depend on the continued existence of a health care industry for as long as people are mortal! Thus, focusing on the industry itself as a bellwether for significant trends is much more dependable than focusing on a single organization.

A second useful feature of industries for trend watchers follows directly from this essential property of industries: they are slow to change. It takes time for a new paradigm of technology to permeate an industry. You can identify and prepare for industry trends more easily than you can for developments in the faster-paced environment of individual organizations. Even within the computer industry, a model of rapid transformation, the core competencies required by any given segment of the industry change more rapidly than those in the industry as a whole.

Unfortunately, few people properly track the emerging trends in their own industry, much less others. In fact, when asked, work teams often find it difficult to agree what industry their own organization is in! This lack of clarity is disturbing from both a leadership and an organization development standpoint. It suggests that people will not recognize critical changes in their industry until they have reached the point where the organization is forced to respond to them. Organizations are also afflicted by this inattention to industry trends. Whole segments of the work force are often allowed to let their skills lag behind the industry standard, until the day arrives when they are dismissed in wholesale lots. This entails a tremendous cost in morale and productivity, as well as a loss of irreplaceable experience. Trend watching is an important leadership skill precisely because it can help to avert this shortsighted waste by encouraging people to prepare themselves for new developments in the industry.

Professions

A profession is a craft or discipline with its own history, core competencies, recognized standards of practice, and expert practitioners. Formal education or training and a protracted period of apprenticeship are usually necessary to master a profession. Unlike individual jobs, which are created and eliminated overnight, professions persist over long spans of time. Consequently, they are among the most stable systems available for trend watching.

The viability of a profession in a particular organization depends on whether or not that profession contributes essential competencies. If the organization is directly dependent on the core competencies of a profession to fulfill its mission, people in that profession have a longer planning horizon for their career. People whose professions contribute competencies that are secondary to the central mission of the organization should be advised to plan their careers in terms of growth within the profession rather than within the organization. For this reason it is always advisable to keep a watchful eye on trends within professions and to consider how these trends relate to the organization's strategic aims.

Given the trend toward smaller organizations with flatter structures, few people can realistically expect to keep moving upward in the organization into jobs with ever-increasing responsibilities and perquisites. Growth within one's profession is a rewarding alternative pathway for career development that a leader can use to enlist the willing collaboration of team members. Tremendous satisfaction and self-esteem can be found in developing excellence in a chosen craft. Staying current with the latest advances in a professional field is a process of continual learning that keeps the mind alert and skills sharp. Acquiring new competencies in a profession increases your team members' portfolio of marketable competencies.

Professions also offer the advantage of *linkage*. Established professions generally promote networks of contact among practitioners.

These contacts occur through a variety of forums, including conferences, journals and other publications, computer bulletin boards, and professional associations. Participation in professional networks links people, information, and career resources beyond the boundaries of the current organization. Networks are valuable resources for the dedicated trend watcher.

Organizations

Organizations are the level of work system that people most often think about when planning their career. This is understandable—organizations are tangible and specific where industries and professions are abstract. Yet, paradoxically, organizations are usually among the *least stable* elements of the entire work and career system for the purpose of trend watching. As a result of the turbulent conditions described earlier, organizations change too quickly to be dependable indicators of the future. The core mission of an organization may remain stable over time, but specific jobs and functional subunits can disappear overnight. Leaders should encourage people to make their plans for the future in a particular organization flexible and contingent. It is important to pay attention to where the organization is heading, but to be prepared for unannounced detours and reversals.

Effective trend watching in an organization requires political skills. It is important to cultivate a network of contacts to widen your sources of information. Stay abreast of events throughout the organization to anticipate shifts in its power structure and strategic direction. Monitor the overall strengths and weaknesses of the organization and its various work units. Developments outside your immediate work area can limit or enhance the career opportunities of your team members.

Jobs

When we plan for our future we tend to think in terms of specific jobs. This connection, which seems so straightforward, conceals a

dangerous pitfall. Jobs are actually the shortest-lived and least stable context for career planning. As more organizations move toward
self-directed teams as their basic work unit, jobs per se are becoming less distinct. Therefore, the trend to watch with regard to work
is where the opportunities for certain types of learning are likely to
become available.

In times of rapid change, jobs are temporary opportunities for
acquiring experience, knowledge, competencies, and contacts.
These portable assets can then be applied to career plans based on
the more stable systems of industries and professions. It takes time
to learn from a job and to create a record of accomplishment. Yet
because jobs are so ephemeral, time is an unreliable resource. By
offering people a chance to develop their strengths in particular
areas that will prepare them for the future, work becomes an incen-
tive in and of itself.

Individuals

Career planning is just one aspect of a larger process of life planning. The career decisions people make should reflect a future they
have designed based on realistic self-understanding. The leader as
a facilitator helps people achieve that understanding. The leader
as a forecaster looks for certain trends in each individual's development with implications for his or her role in the future of the work
team.

What aspects of an individual are pertinent to trend watching?
A person's developmental stage is one factor that must surely be
considered. Earlier we noted that industries and professions both
spring from a ground of basic human needs. These needs are rooted
in a few fundamental life challenges that every adult must deal with
in some manner, such as health, shelter, recreation, work, and family. Although these challenges are constants in our lives, our needs
in each area evolve and change over time. Risks that exhilarated us
during our days of youthful exploration may be unwelcome later in
our career. A passion for personal achievement can evolve into a

desire to mentor a successor to carry the work forward. As family members age we may need to spend more time as caregivers at home and less as problem solvers at work. When you think about your life as it will be ten or twenty years from today, you can anticipate any number of probable changes in your circumstances and needs. Your career plans should be consistent with these trends. As a leader, you can help people direct their efforts toward tasks that will prepare them for what they want or can expect to be going on in their lives in the future.

Another individual factor to consider is a person's portfolio of competencies and skills. Competencies are general areas of proficiency, whereas skills are specific actions or activities that support an overall competency. Competencies and skills are somewhat analogous to professions and jobs. Competencies tend to be durable and require years of continual learning to master; skills are geared to short-term tasks. For example, computer programming is a competency area; familiarity with programming languages such as COBOL or C is a collection of discrete skills. The competency of programming persists, while specific programming languages come and go as technology changes. In most organizations and professions, a limited number of competencies are absolutely essential for success, and others are just "nice to have." As a forecaster, you can help people to analyze the competencies they will need to develop in order to maintain or enhance their marketability.

Trend watching at each of the five levels described above is a vital skill for the leader as a forecaster. It demands a willingness to seek out people, information, and other resources, as well as a healthy dose of speculative imagination. Yet trend watching depends on one's interpretation of what is already present or is likely to occur. Forecasters also need another future-oriented leadership skill. They must be able to *envision* what seems impossible under present circumstances and enlist others to make it a reality.

Gary Hamel and C. K. Prahalad, in their discussion of strategic intent in *Competing for the Future*, provide numerous examples of this process in action. When Canon was a minor Japanese photographic equipment manufacturer, it set the apparently absurd goal of shattering Xerox's global dominance in the photocopier field. Not only did Canon succeed in that quixotic enterprise; it went on to repeat it by patenting and licensing breakthroughs in related areas such as laser printer technology. A vision of the future that is compelling and inclusive enough to absorb the best efforts of committed men and women can literally carry us to the moon. The role of the leader as forecaster is to articulate a future so full of exciting possibilities that no one will be able to rest until it is achieved. No current trends lead inevitably to this envisioned future—it demands a leap of faith and an ungodly amount of hard work.

Here we have what is perhaps the most indispensable of all the leadership roles. Leaders are bridges that connect people to the future. They include others' visions in their own, building alliances and partnerships based on shared aspirations. Taking the long view will make us more effective leaders today and will carry us through our uncertain times to the future we dare to create.

19 RICHARD J. LEIDER

The Ultimate Leadership Task

Self-Leadership

Richard J. Leider is the founder and a partner of
The Inventure Group, a training firm in Minneapolis,
Minnesota. He is the author of Repacking Your
Bags, The Power of Purpose, The Inventurers, *and*
Life Skills. *Leider is a speaker, writer, and seminar*
leader and is a nationally recognized leader in the
career development field.

We live in an era of organizational reengineering. To become or remain competitive, leaders often must realize improvement through radical change, or reengineering. In the context of radical change, what career responsibility, if any, do leaders have to their followers? How can leaders obtain discretionary energy and performance urgency unless they have also created a new relationship with their employees? And how can leaders build such effective relationships unless they have effective relationships with themselves, through self-leadership.

The Soft Stuff Is the Hard Stuff

People cannot be reengineered. Organizations cannot compel individuals to be empowered, and leaders cannot empower people to be innovative or courageous or to choose courses of action that are unfamiliar or uncomfortable. Individuals have to empower themselves. Only individuals can choose to take a new direction or risk their career reputations to achieve a new vision, because all change is self-change. All reengineering demands major self-leadership choices.

For these reasons, and because humans are humans, they have difficulty coping with change. Many organizations and their leaders have discovered that "the soft stuff is the hard stuff" in creating radical change. Often, leaders tend to shy away from the human side of leading change because the people side of the business isn't their strong suit. They're more comfortable with the technical or financial tasks than with the human issues. They say, "I don't want to get into all that soft stuff. I just want to get results."

I sympathize. But two decades of working with leaders in change situations have convinced me of three things:

1. All change is self-change. You cannot get the result you need today without getting into "that soft stuff." All change is choice. There is no way to do change in a nice, tidy manner.

2. With self-change you get emotions. It doesn't take a degree in psychology to help people help themselves. It requires a leadership art with people that makes them felt heard. It requires "that soft stuff"—your heart. The word *heart* is made up of two words: *hear* and *art*. The core of the change process is the art of hearing. Listening is absolutely essential to change.

3. Change requires self-leadership. The trend of the 1990s is for all of us to have more accountability, to take more control of our lives. Leaders must continually look within to decide what they want, what they value, and what they are willing to be courageous about.

Real change depends on the motivation and self-leadership of both leaders and followers. A critical element in sustaining any change effort is reigniting everyone's motivation and talents and providing support in using them effectively in the organization. Even in the new world of teams, individual choice remains the key to creating a high-performing team. You cannot build a great team from a collection of passive parts.

The New Career Reality: YOU, Inc.

In the face of radical change, work is not working for many people today. Employees at all levels, in organizations big and small, don't know where they belong anymore, or if they belong at all. People who historically assumed that their organizations would "look after them" are unprepared when new organizational realities turn their job security into the new career reality—YOU, Inc. They now work for themselves first and their organizations second.

People frequently complain that their work, which they used to love, has become drudgery. Or they're doing twice as much today as they were before, but enjoying it half as much. Nevertheless, they're reluctant to voice these complaints to leaders in their organization, because they feel vulnerable. The new "intrapreneurs" question the meaning of what they are doing and feel little loyalty to corporate authority, yet want to contribute their talents. They're naturally overwhelmed, frustrated, and tired of living in the "aftershock" of change. They're skeptical about new leaders who are embraced as cure-alls for what ails their organization.

The switch from career dependence to career self-leadership is not only imperative but also inevitable in today's reengineered organizations. The leader who can recognize this essential shift to YOU, Inc., and build on it has a huge strategic advantage in recruiting talent to a preferred workplace. And preferred workplaces will attract the critical self-led workers needed for success.

Self-Leadership Is the Essence of Leadership

The YOU, Inc., realities today require a new "career covenant," under which leaders help followers develop and master the portable career skills needed in the twenty-first century and employees embrace a spirit of competitive urgency and performance learning. Self-leadership is the core around which a new career covenant is built. It consists of personal purpose, values, vision, and courage. It is the character each person brings to the leadership role.

Self-leadership is the essence of leadership. It is based on knowing yourself and seeking reliable counsel. Leaders in a changing world need to take stock of their personal attributes that embrace or resist change. Unless they understand the vision that motivates them to lead, the purpose that ignites them, and the values that empower them, how can they make courageous choices in a chaotic world?

Self-leadership is the essence of all individual, team, and organizational change. Visionary leadership demands courage. Team unity demands individual enrollment. Organizational change demands self-change. Thus, leaders need to weave the golden thread of self-leadership through all their change philosophies, processes, programs, and tools from start to finish. This deceptively simple concept elicits lip service from many leaders that contrasts sharply with the time and resources they actually give to it. Many leaders are perceived as all form and no essence, as not "walking their talk." Leaders must continually refer to their own personal purpose, values, vision, and courage. They must deal not only with the external threat of competitive failure, but also with the even greater internal threat of lack of leadership integrity, because in the twenty-first century, self-leadership is the ultimate leadership challenge— a survival skill.

To make matters interesting, things aren't easy for leaders at home these days, either. Families and relationships are full of new challenges that many leaders are not prepared for. Most leaders are working harder longer. Marriages that once would have struggled along with "inner kill," but remained unchanged for years, break up. (Inner kill is the art of dying without showing it; the marriage looks good on the outside but is dead on the inside—no vitality.) Earnings are often in a race with expenses and the expenses seem to be winning. The leaders' challenges today at work and at home are made up of constant and difficult stresses. It's no wonder that many leaders ask themselves if it's all worth it and can't figure out how to manage it all.

Many great thinkers, from Thales ("Know thyself") to William Shakespeare ("To thine own self be true") to Mahatma Gandhi ("You must be the change you wish to see in the world"), have urged us to look within ourselves for leadership guidance. Today more leaders are taking their advice seriously, and for good reason.

Twenty Tips for Self-Leadership

Here are twenty tips for self-leadership today:

1.   The quality and depth of our leadership reflects itself in our relationships with our colleagues and followers; we must be clear about our *values* because they reveal who we really are as leaders.

Tip

Recognize your stress level. Watch for the signs of stress—forgetfulness; chronic fatigue; sleeplessness; changes in appetite; increased colds, headaches, or lower back pain; withdrawal from relationships; or increased mood swings. If you aren't sure you have a problem, ask your family or friends whether they've noticed changes in you.

2.   We are not powerless in choosing our living and working conditions; we do have choices and they are the secret of our *power*; the willingness to exercise our choices is the source of leadership energy.

Tip

Gain control where you can. A leader's job includes stressful forces beyond your control. Look for personal areas in which you can take charge. Schedule time to accommodate your need for exercise or to attend family events.

3. We must recognize our *addictions* to discover if we are being true to our essence or living in a self-imposed prison, driven by others' or our organization's expectations.

Tip

Balance your life-style. Leaders who feel like victims are often perfectionists, idealists, or workaholics who can never truly please themselves. Think of one other area in your life you would like to develop besides your work—your mind? body? spirit?

4. Real changes come from changing our *mental maps*; high energy comes from a clear and passionate personal vision.

Tip

Take a daily solo. An absolute essential for clear pictures is to allow at least fifteen minutes a day to reflect on the big picture and to set or revise priorities according to it.

5. Leadership *assessment* is best done on the basis of our own complete records of what we do rather than anybody else's partial, incomplete records.

Tip

Do what you love, or get career counseling. We may burn up doing what we love, but we do not burn out or rust out. If you're burning out, you may not really love what you do and may need to reinvent your job.

6. We must take *inventory* of our leadership talents if we are to profit in the future from the lessons of the past.

Tip

Examine your job. Keep a notebook for a week in which you jot down everything you naturally love to do and everything you intensely dislike doing at work. Ask yourself honestly, "How much time do I spend doing what I naturally love to do?" Then focus on your strengths and manage your weaknesses.

7.   We must decide personally by which *criteria* we want our leadership legacy measured.

Tip

Renew a relationship with a mentor or coach. A good coach can help by providing insights into obstacles in your work or personal life and by offering a new perspective on your values and criteria for success. Ask yourself, "Who are my teachers today?" "Who is the first person I'd call for leadership advice?"

8.   Reinventing ourselves is a lifelong and *continuous learning process*; we must become comfortable with the reality that satisfaction always leads to dissatisfaction.

Tip

Challenge yourself to get out of your comfort zone. Pursue a non-leadership position in a professional or community organization. Or undertake a new learning experience outside of your element. Risk and challenge can recharge your batteries.

9.   We must establish solid *support systems*—a personal board of directors—that can carry us through the vagaries of change.

Tip

Pick a personal board of directors. Who are the people whose wisdom and personal counsel you value? Who would you select to sit on the advisory team for your personal life, work, and leadership?

10.   We must take *risks* to initiate courageous conversations that will keep us in honest and creative face-to-face dialogue with our colleagues and followers.

Tip

Quit doing something. Busy leaders tend to overcommit themselves. Saying no and meaning it will reduce your stress and give you back your sense of control. Look over your schedule and choose to stop participating in one committee or assignment.

11.   We must be developing a personal *Plan B* even before we have successfully achieved Plan A.

Tip

Design a written Plan B. What would you do if you were fired tomorrow and had to look for customers, not a job? What exactly do you do that people would pay money for?

12.   We must not play "victim" to external forces; we need to *take control* of our calendars.

Tip

Picture your ideal week. Recently, *The Wall Street Journal* wrote about a survey of American attitudes toward time. One of the more interesting questions was this: "Would you sacrifice a day's pay for an extra day off each week?" The results showed that many people would. How about you? What does an ideal week look like for you? Sketch it out on a piece of paper.

13.   We must first make the important *life decisions* that are the raw materials of career decisions.

Tip

Schedule a "heart checkup." When did you last have a real "life priorities" conversation? Or a heart-to-heart visit with someone close to you? Think about your friendships. When was the last time you asked someone how he or she was *and* stopped long enough to hear the answer? Are you worried that you and your partner don't talk any-

more? Schedule a heart checkup with someone close to you this
week.

14.   We must blend our priorities and trade-offs in our personal
life and work or we risk wasting our most valuable currency—time.

Tip

Envision yourself in the year 2000. Where will you be when the clock
rings midnight on December 31, 1999? Discuss your ideal career and
life scenario with someone close to you.

15.   Working from a clear sense of *personal purpose* creates success with fulfillment; a written personal purpose statement reduces
anxiety in times of change.

Tip

Ask the big question. The fact is that many of us are put off by purpose. If we're asked to describe our life purpose, we assume that it
has to be something that can go on a wall plaque, something inspiring, like dedicating ourselves to world peace. Although some leaders
do have an overwhelming sense of purpose, many don't. Nevertheless, it's important to continually ask the big question, "Why do I get
up in the morning?" How would you answer that question for today?

16.   We must live with clear intention and make consistent
contact with a *higher power* greater than ourselves.

Tip

Find a listening point. We spend a great deal of time running around
trying to figure out what to do, but we need to figure out what we
want to *be* first. Make it a point to take regular spirit breaks. Imagine
yourself in a favorite peaceful place—a listening point. Several minutes there will renew your spiritual core. Take four deep breaths, inhal-
ing and exhaling slowly, to deepen your focus. Give your spiritual core
space to grow.

17. Leading from a clear, personal sense of purpose creates *courage*; real courage attracts real followers.

Tip

Review this week's schedule. We're only as good as the commitments on our calendars. How we spend our time defines how we live and lead. Are you spending time with the courageous "change champions" in your organization? Do your meeting agendas allow time for "courageous conversations"?

18. The key to high performance is *integrity*—doing little things consistently. Leadership integrity is built or destroyed by small day-to-day things that become a pattern.

Tip

Actually practice the stress management techniques you know. You probably know many. One simple technique is to leave fifteen minutes early for appointments so you won't have to rush. What's a stress management technique you know and need to get back to?

19. *Overstress* comes mainly from reactive living; stress can break us down or it can energize us; the difference is in how we perceive it.

Tip

Self-leadership is self-care. The way to start self-leadership is to be honest with yourself. How healthy are you? Do you have the energy and vitality you need to last through the race? Schedule a physical checkup soon.

20. People are attracted to what is celebrated; *celebrate* the many faces of celebration.

Tip

Lighten up. Celebration is a building-block process; notice the "baby steps" toward change by phoning, writing notes, and affirming your progress all year long. And refind your smile if you've lost it!

20 DOUGLAS K. SMITH

The Following Part of Leading

Douglas K. Smith is a writer and consultant concerned with organizational performance, innovation, and change. He is author of Taking Charge of Change, *a cutting-edge exploration of the management principles, strategies, and visions essential to behavior-driven performance and change. He is also coauthor of* The Wisdom of Teams, *which is widely acknowledged as the leading book written on the discipline required for team performance. Smith is co-creator of the "Horizontal Organization," a set of principles for designing organizations that* Fortune *magazine has called the "model for the next 50 years."*

In the twenty-first-century organization, all leaders must learn to follow if they are to successfully lead. Profound and continuing changes in technology, demographics, government, and economics have made the omniscient leader obsolete. Yes, leaders must continue to set direction, make tough decisions and choices, and inspire commitment from those who follow them. They must find ways to "go first" and, in doing so, to put their own unique stamp of personality and talent on the enterprise. But that is no longer enough.

Leaders at all levels and in all situations must pay close attention to situations in which their most effective option is to follow—not because the hierarchy demands that they "obey," but because performance requires them to rely on the capacities and insights of other people.

Most of us, of course, have known and honored people who "led from behind." Too few of us, however, have sought to emulate them. Rather, we have considered them as unusually "good" people, admirable souls who surely were exceptions in the rough-and-tumble, Darwinian environment of organizations. Such judgments were perhaps accurate for most of the twentieth century. But today's most critical performance challenges demand that we rise from the comfortable couch of "good-versus-bad" moral judgments to a more proactive and practical outlook and ask, "What must leaders do to ensure results?" More than ever before in history, the answer lies in following—following our vision and purpose, following our principles for managing toward that purpose, and following *all the people* who will make an organization's vision happen.

Why Following?

Organizational performance is no longer a well-ordered affair. Ten or twenty years ago, if you asked how a private sector organization was performing, your respondent would tick off financial and market indicators, followed by functional and then individual contributions. All metrics would be quantitative, expressed in monetary or volumetric units, and would reflect periodic (annual, monthly, weekly, daily) accomplishments. If you asked how a nonprofit or government organization was performing, at best you would hear about the scope of its purpose, again quickly followed by functional and individual contributions.

In this world, leaders and followers were strictly divided. The command-and-control hierarchy required front-line employees to follow and the CEO or executive director to lead. Everyone in between led those below and followed those above. Leading meant making decisions and providing direction; following meant obeying. Organizations were machines. The best organizations were the best-oiled, most efficient machines. People—whether leaders or followers—were cogs.

Today, if you ask how an organization is performing, as often as not your respondent will condition any description with caution and uncertainty. "Who knows?" colors any answer that is forthcoming. Most of us understand that the elegant blueprint of financial, market, functional, and individual indicators is no longer enough. Shareholders are not king. Nor are customers. Instead, all organizations must continually balance their performance in favor of every constituency that matters. In the for-profit sector, that always means shareholders, customers, and employees. In government and nonprofit organizations, it means beneficiaries, funders, and employees. And in both, *employees* means everyone who works for the organization, not just people who are below the top. The CEO is an employee, too.

Delivering balanced performance now requires both functional and cross-functional ("process") excellence built on both individual and team contributions. Goals and accomplishments must be continuous as well as periodic. And what matters most can be qualitative (for example, morale) as well as quantitative. Finally, speed (cycle time) and specificity (zero defects) have joined volume and money as key metrics.

Viewed as a blended whole, this "both/and" performance agenda demands both/and organizing approaches. Today, the people in an effective organization must both think and do, both manage others and manage themselves, both make decisions and do real work. They must figure out the best way both to divide up labor and to reintegrate it. And they must do so in a manner that ensures the advantages of both fixed routine and flexibility. Finally, they all must know when to hold themselves both individually and mutually accountable for results.

Few people who only follow will contribute to such organizations. Nor will many who only lead. Instead, all must learn how to both lead and follow. It is common wisdom that the person who does the job knows best how to make that job more responsive to customers and other environmental factors. That person's supervisor had better know when and how to follow. More and more performance challenges demand the real-time integration of multiple skills and perspectives among small numbers of people working as a team. The best team leaders know that team performance depends on the team being in control, not just one individual on the team. Therefore, team leaders—like all other team members—must know when to follow.

When an organization's performance depends more on getting continuously better at cross-functional excellence than on improving functional excellence, all the people who contribute to that process must know how to follow and serve those who are "upstream" and "downstream" from them. What, after all, are internal customers other than people whose needs we must follow and attend to? Finally, top leaders who hope to set the energies and performance of people on fire through rich, promising visions must know when to follow their people's interpretation of those visions in order to truly benefit from the creativity and meaning that any vision-driven enterprise requires.

Today's most successful organizations are purposeful. But how can a purpose drive an organization if the people within it do not know when and how to follow it? Today's most effective organizations operate according to a handful of powerful principles instead of thick manuals of policies and rules. But how can people apply those principles if they do not know how to follow them? Today's most powerful organizations make real the notion, "People are our most important asset." But how can they do so unless everyone both leads and follows?

The Problem with Following

Following suffers from a serious image problem. Few children aspire to grow up to become followers. Following is not included in selection criteria for colleges, professional schools, scholarships, or awards. In fact, at school, in books and newspapers, in the movies, and on television, following is often condemned as a mindless denial of basic humanity. We are treated to a steady diet of groupies, cult members, and brainwashed masses and are bluntly warned against the horror and destitution of following.

The first time most of us bump into this paradox is when we apply for an entry-level job. After being hired and quickly learning the paramount importance of following directions from above, we nonetheless find that the public discourse within the organization is all about leadership. The corollary to "People are our most important asset" is, inevitably, "We want everyone to be a leader." How many companies, nonprofit organizations, or government institutions have training courses in "followership"?

In some respects this is odd. Even before the world completely changed, most people were, in fact, followers. Indeed, it is a point of pride in mature adults to recognize the dignity and utility in being loyal subordinates, dependable people who know their role and upon whom the boss or leader can always count to deliver. But the honor in this has always been rather private, evoking images of handshakes and gold watches more than stirring, in-your-face headlines. "Real leaders," we believe, are made of sterner, more iconoclastic stuff. Consequently, even in its most admirable aspects, following has remained a dirty secret, a closet phenomenon that few of us enthusiastically or consistently embrace and celebrate.

In what is now a both/and world, following continues to bear an either/or burden at the center of which lies self-interest. Either you are a leader or you are a follower. At times, self-interest dictates that you follow because you have no choice. It is in your job description. But you are always looking for "advancement," for the opportunity to break the bonds of following by advancing to a position as a leader. One need only look at an organizational chart to see who are the leaders and who are the followers.

The only individuals standing apart from this position-based pattern are those special people who are so selfless that, in following others, they actually take a higher ground of leadership. And do not assume that I am only describing historical figures like Gandhi here. All of us have known comparable organizational "saints" who, in always ignoring their own self-interest, garner a moral base for, in fact, leading. The opinions and influence of such people are always sought out in support of any critical change or initiative. Put differently, pure following is a subtle act of leadership.

Of course, very few such people exist in organizations. Self-interest is too strong a force. And therein, I believe, lies a large measure of the answer to the question of how to shift the image and practice of following from the ineffective either/or past to a more promising both/and future. Performance now demands that we all learn *how and when we most effectively advance our self-interest by following.* In fact, I would state this even more strongly. In the complex interdependent reality we now inhabit, our self-interest— indeed our survival—demands that we become as adept at following others as we are at getting them to follow us.

Our self-interest demands that we learn the both/and reality in following and leading. This starts with abandoning a positional reference to the issue of who are followers, who leaders. Position was a powerful engine for organizations that depended on people as cogs. But today's organizations require fast and flexible networks of engaged and empowered people, not human robots who contribute coglike efficiency to organizational machines. Today, performance challenges—not position—should determine when you should follow and when you should lead.

The Following Part of Leading

Everyone must learn both when and how to exercise the following part of leading and the leading part of following. Knowing when to follow is not a bimodal, either/or affair. Unlike position, which remains static for significant periods of time, performance goals and demands constantly shift. Performance happens in real time, not organizational time. As a result, learning when to follow is a constant challenge that coexists *simultaneously and in parallel* with knowing when to lead. Consider, for example, the indicators of when a leader must follow in each of three common performance situations:

1. *Individual performance:* As a leader, you must follow another individual, regardless of hierarchy, if

   That individual, through experience, skill, and judgment, knows best

   That individual's growth demands that you invest more in his or her skill and self-confidence than in your own

   Only that individual, not you, has the capacity (the time and opportunity) to "get it done"

2. *Team performance:* As a leader, you must follow the team if

   The team's purpose and performance goals demand it

   The team, not you, must develop skills and self-confidence

   The team's agreed-upon working approach requires you, like all the others, to do real work

3. *Organizational performance:* As a leader, you must follow others, regardless of hierarchy, if

   The organization's purpose and performance goals demand it

   The need for expanding the leadership capacity of others in the organization requires it

   "Living" the vision and values enjoins you to do so

How can you exercise the following part of leadership? How can you go beyond just good listening to actually following? These are some of the critical behaviors and skills that can make you an effective follower:

- *Asking questions instead of giving answers:* By asking such questions as "What do you think we should do?" or "How do you suggest we proceed?" you take a step behind another person. Whether you stay behind, of course, depends on your intention to actually follow the suggestion or answer of that other person.

• *Providing opportunities for others to lead you:* This goes beyond the traditional notion of looking for growth opportunities for other people. Unless the opportunity in question bears a real risk for your personal performance outcome, you are not actually positioning yourself as a follower.

• *Doing real work in support of others instead of only the reverse:* Rolling up your sleeves and contributing "sweat equity" to the efforts and outcomes of other people earns you their appreciation as someone upon whom they can depend, regardless of the relative hierarchical or functional position each of you holds.

• *Becoming a matchmaker instead of a "central switch":* In addition to following other people yourself, you must learn to help them follow each other. This requires you to get beyond considering yourself the "central switch" through which all decisions flow. Instead, you need to look for every possible chance to help people find their best collaborators. "Have you asked Sally or Rasheed what they think?" is often the only input required to facilitate the effort at hand—although you then must submit your effort and support to whatever the people in question suggest.

• *Seeking common understanding instead of consensus:* The pejorative meaning associated with consensus management has nothing to do with either effective leading or effective following. Leaders who know when and how to follow build deep common understanding, not superficial consensus, around the purpose, goals, and approach at hand. They submit themselves and others to the discipline of ensuring that all sides to any disagreement are fully understood by everyone, recognizing that mutual understanding is far more powerful than any particular decision to choose path A over path B. All people will follow strong, commonly understood purposes and goals more easily than the "put-up jobs" associated with consensus.

Conclusion

Few of us need to be persuaded about the contributions we must make as leaders. Following, however, presents a more complex dilemma on the eve of the twenty-first century. Neither we nor our colleagues will succeed if we continue to divide ourselves mechanically into leaders and followers. Instead, we must find opportunity, contribution, and honor at *all times in both roles*. That will require us to strip out any untoward associations with following and replace them with sound, performance-oriented meanings.

I do not believe we can pull this off with "newspeak" that portrays everyone as leaders and no one as followers. Such puffery fools few adults for very long. Common sense tells us that, in all situations, some must lead and some follow. "Too many cooks," we all know, "spoil the broth." Moreover, when organizations flatter themselves by saying, "Everyone is a leader," they ignore the hard, substantive learning about following that all hierarchically appointed leaders must acquire in order to make the promise of leadership in others come true.

We need to craft a different organizational culture, one that self-consciously practices and celebrates both the following and the leading skills in all of its people. In this culture, people are not "assets." They are continually shifting collaborations of individuals who make performance and change happen. In those collaborations, individuals forever both follow and lead one another in whatever combination works best for the task at hand, then recongeal around different followers and leaders for the task coming on its heels. In those moments when some are following, they do so neither as saints nor serfs, but as human beings trying to make a difference.

21 DAVE ULRICH

Credibility × Capability

*Dave Ulrich is professor of business administration
at the School of Business, University of Michigan, and
a partner in the Global Consulting Alliance. He is
coauthor of* Organizational Capability: Competing
from the Inside/Out, Human Resources as a Competitive Advantage: An Empirical Assessment of
HR Competencies and Practices in Global Firms,
and The Boundaryless Organization. *Ulrich is the
editor of* Human Resource Management. *He is a
fellow in the National Academy of Human Resources
and has been listed by* Business Week *as one of the
world's top ten educators in management and the top
educator in human resources.*

The computer I am using to draft this chapter is both complex and simple. Complexity comes from the intricately designed and manufactured memory chips, software code, and other techno-logical advances. Few fully understand all the intricate parts that must come together to make this computer work. But, for me it is simple. I turn it on, I see the screen, I punch keys and letters appear on the screen, I hit other keys, and my document is stored so that I can print it later. Frankly, I do not understand all the mathematics, engineering, and science that makes the computer work, but I can still use it productively.

Likewise, leadership is both complex and simple. The complexities of leadership are paradoxical: it is an art and a science, it involves change and stability, it draws on personal attributes and requires interpersonal relationships, it sets visions and results in actions, it honors the past and exists for the future, it manages things and leads people, it is transformational and transactional, it serves employees and customers, it requires learning and unlearning, it centers on values and is seen in behaviors. Leadership, like the inner workings of a computer, is a complex set of relationships, systems, and processes that few fully master.

However, in a world of unparalleled change, immediate information, global networks, and rising employee and customer expectations, the leaders of the future must discover simple models that access the complex underpinnings of successful leadership. Here, my focus is on the keyboard, the oversimplified but useful model of the leader of the future. Following this logic, leadership in the future (1) works to turn aspirations into actions, (2) rests on five assumptions, and (3) requires both personal credibility and organizational capability.

Leadership Purpose: Turning Aspirations into Actions

The outcome of effective leadership is simple. It must turn aspirations into actions. Aspirations come in many forms: strategies, goals, missions, visions, foresight, and plans. Regardless of the term, leaders create aspirations. Successful aspirations have certain defining characteristics:

- They focus on the future by visualizing what can be.

- They connect and integrate the entire value chain of a

firm (suppliers, customers, and employees) rather than
what goes on inside the firm.

- They create energy and enthusiasm about what can be.

- They engage employees' hearts (emotion), minds (cog-
  nitions), and feet (action).

However, the leader's job is not just to aspire, but also to act.
Turning aspirations into action translates a statement of intent into
a series of behaviors. Leaders in the future will not just "want to
become the preeminent global provider" or "anticipate changing
customer values through dedicated employees." Instead, they will
intentionally and purposefully create actions that cause these aspirations to happen. It will not be enough to write value statements;
these statements will have to create value. It will not be enough to
run visioning workshops; the visions will have to be reflected in
daily behaviors. It will not be enough to declare an intent; leaders
will have to deliver results.

Leadership Assumptions

To turn aspirations into actions, assumptions about future leaders
will have to change in five ways.

From Leadership at the Top of the Enterprise
to Shared Leadership

Most articles and books on leadership have highlighted the role of
the CEO or senior individual in an organization as *the* leader who
makes things happen. We like to be able to identify our heroes and
leaders by name: Jack Welch is creating culture change at General
Electric; Louis Gerstner is reinventing IBM; Arthur Martinez is

transforming Sears, Roebuck; Larry Bossidy has energized Allied-Signal; George Fisher is fundamentally reshaping Eastman Kodak; and so on.

The future and real heroes of business will be unnamed leaders who turn aspirations into actions inside companies. (See *The Real Heroes of Business and Not a CEO Among Them,* by Bill Fromm and Len Schlesinger, 1993; and *Winning the Service Game,* by Benjamin Schneider and David E. Bowen, 1995.) These leaders will probably not get on the cover of *Business Week, Fortune,* or *Forbes*. They will be the individuals who turn aspirations into actions in a daily way. They will be the employees who go the extra mile in customer service by quietly and consistently exceeding customer expectations. They will be the middle-level managers who engage and care about employees without fanfare. Future leaders will be less visible and identifiable by public acclaim, but more important to the individual customer. I have fewer dealings with Sears executives than with the store associates who meet my needs and care about me.

From One-Time Events to Ongoing Processes

Leadership has often been framed in terms of single events, such as leadership or office conferences, videos, strategic planning sessions, or other event-driven activities. As leadership becomes more ingrained within the firm and less resident only at the top, one-time events need to be replaced with ongoing processes. Rather than holding meetings off-site to debate and make major decisions, leaders in the future will take part in a "natural act in a natural place." (Steve Kerr coined this phrase when working with General Electric's cultural change effort called "Workout.") They will have to master the art of engaging employees and making decisions in staff meetings, site visits, daily communication with employee groups, and other on-site situations.

Future leaders will be less concerned with saying what they will deliver and more concerned with delivering what they have said they would. Symbolic leadership will always be important, but consistent, reliable, predictable delivery on promises will be the foundation of leadership.

From Individual Champions to Team Victories

In an increasingly interdependent world, leadership must be created through relationships more than through individual results. Leaders of the future will have to master the art of forming teams and learning to work with boundaryless teams. Instead of coming from individual heroes, future successes will come from teams that share resources and that learn to overlook personal ambition for the sake of the team. Leaders who learn to collaborate through teams rather than directing through edicts see the value of team success. In almost every team sport, good teams will beat good talent. The best athlete in the league seldom is on the team that wins the most games.

Future leaders will have to master teamwork. They will have to understand how to work with and through others because no one person can possibly master all the divergent sources of information necessary to make good decisions. Thus, diversity, as evidenced by teams that are composed of individuals with different talents, becomes a competitive advantage.

From Problem Solvers to Pioneers

Two individuals want to cross a river. The first carefully identifies where she wants to come out, then identifies each stone she will step on before taking the first step. The second examines the other bank of the river and identifies in general where he will come out, then finds the first few stones and gets going. The first individual is the problem solver. Leaders traditionally have been taught to be problem solvers, defining where they are headed in explicit terms (for example, financial results or market share gains) and making sure that all the steps to the end are detailed before acting. In the future, because of the enormous pace of change, the end state can never be precise. Leaders have to shape a direction, then take steps toward that direction with the confidence that they will continually make progress. These leaders are like the pioneers who moved West without specific location as an outcome, but with a conviction that the direction in which they were headed was right.

Future leaders will need to be pioneers who take risks, create new paths, shape new approaches to old problems, and have strong values and beliefs that drive their actions.

From Unidimensional to Paradoxical Thinking

The traditional world of leadership thinking is bounded by right answers. Leadership skills are neatly laid out and packaged so that the individual can become more effective. In the complex world of the future, the bounds must be unshackled and leaders must learn to live with and master persistent paradoxes. Paradoxes occur when two competing demands pull someone in seemingly opposite directions. Leaders will be expected to satisfy customers and employees, to cut costs and grow businesses, to innovate with new products and increase share of old products, to serve local market needs and respond to global conditions, to shape a vision and create action. Learning to serve multiple stakeholders and to manage ongoing paradoxes will be the new challenge of future leaders. These leaders will need to learn to live in ambiguity and to balance competing demands

Ultimately, these new assumptions about leadership—that it is shared, involves ongoing processes, focuses on team victories, requires pioneers, and accepts paradox—will form the framework for the leader of the future. These assumptions will force leaders to learn, unlearn, and relearn continually. When leaders grasp the implications of these assumptions, they can respond to the leadership challenge of the next century.

Leadership Charge: Credibility × Capability

A simple charge for leadership that fulfills the goal of turning aspirations into actions, based on the defined assumptions, comes from the concept *credibility × capability*. Successful leaders of the future must be personally credible. Credible leaders have the personal habits, values, traits, and competencies to engender trust and commitment from those who take their direction. Perhaps one of the best examples of this personal credibility is the leadership of Mahatma Gandhi, who claimed, "My life is its own message." He said, "You must watch my life, how I live, eat, sit, talk, behave in general. The sum total of all those is my religion" (quoted in Keshavan Nair, A *Higher Standard of Leadership*, 1994, p. 15). Gandhi believed that his personal life gave him the credibility that enabled him to be a successful leader.

Successful leaders of the future must also be able to create organizational capability. Capability comes from leaders who are able to shape, structure, implement, and improve organizational processes to meet business goals. Many great leaders have the ability to shape organizations. Rich Teerlink at Harley-Davidson has worked to create a stronger organization through training and organizing his work force. He said, "If you empower dummies, you get dumb decisions faster." His view is that capable organizations come from more talented *and* more committed employees.

In this simple model, a leader must engender personal credibility and create organizational capability (see Figure 21.1). Some leaders are taught to be personally credible, to develop good habits, to live virtuous lives, and to build moral character. All these personal attributes are noble and worthy. However, being only a credible individual will not be sufficient for the leader of the future. I may like, trust, respect, and enjoy the company of an individual, but this personal affinity will not sustain leadership.

On the other hand, some leaders are gifted at aligning and adjusting organizations. They mobilize resources, shape visions,

Figure 21.1. Leadership Charge: Credibility × Capability.

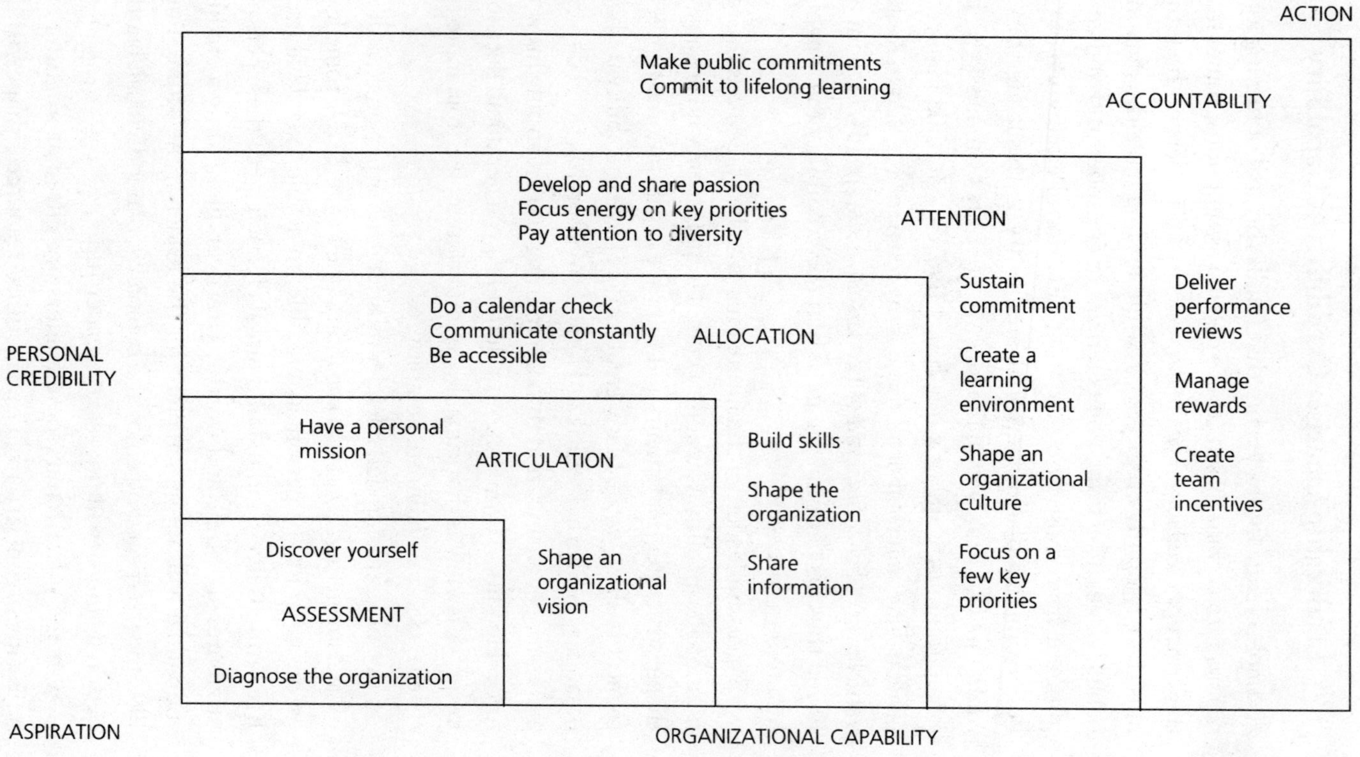

ACTION

ACCOUNTABILITY

Make public commitments
Commit to lifelong learning

Deliver performance reviews

Manage rewards

Create team incentives

ATTENTION

Develop and share passion
Focus energy on key priorities
Pay attention to diversity

Sustain commitment

Create a learning environment

Shape an organizational culture

Focus on a few key priorities

ALLOCATION

Do a calendar check
Communicate constantly
Be accessible

Build skills

Shape the organization

Share information

ARTICULATION

Have a personal mission

Shape an organizational vision

ASSESSMENT

Discover yourself

Diagnose the organization

PERSONAL CREDIBILITY

ORGANIZATIONAL CAPABILITY

ASPIRATION

design processes and systems, and build in accountabilities. These leaders make organizations competitive, but if they do not build personal credibility, they will also fail. They will not be able to create the emotional bond needed in times of rapid and turbulent change.

In this view of leadership, two generic diagnostic questions can be asked to assess leadership quality:

1. *Credibility*. Does this leader have credibility with those he or she works with? Do individuals trust, respect, admire, and enjoy working for this leader? Do those who work with this leader as subordinates, peers, customers, or supervisors feel a personal and emotional bond with him or her?

2. *Capability*. Does this leader have the ability to make the organization succeed? Does she or he have the ability to shape a vision, create commitment to the vision, build a plan of execution, develop capabilities, and hold people accountable for making things happen?

On these two simple dimensions should rest many leadership requirements of the future. Leaders who demonstrate both credibility and capability will engender passion and performance, resolve and results, commitment and competence. They will be individuals who have strong characters and who also build strong organizations that do not depend on their characters for success.

Figure 21.1 shows five steps these leaders will need to take to turn aspirations into actions at both the personal (credibility-building) and organizational (capability-building) levels:

1. *Assessment*. Leaders need to assess their personal and organizational strengths and weaknesses. This candid assessment should help them to see the world as it is, not as they would like it to be. Acknowledging weaknesses and being able to leverage strengths

enables leaders to know themselves and their organizations well enough to make progress.

2. *Articulation*. Leaders need to articulate their personal and organizational goals and directions. Personal missions and organizational visions become useful means for articulating a direction.

3. *Allocation*. Leaders need to allocate resources. Personal resources include time and accessibility. Leaders who do not manage their calendars fail to build credibility because they never have time for anyone or anything. Likewise, leaders need to allocate resources within an organization to strengthen it. Building competencies through training, shaping teams and reengineering work processes, and sharing information become means of allocating organizational energy.

4. *Attention*. Leaders need to focus their attention. They gain credibility by having passion about a few priorities and by paying attention to those whose interests may not be met by majority rule. Leaders help organizations to focus attention by specifying a few key priorities, relentlessly pursuing those priorities, and building an organizational culture of resolve.

5. *Accountability*. Leaders need to ensure accountability. Without a "return-and-report" process, personal goals become wishes, not realities. Likewise, building a performance management system where organizational behaviors are expected and accounted for becomes critical.

Personal credibility and organizational capability are the primary factors that drive these processes. Turning aspirations into actions becomes the leader's task.

Leadership of the Future

Given the purpose, assumptions, and charge for leaders of the future, a simple question remains: Would I know one if I saw one? The leaders of the future will be known

- Less for what they say and more for what they deliver

- Less by their title and position and more by their expertise and competence

- Less by what they control and more by what they shape

- Less by goals they set and more by mind-sets they build

- Both for great personal credibility and for exceptional organizational capabilities

These are simple axioms that shape the leadership path for the future but that will require complex insights by leaders in order to stay on the path. They are the keyboard for the more complex dynamics of successful leadership, but with these keys, leaders will be successful.

22 WARREN WILHELM

Learning from Past Leaders

Warren Wilhelm is vice president of corporate education for AlliedSignal Inc. and has over twenty-five
years' experience in the management of human
resources. He has taught human resource management in the graduate business schools at Harvard
University, the University of Colorado, and Babson
College and founded and managed a consulting firm,
The Human Resource Consulting Group, from 1981
to 1989. From 1989 to 1993, he was head of organization and management development for Amoco
Corporation, where he was responsible for corporate
culture change. Wilhelm also serves as president of
the Global Consulting Alliance.

Leaders in the future will be different from leaders of the past and
from today's leaders. True or false?

The answer, of course, is both. Certain characteristics of effective leadership appear to be ubiquitous and ever enduring, whereas
others appear to change with the times. By defining what seem to
be the core characteristics of effective leadership, we can draw the
continuity thread through time. And by embellishing the thread

with the timely perturbations caused by technical advances, societal change and reconfiguration, wars, natural events, and other passing phenomena, we can identify the dynamics of leadership that make it more or less effective at any given point in human history.

Merely to identify the characteristics of effective leadership and leaders is insufficient to define leadership in the future, but it is a place to start. As has been true through the ages, effective leaders of the future will possess certain core competencies or characteristics that allow them to be effective. Built onto these core characteristics must be learned dynamic capabilities that allow the raw talent to take shape in ways that cause others to follow willingly and often excitedly.

The core characteristics, the sine qua non of effective leaders in the future, will be much the same as they have always been. They include basic intelligence, clear and strong values, high levels of personal energy, the ability and desire to grow constantly, vision, infectious curiosity, a good memory, and the ability to make followers feel good about themselves. Each of these, and the integrated bundle of characteristics they form, will be necessary but insufficient for effective leadership in the future. I will first examine each of the core characteristics, then describe the dynamics that allow them to be wrapped together with behavior to produce that small proportion of the human population who become true leaders.

Intelligence is the most basic leadership characteristic of all. The ability to see more and faster, to reason more effectively, to associate all the learnings of one's life so far causes others to be drawn to the leader and attach themselves in symbiotic relationships. The argument can be made that raw intelligence per se is insufficient for leadership, that leaders must also be skilled at applying their intelligence to real-world, day-to-day activities. Although this is true in most cases, raw intelligence, applied or not, is the basic building block of leadership.

Leadership without direction is useless. Uninformed by ideas about what is good and bad, right and wrong, worthy and unworthy, it is not only inconsistent but dangerous. As the pace of change in our world continues to accelerate, strong basic values become increasingly necessary to guide leadership behavior. Such values act as social constructs. They allow leaders to make decisions about the direction in which to lead and how to proceed. Without values, otherwise effective leadership can be grossly destructive socially, as proved by dictators such as Hitler and Saddam Hussein. It is the interactive combination of intelligence and sound social values that allows leaders to nudge forward the positive progress of humankind.

As always, the future's most effective leaders will have high and persistent levels of energy. Leadership is tough work. Although basic energy levels seem to be genetically determined, it is almost always true that effective leaders have and operate at high levels of personal energy. Not only is energy consumed by good leaders; it is also reinvested, compounded, and used to fuel constant personal growth.

Leaders have always needed to grow constantly as intellects, repositories of information, and guides of behavior, basing this growth on their collected wisdom. As the world produces information more rapidly and our ability to transmit and communicate information increases at an accelerating rate, it is necessary for leaders to be able to absorb and use that information to better understand the world and lead more knowledgeably.

Effective leaders have the vision required to see things differently from others. They collect and arrange the same data we all see in ways that allow them to conceive of new and unseen phenomena. A core characteristic of all effective leaders is the ability to have a vision of where they are trying to go and to articulate it clearly to potential followers so that they know their personal role in achieving that vision.

As our planet shrinks and information moves virtually instantaneously around the globe, it is necessary for effective leaders to form and constantly modify their view of the world. Their thinking and actions will be determined by their worldview, and it is essential to think as broadly as possible and to be current up to the minute. Building and constantly modifying a worldview will be more difficult in the future than in the past simply because of the pace of change and the increased availability of information.

To fuel this worldview and keep it constantly up-to-date will require a massive curiosity, an insatiable desire for information. Leaders will be required to continually seek out vast amounts of information, process it, and modify their leadership activities based upon it. Curiosity and the desire for information seem to be self-regenerating phenomena. That is, the more we know, the more we want to know. The effective leader will always find ways to receive and process increasing amounts of information. This processed information then informs behaviors and persuasive activities that convince others that the leader's chosen directions are the best ones to pursue.

A long-term high-capacity well-honed memory will be as necessary for effective leaders in the future as it has always been. Not only does memory support information gathering and processing, it also allows leaders to build the interpersonal bonds so necessary for leadership continuity. A leader's ability to remember aspects of followers' personal lives, thereby showing his or her interest, is one of the glues that cause followers to continue to bond to the leader.

Effective leaders must be easily "referable." That is, followers feel good about their leader because she or he makes them feel good about themselves. Referent power is the power derived by leaders from their followers when the followers are self-enhanced by their relationship with the leaders. Often called charisma, and enduringly resistant to scientific explanation, this referability of leaders is nevertheless an important component of their effectiveness.

I have described here the basic characteristics that will be needed for effective leadership in the future. These characteristics, though necessary, will be insufficient to produce effective leadership by themselves. It is the weaving together, the dynamic interaction, of the characteristics on a day-by-day, minute-by-minute basis that allows truly effective leadership. Built on the foundation characteristics are enabling behaviors that allow those who possess the raw material of leadership to transform it into effective leadership action. These enabling behaviors include empathy, predictability, persuasive capability, the ability and willingness to lead by personal example, and communication skills.

The best leaders have always been able to put themselves in the minds and situations of others. This empathy both allows the leader to understand and predict another person's behavior and causes the other person to realize that the leader appreciates his or her situation. The leader can then take action based on the predictable behaviors and responses of those who are being led.

All of us have a natural tendency to reduce unpredictability in our world so that we can increase personal control over our lives. It is easier for others to follow leaders who are predictable and who exhibit consistent behavior than leaders who are unpredictable. The leader-follower relationship infers that the leader will have some power over the follower. No one in a position of lesser power relative to another wants the behavior of the more powerful other to be unpredictable. That situation is dangerous and unsettling; rational people try to get out of such situations as quickly as they can.

Effective leaders are persuasive. They ingest and digest large amounts of information and reprocess that information so that it can be formed into persuasive arguments. They then use these arguments to persuade others of certain values or actions. Most persuasion is done in the absence of other forms of power over those who are being persuaded, so the ability to persuade is in itself a major source of leadership power.

Leadership by personal example has always been one of the most effective forms of leadership. It is also one of the most difficult. As we see on a daily basis in our public and political arenas, followers demand of their leaders significantly higher standards of personal conduct than they demand of themselves. Therefore, leaders have fewer degrees of behavioral freedom than those they are leading. Effective leadership requires a degree of control over libidinous impulses and some denial of personal gratification, which many people are unwilling to endure. This diminished personal freedom is a price of leadership. Those who are unwilling to pay it, however qualified they might be otherwise, are quickly denied the right to remain in their leadership role.

Finally, at the core of effective leadership is the ability to communicate. All forms of communication must be mastered by the effective leader: written and oral, electronic and digital, communication by graphics and behavior, by art and music, by expressed emotion, and more. Such mastery often requires almost an entire lifetime to achieve. But the studied master of communication becomes a more effective leader, justifying the investment necessary to reach this state.

Against the backdrop of the canvas of all humanity, I have painted a picture of that tiny proportion who become our most effective leaders. As we view the picture, we find that tomorrow's leaders will not be all that different from yesterday's; the common threads of leadership competence seem to stretch from the beginning of recorded history to as far as we can see into the future. Some characteristics of leaders appear to be genetic; others have to be carefully learned. It is the bundling together of the basic characteristics of effective leaders and the dynamics of their behaviors that produces effective leadership, no matter how it is defined. So our advice to aspiring future leaders should be to study effective leaders of the past. Analyze their intellectual, moral, and behavioral makeup. Look for common ingredients. Then add those ingredients to your own mix, build on them, and grow your leadership capabilities into what can only be a minute extension of the combined capabilities of the millions of leaders who have gone before.

23 MARSHALL GOLDSMITH

Ask, Learn, Follow Up, and Grow

*Marshall Goldsmith is a founding director of Keilty,
Goldsmith & Company (KGC), a consulting firm
based in San Diego, California; a partner in the
Global Consulting Alliance; and a member of the
board of governors of the Drucker Foundation. His
clients have included many of America's leading corporations, and the leadership feedback processes that
KGC has helped to develop have been used by more
than one million people in seventy different organizations around the world. In 1974 his firm was
recognized for being co-designers of one of America's
most innovative leadership development programs.
Goldsmith was rated by* The Wall Street Journal *as
one of the top ten consultants in the field of executive
development.*

In a talk to the Drucker Foundation Advisory Board in 1993, Peter
Drucker said, "The leader of the past was a person who knew how
to *tell*. The leader of the future will be a person who knows how to
ask." The traditional hierarchical model of leadership will not work
effectively for major organizations in tomorrow's changing world.

In the "old days," a person was hired into a position, learned the job, and—usually because of some form of functional proficiency—received a promotion into management. Then, as a manager, this same person could tell a *few* people what to do. Next, if the person was skilled and/or lucky, more promotions followed until he or she eventually became an executive who could tell *lots* of people what to do.

In most cases, the leader of the future won't *know* enough to tell people what to do. The world is changing too rapidly. No one person will be smart enough to keep up. As Edgar Schein notes in this volume, leaders will need to effectively involve others and elicit participation "because tasks will be too complex and information too widely distributed for leaders to solve problems on their own."

If leaders will not be able to keep up with the rapidly changing world, detailed policy manuals don't have a chance! Many organizations have historically operated on the "there is one best way" school of management. A classic example was the old Bell System. The basic philosophy was very clear: "There is one best way to do things. Let's figure out what it is, put it in a manual, and make sure everyone does it that way." One former Bell System executive, who later became a high-level executive in a "Baby Bell," jokingly remarked, "In the old Bell System we had rules, regulations, and guidelines on how to do everything but go to the bathroom—and they probably had a task force assigned to study that!" He went on to note that this regimentation was the philosophy of *yesterday*, not the philosophy of *tomorrow*.

Did the old Bell System, complete with its shelves of policy manuals, work? Pretty well! It worked in a relatively stable world without aggressive competitors. However, as leaders in the new AT&T now realize, the old command-and-control model of leadership will not encourage the creativity and responsiveness needed to get tomorrow's job done.

A classic example of a new-world organization is AT&T Wireless Services (formerly McCaw Cellular Communications); which

AT&T paid twelve billion dollars to acquire. In the changing world of cellular communications, a company can go from state of the art to dinosaur in a matter of months. For example, imagine that AT&T Wireless needed to make major changes because of problems in a local market, but before the changes could be made:

1. Employees had to "bubble" their concerns through each level in the AT&T system

2. A task force had to be assigned

3. New policy manuals had to be written

4. The new procedures had to be disseminated down the chain of command to the local employees

What would happen? The local market would be lost, the bright, entrepreneurial employees would leave the company to work for competitors, and AT&T would lose an important part of its twelve-billion-dollar investment. AT&T is a great example of an organization that has realized that success in the past does not guarantee success in the future. In today's AT&T, leaders are trained to "break the mold," empower people, and consistently reach out to acquire new insights.

How will the leader of tomorrow differ from the leader of yesterday? The thought leaders represented in this book describe a variety of differences; I will describe one key process. The effective leader of the future will consistently and efficiently *ask, learn, follow up,* and *grow.* The leader who cannot keep learning and growing will soon become obsolete in tomorrow's ever-changing world.

Ask

The effective leader of the future will consistently ask—to receive feedback and to solicit new ideas. Tomorrow's leader will ask a variety of key stakeholders for ideas, opinions, and feedback. Vital sources of information will include present and potential customers, suppliers, team members, cross-divisional peers, direct reports, managers, other members of the organization, researchers, and thought leaders (see Figure 23.1). The leader will ask in a variety of ways: through leadership inventories, satisfaction surveys, phone calls, voice mail, e-mail, the Internet, satellite hookups, and in-person dialogue.

The trend toward asking is already very clear. Twenty years ago very few top executives *ever* asked for feedback. Today the majority of the most highly respected leaders in North America *regularly* ask for feedback, in companies such as American Express, General Electric, Eastman Kodak, McKinsey & Co., Merck, Motorola, Nortel, and Pfizer. This trend is also growing rapidly throughout the world.

One global leader who spends a great deal of his life asking is George Weber, the secretary-general of the International Federation

Figure 23.1. The Challenge: Reaching Out for Input, but Not Drowning in a Sea of Information.

of Red Cross and Red Crescent Societies (IFRC). With a worldwide staff that contains representatives from ninety-five countries and a customer base that spans the globe, George is continuously asking key stakeholders for ideas on how he and his organization can better meet the needs of the world's most vulnerable people. He believes that the IFRC can only remain viable through consistent internal and external asking.

Aside from the obvious benefit of gaining new ideas and insights, asking by top leaders has a secondary benefit that may be even more important. The leader who asks is providing a role model. Sincere asking demonstrates a willingness to learn, a desire to serve, and a humility that can be an inspiration for the entire organization.

Learn

Peter Senge has written extensively about the future importance of the learning organization. The learning organization will need to be led by people who model continuous learning in their own day-to-day behavior. Two keys to learning are (1) effective listening and (2) reflection after asking for and receiving information. Asking for input and then "shooting the messenger" who delivers the bad news is worse than not asking at all. Leaders will need to provide recognition and support for people who have the courage to tell the hard truth before issues become disasters. Another major challenge for the leader of the future will be prioritization. Leaders will face the danger of drowning in a sea of information (see Figure 23.1). There is more to learn than any human can effectively process. One leader in Sun Microsystems reported that he received approximately two hundred e-mail messages *per day*. Leaders will need to focus on the vital few areas for change from each important source of information.

Although the leader of the future will need to receive input more frequently and from more sources, the time available to process this information may actually be declining. Today leaders exist in a world that is characterized by downsizing and ongoing reengineering. They need to get more work done, get it done faster, and get it done with considerably less support staff. In the private sector, there are no indications that global competition will *decrease* in the future or that leaders will have more time and more staff. In the social sector, there are no indications that human needs will decrease, or that government will take care of more social problems. Leaders who can ask, process information, and learn in a highly efficient manner will have a tremendous competitive advantage over their slower and less proactive competition.

Follow Up

Keilty, Goldsmith & Company recently conducted a study on the impact of asking for feedback and following up with over eight thousand leaders in a Fortune 100 company. Each manager in the company asked for feedback from direct reports, using a Leadership Inventory that had been designed to reinforce the company's new values. After receiving a confidential summary feedback report, each manager was asked to:

1. Pick one to three key areas for improvement and develop an action plan for desired change

2. *Respond* to the co-workers by thanking them for the feedback, discussing the action plan, and involving them in the change process

3. *Follow up* with co-workers to check on progress and receive further assistance

Managers were asked to spend only five to fifteen minutes responding in a focused two-way dialogue. They also were asked to spend only a few minutes following up by asking for a "progress report" and further suggestions.

Approximately eighteen months after initially providing feedback, co-workers were asked to again provide feedback to their managers using the Leadership Inventory. Two additional questions were added to the inventory concerning:

1. The manager's degree of change in leadership effectiveness
2. The manager's degree of follow-up

The findings of the study were dramatic but not surprising. The degree of change in perceived leadership effectiveness was clearly related to the degree of follow-up (see Figure 23.2). Managers who were seen as *not following up* were perceived as only slightly more effective as a group than they were eighteen months earlier. Although 46 percent were rated as more effective, over half were rated as unchanged or less effective. Managers rated as *doing some follow-up* experienced a very positive shift in scores, with 89 percent being rated as more effective. Almost half of the leaders in this group (45 percent) were rated in the highest two categories (+2 or +3) and almost none (3 percent) were seen as less effective. *Consistent or periodic follow-up* had a dramatic, positive impact. Over half the leaders (55 percent) were rated in the highest possible category, with 86 percent rated either +2 or +3.

Studies similar to this one are being completed in six other major corporations with leaders from over twenty countries. So far, the results have been remarkably consistent. Studies have also been conducted concerning the impact of asking for feedback and following up with team members and external customers. Results point to a very similar pattern: team members and suppliers who ask for feedback, respond in a positive manner, and follow up are seen by their fellow team members and external customers as dramatically increasing in effectiveness.

Follow-up will be a key challenge for the leader of the future. For "real-world" leaders, asking and learning will have to be more than an academic exercise. The process will have to produce meaningful, positive change. By learning how to follow up efficiently and effectively in an extremely busy world, leaders will enable key

Figure 23.2. Findings on the Relationship Between Follow-up
and Perceived Leadership Effectiveness.

Managers Who Did No Follow-Up

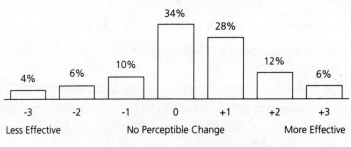

Change in Leadership Effectiveness

Managers Who Responded and Did Some Follow-Up

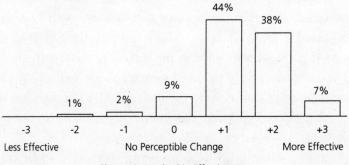

Change in Leadership Effectiveness

Managers Who Responded and Did Consistent (Periodic) Follow-Up

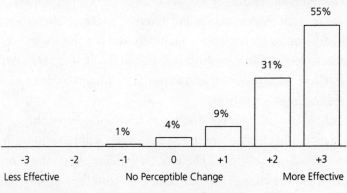

Change in Leadership Effectiveness

stakeholders to see the positive actions that result from the input they were requested to provide.

Grow

The leader of the future will have to change and grow on the job. Can this happen? Definitely, yes! Leaders who reach out, ask for input, learn, respond in a positive manner, involve key stakeholders, and follow up will almost invariably be seen as becoming more effective and as growing over time.

As demands on leaders increase, effective leadership growth and development will become more important than ever. However, the methodology of leadership development may radically change. Historically, leadership development efforts have tended to focus on the "front side" of the development process: impressive training, well-designed forms, clever slogans, and lots of "flash." They have not focused on the "back side" of the process: the ongoing application of what is being learned. Follow-up studies have validated the obvious. What leaders do back on the job will be more meaningful than what they do in classrooms.

Future leadership development will not be like *getting* in shape. It will be like *staying* in shape. Recent research has indicated that the "program-of-the-year" approach to leadership development has the same impact as the crash-diet approach to physical fitness. The results don't last! Many organizations have spent millions of dollars on programs and almost nothing on follow-up. In the future, far more effort will be placed on developing the processes required to ensure positive, ongoing leadership growth. By developing processes that ensure ongoing asking, learning, and follow-up, leaders will grow in a manner that produces a positive, measurable impact.

Conclusion

The leader of the future will face different and in many ways more challenging demands than the leader of the past. Global competition will rapidly increase, organizations will continue to downsize and reengineer, leaders will have less support staff, workloads will probably increase, and the pace of change will accelerate. The need for human services will continue to increase at a rate greater than the government's ability to meet the need. Traditional hierarchies will break down and the number and fluidity of stakeholder relationships will keep growing. The leader who tries to know it all and to tell everyone what to do is doomed to failure. The leader who believes that there is only one best way and attempts to write detailed procedures has no chance.

Almost all of the thought leaders represented in this book believe that the leader of the future will need to continuously involve and learn from others. Unfortunately, as this need is increasing, the time available to do it is decreasing. As the amount of information made available to the leader is increasing, the time to process it is decreasing. The leader of the future will need to be able to effectively focus and prioritize. In a period of rapid change, focus and the frequency of interactions may become more critical than the duration of the interactions.

Recent research has shown that leaders who ask for input from key stakeholders; learn with a positive, nondefensive attitude; and follow up in a focused, efficient manner will almost invariably grow and develop in terms of increased effectiveness. Learning from input and increasing leadership effectiveness is a lot like getting a physical exam and changing one's life-style. The doctor usually suggests, "Go on a low-fat diet and work out every other day." The challenge is not in *understanding* this advice, but in *doing it*. As Arnold Schwartzenegger once said, "Nobody ever got muscles by watching *me* lift weights."

I leave you, the reader, with a final challenge. By reading this book you have already demonstrated one characteristic of the effective leader of the future. You have reached out to get the latest information from a variety of sources. Read the articles with an open mind. Try to see the value of opinions that may differ from your own. After completing this book, develop the profile of the leader of the future that *you* want to be. *Ask* for input from your key stakeholders on how your behavior and activity match your vision, *learn* from what people tell you about yourself and your opportunities for the future, prioritize and focus on a few key areas for change, and *follow up* to ensure effective implementation. Completing these key steps can help you to *grow* and become the leader of the future that you want to be.

Part IV

Executives on the Future of Leadership

24 C. WILLIAM POLLARD

The Leader Who Serves

C. William Pollard is chairman of The ServiceMaster Company, which has been recognized by Fortune magazine over the past ten years as the number-one service company among the Fortune 500, and by The Wall Street Journal in its 1989 centennial issue as a "star of the future." Pollard serves as a director of Herman Miller, Provident Life and Accident Insurance Company, and Trammell Crow Company. He also serves as a trustee of Wheaton College, the Hospital Research and Educational Trust, The Drucker Foundation, and several other educational and not-for-profit organizations.

Will the leader please stand up? Not the president, or the person with the most distinguished title, but the role model. Not the highest-paid person in the group, but the risk taker. Not the person with the largest car or the biggest home, but the servant. Not the person who promotes himself or herself, but the promoter of others. Not the administrator, but the initiator. Not the taker, but the giver. Not the talker, but the listener.

We live in a world of accelerated change and choice, dislocation and discontinuity. The changes in the politics and economies of the former Soviet Union, Eastern Europe, and China have affected the lives of millions of people. There is more freedom and choice in the world today, and definitely more confusion. The restraints that suppressed age-old conflicts between some religious and cultural groups are no longer there, and old hatreds have come to the surface. The only thing certain about tomorrow is that it will be different from today. And tomorrow's challenges require that its leaders be *servant* leaders.

Peter Drucker refers to our times as the postcapitalist society. He concludes that information, not capital, will be the critical resource of the future. Charles Handy refers to it as the Age of Unreason and says that we need more upside-down thinking. The upside-down thinker wonders why roads are free and railroads are expensive, or why a national curriculum is needed when people learn as individuals. The upside-down thinker tries to plan for a world in the future where less than half the work force will be in full-time jobs. The rich and talented will have to work harder and will have less time for leisure, and the poor will have more time for leisure and less money for satisfaction. The wars and battles of the future will be between groups of people, not nation-states.

Some people in our universities and centers of learning discuss our period of time in terms of postmodern and deconstructionist thinking, where everything is relative and there are no standards or meaning. They say that the university is no longer a place for the pursuit of knowledge. In postmodern thought it becomes a place to pursue pleasure and desire and should be more erotic than cerebral. Words no longer have a common meaning. Interpretation is in the eye of the reader or listener, but however we view or label this rapidity of change and choice and the lack of predictability in the events that swirl around us, I believe that this crucible of uncertainty provides a great opportunity for positive direction, provided that those who have been trained to think also *lead*.

Samuel Beckett and James Joyce were friends and confidants.

Although the writings of Joyce received more fame and publicity, Beckett won a Nobel Prize for literature in 1969. His short stories, novels, plays, and radio and television scripts are generally obscure and esoteric works that stress the absurdity and despair of life. His characters typically engage in meaningless tasks to occupy their time but have no purpose or mission and accomplish nothing. In speaking with unflinching honesty about the emptiness of a life without direction or purpose, he may well have been describing the modern-day person in an environment of accelerated change and choice without leadership. This is not how things have to be. A leader who is willing to serve can provide hope instead of despair and can be an example for those who want direction and purpose in their life and who desire to accomplish and contribute. This leader is the leader of the future.

Now, as I ask these fundamental questions about leadership and the future, I do so not as a philosopher or educator, but simply as a businessman, someone who is seeking to lead, along with my partner Carlos Cantu, a fast-growing, dynamic service company that we call ServiceMaster. We have experienced rapid growth, doubling in size every three and a half years for the past twenty years, with revenues now in excess of $4 billion. We employ or manage more than 200,000 people, and provide services in the United States and twenty-nine foreign countries. We are a public company, with our shares listed and traded on the New York Stock Exchange. Yes, I live in one of those pressure-cooker environments where earnings and profits must be reported every quarter, and where they have been up every quarter for the past twenty-four years. The shareholders to whom Carlos and I are responsible as leaders vote every day on our leadership. They have the choice to buy, hold, or sell their share of ownership.

Much about our business may be classified as routine or mundane. We often deal with people in entry-level positions who are unskilled, frequently uneducated, and, more often than not, unnoticed. We do such things as clean toilets and floors, maintain boilers and air-handling units, kill bugs, provide maid service, and maintain and repair home appliances. The task before us is to train, motivate, and develop people so that they will do a more effective job, be more productive in their work, and, yes, even be better people. This is both a management and a leadership challenge. For us in ServiceMaster, it is more than a job or a means to earn a living. It is, in fact, a mission—a way of life. Our company objectives are simply stated: to honor God in all we do, to help people develop, to pursue excellence, and to grow profitably. The first two objectives are end goals. The second two are means goals. As we seek to implement these objectives in the operation of our business, they provide us with a reference point for what we do and how we determine what is right and seek to avoid what is wrong. In effect, they define our mission.

First, we seek to recognize the dignity and worth of all people because they have been created in God's image. Thus, our role as leaders involves more than just what people do on the job. We also must be involved in what they are becoming as whole people and how the work environment is contributing to the process. Are these people growing as individuals who can contribute at work, at home, and in the community? And do we, as leaders, have a positive influence on their growth? Stressing this value, as you might anticipate, affects our view of the importance of training and involves more than teaching people to use the right tools or to complete an assigned task within a defined period. We must consider how they feel about their work and about themselves and how they relate to others in the work environment and at home.

Servant leaders must be committed. They are not bystanders or simply holders of positions. Their leadership responsibility is for the long term and not for their own short-term benefit. No enterprise can function to its capacity unless its people can rely upon the covenants and commitments of their leaders. This is more than just something formalized into a written agreement, and it goes far beyond the covenants that are usually contained in any legal document. It extends to the people who are relying upon the leader for their future. It fulfills our campaign promises.

Our word and the promises we make to each other provide the framework for relationships to grow. Leaders must keep their promises to the people they lead, even if it is at their own personal risk and sacrifice. It is their obligation. To understand the extent of this obligation, one can picture it as a debt—a liability—on the balance sheet of every leader. The opportunities, jobs, and families of the leader's followers need to be considered a debt in the same way that a mortgage is considered a debt. It is every bit as real, every bit as important.

Too often, leaders sit in large offices with big staffs and think they know and understand the people they lead because they have achieved some successes in their life and can read the reports that others provide for them. Servant leaders listen and learn from those they lead. They work at making themselves available. Their door is always open. They are out and about talking and listening to people at all levels of the organization. They must be willing to walk a mile in the other person's shoes. As they listen, they learn. They become frantic learners and avoid the trap that so many so-called successful leaders experience—the arrogance of ignorance.

Leaders make things happen. They are responsible for initiating and, in some cases, creating disequilibrium in order to maintain the vitality of the organization they lead. Too many organizations, including governments, are crippled by the cancer of bureaucracy, with people caught up in the activities and layers of management but not in results, defending the status quo and preserving a position but not serving and creating value. Because leaders make things happen through others, they must be generous in their delegation of authority and responsibility. It is a grave wrong and injustice for a superior to steal the ability to make a decision from a subordinate.

Servant leaders are givers, not takers. They never hold on to a position or title. They have the job because they can live without it. This requires all good leaders to have a plan for succession and for the development of future leaders. Servant leaders want to serve only until a successor is identified and ready and not one moment longer. It is the availability and readiness of the right person for the future that should determine whether a leader steps aside and not a predetermined date or age or any other artificial criterion.

Servant leaders promote diversity, recognizing that people's differences can strengthen the group. They learn to accept these differences and seek to provide an environment where different people contribute as part of the whole. As groups of different people work together under effective leaders, we are confronted with the reality that no one person can accomplish the task alone. An individual standing alone contributes less than he or she does as a member of the whole. In the words of Ecclesiastes: "Two can accomplish more than twice as much as one, for the results can be much better. If one falls, the other pulls him up; but if a man falls when he is alone, he's in trouble. . . . And one standing alone can be attacked and defeated, but two can stand back-to-back and conquer; three is even better, for a triple-braided cord is not easily broken" (Ecclesiastes 4:9–12, *The Living Bible*). As servant leaders, we can provide an environment in which people can learn and grow as they work and share together.

During a trip to Leningrad in 1989, I met a custodian named Olga. She had the job of mopping a lobby floor in a large hotel. I took an interest in her and her task and engaged her in conversation. Olga had been given a T frame for a mop, a dirty rag, and a dirty bucket of water to do her job. She wasn't really cleaning the floor; she was just moving dirt from one section to another. The reality of Olga's task was to perform the fewest motions in the greatest amount of time until the day was over.

Olga was not proud of what she was doing. She had no dignity in her work. She was a long way from owning the result. But Olga had great untapped potential. I'm sure you could have eaten off the floor in her two-room apartment. But work was something different. No one had taken the time to teach or equip Olga or to care about her as a person. She was lost in a system that did not care. Work was just a job that had to be done. There was no servant leader for Olga.

By contrast, I had an experience just a few days later while visiting a hospital that ServiceMaster serves in London, England. As I was introduced to one of the housekeepers as the chairman of ServiceMaster, she put her arms around me and gave me a big hug. She thanked me for the training and tools she had received to do her job. She then showed me all that she had accomplished in cleaning patient rooms, providing a detailed "before and after" Service-Master description. She was proud of her work. She had bought into the result because someone had cared enough to show her the way and recognize her efforts when the task was done. She was looking forward to the next accomplishment. *She was thankful.*

The difference between these two women was that one was proud of what she was doing. Her pride affected her personal development. The other was not proud and had a limited view of her potential and worth. The difference, I suggest, had something to do with servant leadership of the lack thereof.

Servant leaders must be value driven and performance oriented. They must think through what is right and what is wrong in executing their responsibilities. They must lead people to do things the right way and to do the right thing. It is our belief at ServiceMaster that leaders must provide an example by their actions and conduct, maintaining a continuing expectation and standard for the people of the organization. Truth cannot be compromised. The truth of what we say is shown by what we do. As the founder of Service-Master used to say, "If you don't live it, you don't believe it."

But in a pluralistic environment with a great diversity of views, can there be a right or wrong? Where is the reference point for leadership? The reference point at ServiceMaster begins with our first objective: to honor God in all we do. We seek to discover and apply those God-given standards, God-given limitations, and God-given freedoms.

As leaders, we recognize that we are all prisoners of our hope. Our hope sustains us. Our vision of what could be inspires us and those we lead. In implementing our vision, we accept the reality that we don't have all the answers. A servant leader's results will be measured beyond the workplace, and the story will be told in the changed lives of others. There is no scarcity of feet to wash. The towels and the water are available. The limitation, if there is one, is our ability to get on our hands and knees and be prepared to do what we ask others to do.

25 ALFRED C. DECRANE, JR.

A Constitutional Model of Leadership

Alfred C. DeCrane, Jr., is chairman of the board and chief executive officer of Texaco Inc. DeCrane is a director of CIGNA Corporation; Dean Witter, Discover & Co.; CPC International, Inc.; and the American Petroleum Institute. He is a trustee of the Committee for Economic Development and The Conference Board and a member of the National Petroleum Council and The Business Roundtable. In addition, DeCrane is a member of the board of trustees of the University of Notre Dame and a managing director of the Metropolitan Opera Association.

It is a challenge, as well as something of a presumption, to allege sufficient understanding of both leadership *and* the future in order to offer useful ideas on the business leader of the future.

The Socratic approach would say that we should focus initially on analyzing just what the future of business is likely to be—the context and environment within which this individual will be called to lead. Having identified this context, we might then begin to delineate the necessary qualities, characteristics, and approaches for leadership success in that very specific environment.

Future-oriented analyses, like those of Herman Kahn, Alvin Toffler, and Peter Drucker, offer some compelling concepts about the directions in which this country and the world may move, and the skill-sets that might be critical for success. But even the most sophisticated trend analysis, projection, and forecasting techniques have real limits, and we are left with a timeless lack of certitude about what the long-term future will bring.

There is, however, a model that can help us put forth some meaningful concepts regarding future leadership in business. I think of it as the *constitutional model*. James Madison and the framers of the U.S. Constitution constructed a document embodying certain core principles to guide the lives of the American people and to establish the framework of governance. They understood that the Constitution had to be clear and specific enough to help create the type of enduring society they desired. But they also understood that the Constitution and the Bill of Rights had to be worded broadly and flexibly enough to be relevant and effective for an endless variety of specific daily issues, changing conditions, and challenges that they could not even envision. Today, we see that the fundamental principles guiding the Constitution survive, even with more than two centuries of amendments and the rigor of interpretation and application.

Similarly, I think we can identify qualities that are a de facto set of core leadership competencies. Although they can be modified and applied as conditions change and new challenges arise, the really basic qualities remain—solid, broad, and relevant. My experience observing and dealing with global commercial organizations of every size and reach, governments, and international associations has reinforced my belief in a set of core qualities.

Throughout the years, I have tried to define and record the core leadership competencies of those I've admired and have sought to identify individuals with these core competencies in my own organizations. I've noted numerous variations in leadership styles and modifications in approaches, but the fundamental qualities have largely remained constant. I've placed these core qualities into four basic areas: character, vision, behavior, and confidence.

Character

At different times, leaders are judged on what they seek to do, how they pursue their goals, and what they accomplish. More than anything, these criteria are outgrowths of the fundamental measure of a leader: the content of his or her character. And even though the personalities and goals of leaders vary widely, I have observed constants in their character.

Leaders, in the words of the ancient Greek, Thucydides, have "knowledge of their duty, and a sense of honor in action." Real leaders are fair and honest, and not just because of laws and regulations; they are ethical, open, and trustworthy. These basic roots of character, perhaps more than any others, garner the respect that is needed in order for an individual to be called a leader. I've been in business long enough to see that short-term "wins" can be achieved without these qualities, but I've also seen that lasting leadership and success—at whatever level—is impossible without them.

These key and basic traits cascade into other characteristics. Leaders are also:

- Infused with humor and humility, and by nature inclined to treat individuals in their organizations equally, without "smiling up and kicking down"

- Self-aware, and honest with themselves as to their own strengths, weaknesses, and sincere efforts to improve

- Inquisitive and approachable enough so that others feel safe offering honest feedback and new ideas

- Open-minded and capable of respecting their competitors or adversaries and learning from them, in both leadership situations and general business conditions

- Action-oriented, which surfaces not as a desire to
  move for movement's sake but to move directly toward
  a clear goal with a relentless follow-through

Effective leaders, it is important to note, do not pursue their objectives at any and all cost, or without regard to *how* they achieve their goals. Leaders remain committed to core values that are uncompromised by a relentless attempt to achieve aims—again underscoring the importance of character to leaders of any era.

Thus, for a leader in business or any other field, integrity of character is paramount. As a former head of the New York Stock Exchange once said, "The public may be willing to forgive us for mistakes in judgment, but it will not forgive us for mistakes in motive."

Vision

Leaders who can spark the imagination with a compelling vision of a worthwhile end that stretches us beyond what is known today, and who can translate that to clear objectives, are the ones we follow. The Federalist Papers confirm that Madison and his colleagues understood that the most elegant documents and structures were irrelevant if they did not help the readers form a vision, an outcome, through clearly stated, overarching objectives.

Successful business leaders develop goals to achieve their vision. Their commitment to the goals, and thus to the vision, is made obvious by both their actions and their repeated communication of what must be done, and why.

Behaviors

With clear objectives in mind, the issue then becomes what a leader will *do*, how he or she will behave while working with and through people in pursuit of the end goal. Although leaders must adapt to a specific and ever-changing set of circumstances, the most successful leaders exhibit a common set of behaviors. Those leaders will:

- Act and be unwilling to rationalize inaction, with relentless follow-through to ensure that the action is implemented

- Create and shape change, rather than passively accepting it, and challenge the status quo, refusing to accept the response, "We've never done that before"

- Seize the opportunities of the present without compromising the need to invest and build for the future

- Flourish in a boundaryless work environment by focusing on results, knowing that much can be done if it doesn't matter who gets the credit

- Evaluate and deploy people based solely on strength, performance, and potential

- Think positively, never give up, seek out the opportunity that lurks in every challenge, and realize that things are never as bad as they seem

- Be detail-oriented enough to know whether the objectives are being met or the course is correct, but not so detail-oriented that they "miss the forest for the trees"

- Seek consensus without being paralyzed by the thought of making a mistake or intolerant of those who make them

- Communicate constantly—influencing, encouraging, critiquing, and *listening*

Strength of character and foresight matter not a whit if people are not willing or able to follow someone. A title alone cannot inspire others to work toward a common end, lending all their energy, ideas, and commitment to the endeavor. But frequent, open, and honest communication does inspire others to follow, including those without the benefit of a title.

With the utmost clarity, leaders convey:

- Well-articulated expectations of high performance for each and every member of the organization and the belief that everyone, including the leader, will be evaluated against those expectations on the basis of performance

- An understanding that communication is a two-way process in which leaders listen, hunger for feedback and new ideas, and are driven by a need to compel and to influence, not to command and control

- An appreciation of the principle that well-informed team members are the most motivated and strongest achievers, and a willingness to communicate with teams and to follow through

- Confidence and trust in employees, and a desire to give opportunities to any individuals who are eager to accept the accountability that necessarily goes with responsibility

Confidence

Leaders share another attribute that is critical for success: self-confidence. Sharply distinguished from arrogance or egotism, a healthy level of self-confidence enables the leader to undertake the difficult ventures necessary to meet his or her goals.

It is this self-confidence that makes it possible for leaders to be willing, prudent risk takers who encourage others to take similar risks. Leaders take responsible risks, risks that stack up appropriately with potential rewards. True leaders understand what is needed to reach their visions and goals, even if this means that they must refuse to "go with the flow." When businesses and other organizations stumble or fall behind in tactics or technology, it may be because their leaders are too timid and send signals that discourage risk taking.

Media stories love to focus on executive "blunders." But Thomas Watson, Jr., of IBM had the appropriate perspective on risk. Once, when discussing IBM's competitive challenges, he said, "We don't have enough people out there making mistakes." Responsible risks need to be taken, particularly by leaders. That's why leaders must have sufficient self-confidence to be willing to experience failure—in order ultimately to experience success. No real leader gets it all right.

Self-confidence in a leader also enables that individual to have confidence in, and support the advancement of, the people in his or her organization. Believing in the enormous capacity of empowered people, leaders unleash that capacity by encouraging their teams not only with sincere praise and recognition, but also by providing constructive critiques and by applauding responsibly undertaken "bold tries" as well as true victories.

I have found that self-confident leaders are not threatened by the success of others in the organization. They are quick and genuine with their praise for others' successes and don't waste energy worrying about their status or that of their peers in the organization. Achieving the vision and the goals consumes their thinking.

Who Are Your Leaders?

Effective leaders in business, if they are to build their organizations for the long term, must have the capacity to cultivate the next wave of leaders, or their contributions are unlikely to last much longer than their physical presence within the company. Identifying leaders in an organization is challenging. We have difficulty distinguishing between current performance and future leadership potential. Too often, I have found that when unit heads are asked to provide "short lists" of leaders with the potential to go further, and I ask who on that list could deal with a challenging assignment, I am met with hesitancy and backtracking, even from the person who submitted the names. In most cases, this seemingly strange phenomenon can be explained by a failure to distinguish between the project manager or team player who delivers results and the leader who displays the character, vision, behavior, and confidence I've described.

We frequently fall into the habit of associating leaders and leadership characteristics only with the top of the organization: senior business executives, political figures, military top brass, sports team captains, and coaches. It is a natural tendency, since they are the most visible and highest-profile leaders. However, in the past, the present, and certainly in the future, true leadership is needed across and throughout all types of organizations. The character and qualities that are found in true leaders are essential at all levels of responsibility.

The core competencies of leadership may mature, broaden, and be honed as the individual's scope of responsibility increases, but the basic leadership principles I have identified and noted over my career help individuals at all stages of responsibility to *lead*. And, as our constitutional model suggests, leaders of the future will surely be doing the same—adapting these core competencies to the challenges of their time and the scope of their responsibilities.

26 ALEX MANDL
DEEPAK SETHI

Either/Or Yields to the Theory of Both

Alex Mandl is executive vice president of AT&T. As CEO of its Communications Services Group, he heads the company's core long-distance, on-line, and multimedia services groups. He also oversees AT&T Wireless Services and the company's Universal Card unit. In addition, Mandl is president and chief operating officer-designate of the new AT&T. He will assume his new role at the time AT&T completes its restructuring. Before joining AT&T, he was chairman and CEO of Sea-Land Service, the world's largest ocean transportation and distribution services company. Mandl received his BA degree in economics from Willamette University and his MBA degree from the University of California at Berkeley. He is a member of both the Warner-Lambert Company board of directors and the United States National Information Infrastructure advisory council.

Deepak (Dick) Sethi is assistant director of executive education at AT&T, responsible for the develop-

*ment of the company's high-potential managers. Prior
to joining AT&T, he worked for Control Data Corporation. He is a member of the advisory board of the
Institute for Management Studies and the New York
Human Resource Planners. He holds an MBA
degree in marketing from Pennsylvania State University and has taught at New York University.*

Ogden Nash once said, "Progress might have been all right once, but it has gone on too long." It's a view shared by many, given the discontinuity and unrelenting pace of the changes we've witnessed just in this decade. Yet clearly, the future will be fanned by greater change, not less.

Some insightful minds are already anticipating its contours. Futurist Alvin Toffler believes that we're in a sea change of civilization that will bring increasingly customized production, micromarkets, and infinite channels of communication. AT&T Bell Labs scientist Greg Blonder, noting that every thirty months a dollar's worth of computer buys twice the processing power, predicts that computers will match human beings in skills and intelligence by 2088. Two years after that date, he says, "the computer will be twice as smart and twice as insightful as any human being" ("Faded Genes," *Wired*, Mar. 1995, p. 107). Meanwhile, *Wired* editor Louis Rossetto, who believes that society is organized by a "hive-mind consensus," says that today's digital revolution may let us fulfill Marshall McLuhan's prophecy to "make of the entire globe, and of the human family, a single consciousness" ("The Digerati," *New York Times Sunday Magazine*, May 21, 1995, p. 38).

Such future visions will no doubt be joined by a rash of predictions from millennium watchers, so it's wise to remember Ralph Waldo Emerson. Warned that the world would end in ten days, he calmly replied, "No doubt we will get on very well without it." A future divined, after all, is often a tomorrow never seen. But whatever the future's final shape, it's clear that things just aren't going to be the same anymore.

Indeed, tomorrow's advance guard is already transforming the very nature of communications, community, and commerce. And that, in turn, is calling into question some basic assumptions that just yesterday were considered givens. Key among them is our view of leadership, for a world upended demands a leader redefined. Determining what skills will be needed to lead in a future that can't reliably be foretold is a bit like trying to herd cats. Yet there are some signposts today that may illuminate tomorrow. And that presents an opportunity not unlike the one described by an AT&T human factors expert who asked, "How do you build a frog? Do you study the croak, the prodigious leap, the hyperbolic eyes?" "No," she concluded, "you study the pond."

The environment or pond that tomorrow's leaders will be expected to excel in is already being reshaped by three converging upheavals: (1) globalization, (2) constant and often discontinuous change, and (3) a revolution in information technology. Each is altering not only the essence of business but also the skills necessary to lead it.

The vision of a global village, for instance, is close to reality. Financial markets already electronically move one trillion dollars a day, crossing borders as they please. And work now follows the sun, in a global baton pass that shifts from time zone to time zone. In the process, the game and the players change. Today's global business, after all, is open to all comers, not just the largest firms or most advanced nations. John Naisbitt estimates that half of all U.S. exports are produced by companies with nineteen or fewer employees.

Meanwhile, the sixteen largest developing nations are setting the pace for global expansion. Their economies are growing at more than twice the rate of the mature economies of North America, Europe, and Japan that traditionally dictated global maneuvers. In turn, global competition is accelerating. According to the U.S. Department of Commerce, between 1990 and 1994, the historical cost of U.S. direct investment in other nations topped $612 billion, an increase of 42 percent. The cost of foreign direct investment in

America, meanwhile, increased more than 27 percent, to $504 billion.

But numbers don't paint the whole picture. "Hot money," for instance, is the latest Wall Street buzzword used to help define the massive change in global financial markets. It refers to the billions of dollars that investors can move in and out of a country in a moment and on a whim; the billions of dollars that, in the stroke of a keyboard, can undermine a nation's economy; the instantly movable money that can give investors, rather than foreign policy makers, the power to control a nation's economic vitality. "Hot money" is also indicative of the cascade of events that have sped things up, obscured a few pertinent details, and sent business as usual packing. A wag once lamented that he'd rather cope with sameness for a while. But today's only constants are the unfamiliar, the uncertain, and the unpredictable.

We're already smudging all manner of lines, from those separating technologies and industries to those dividing markets and products. Meanwhile, partners in one endeavor are at the same time competitors in others. In a world grown economically interdependent, a company's fate is often linked more to a competitor continents away than to the business that happens to share the same block and national economy. In such a world, the classic need for deep harbors and broad highways is yielding to the need for data ports and electronic speedways. Information technology is obliging.

The technologies of communications and computers are already inseparable. Now they are looking to merge with consumer electronics and entertainment to create a whole new industry called interactive multimedia. This hybrid mix of media is scrambling tradition and long-held assumptions, and it may yet have us watching the telephone and answering the TV. It includes the five hundred television channels we keep hearing about and video on demand, wristwatch phones and follow-you-everywhere phone numbers, videophones and the ability to see someone on your computer screen while you collaborate on shared documents, and electronic valets in hand-held communicators that will find addresses, make dinner and airline reservations, and remember bank, social security, and PIN numbers.

Interactive multimedia is also key to the advances in information technology that take power away from large centralized bureaucracies and put it in the hands of individuals. In the process of distributing information and talent throughout an organization, information technology—particularly networking—undercuts hierarchical management systems. The hierarchy traditionally served as an organization's official channel, even though it was joined by informal networks of "old boys," rumor mills, and subterranean contacts who could get things done despite the bureaucracy. Today, information technology is giving those informal networks a new reign, creating, if you will, a grapevine with cachet.

From electronic mailboxes to videoconferences, information technology is redirecting the flow of information and creating a fungible organization unrestrained by the tether of time, distance, and departmental persuasion. This freedom provides the speed, agility, and flexibility demanded in a highly competitive global market. It also alters the very nature of work and managerial authority. After all, if the hierarchy is subsumed, so, too, are its functionaries. The drill of command-and-control, for instance, is giving way to new bonds of trust and support. Vertical structures are lying down on the job to accommodate the lateral, informal, and inherently horizontal essence of a networked organization.

The democratization of information is replacing the power-hoarding concept of "need to know." Shared work is nudging out strict functional autonomy, even as performance is appraised more on overall results than direct supervision of work. And managers, once aligned in a chain of command, are navigating instead a web of interdependent people and interwoven parts. Disturb it anywhere and it vibrates all over.

If anything, these trends will only accelerate in the future, and they are sure to be joined by an even greater crunch of time, an even greater infusion of ambiguity. That, in turn, calls for a new breed of leaders, not just managers. Unfortunately, leadership skills as traditionally practiced aren't up to the task. Managing by the book, for example, will be futile. Innovators will swamp with regularity those who are beholden to the status quo. And leaders who focus on systems and structures will miss the point that tomorrow's most important capital will be intellectual.

This is not to say that the past holds no leadership lessons. Indeed, the future will require a wider, more inclusive lens. In short, we should be speaking not in terms of either/or but both. After all, the future doesn't lie in either communications or computers but both. It won't be shaped by either domestic or global trends but both. It won't be fueled by either established world leaders or upstart entrepreneurs but both.

In this context, leaders can adapt to a mercurial future and use it to their advantage by cultivating the creative tension that comes from balancing extremes—looking at the world from both sides now. The theory of both combines short-term fire fighting with an eye toward long-term payoffs and consequences. It fuses traditionally separate strategic and tactical skills, because both will be required of tomorrow's leader. A domestic and global perspective, already prized, will take on a local component, and the hard side of business will meld with the soft, acknowledging the interdependence not only in the workplace but of financial, employee, customer, and shareowner interests as well. Leadership roles will also straddle extremes, incorporating the skills of the generalist and the specialist, the visionary and the operational whiz.

Tomorrow's leader will be both teacher and student, technologist and entrepreneur, "with the program" in terms of the company's overall objective yet also defined by inspired heresy. The team player, who will prove critical in open, instantly reconfigurable work groups, will also have to be a self-starter. And the leader who will have to be truly wired will also have to manage by walking around, for despite its riches, information technology augments but does not replace the human dimension and its possibilities for sharing, vulnerability, and trust.

There is, however, a singular aspect to the theory of both: a core set of givens that should steer every action and serve as tiebreakers in the leader's ongoing balancing act. The leader of the future will have to be adept at articulating a vision and inspiring others with an imagined future. He or she will find in shared values and beliefs the foundation for commitment, context, and creativity. And finally, the leader will delegate real responsibility and accountability—and expect employees to use it.

These givens speak more to spirit than to skills and, as such, perhaps best define the challenges facing tomorrow's leaders. Simple in theory, they are the hobgoblins of the everyday. Indeed, living with them is much like H. L. Mencken's description of living with a dog or an idealist—it is messy. Yet they are also the mooring that in tomorrow's sea of change can ensure an organization's ability to cope with, and even conquer, that change.

27 WILLIAM C. STEERE, JR.

Key Leadership Challenges for Present and Future Executives

William C. Steere, Jr., is chairman of the board and CEO of Pfizer Inc. He began his career with Pfizer in 1959 as a medical service representative and moved through a variety of marketing and management positions until his appointment as president of Pfizer Pharmaceuticals Group in 1986. He was elected president and CEO of Pfizer Inc. in 1991 and chairman in 1992. Steere is a member of the board of directors and executive committee of the Pharmaceutical Research and Manufacturers of America. He is a member of the board of overseers of the Memorial Sloan-Kettering Cancer Center and the Business Roundtable and is on the boards of the Council on Competitiveness, the New York University Medical Center, the Federal Reserve Bank of New York, WNET-Thirteen, the Business Council, the Business Roundtable, Texaco Inc., Minerals Technologies, Inc., and the New York Botanical Garden.

In a few years, Pfizer will be 150 years old. Our company's culture and management today share many traits with their counterparts of years gone by, including a commitment to innovation, quality, human health, the community, and our employees. However, as in many other companies, our products and technology have become part of a constant and increasingly rapid cycle of discovery, renewal, and obsolescence. The scope of our operations has also changed dramatically, and the environments in which we operate have undergone many transformations.

The forces that require large companies to keep changing and improving constantly are dramatically increasing. They include (1) the increasing globalization of the world economy; (2) the shifting sands of deregulation and reregulation in major industries; (3) the competitive challenge of emerging companies, whether in biotechnology, electronics, software, retailing, or other areas; and (4) the accelerating rate of technological progress, which is reshaping the boundaries of markets. Occasionally these forces achieve a crisis status, as has been the case recently in America's health care industry, resulting from a confluence of rapid, interdependent, evolutionary changes and political shifts in the industry. I would like to discuss the challenges of leadership during these times with regard to three key areas: (1) the role of leadership and corporate culture in a large company today, (2) the importance of consistent execution of a leadership approach, and (3) the role of the leader in the future.

The Role of Leadership and Corporate Culture

The effective leadership of any company can be molded and measured in at least three ways: through the company's business results, its organizational structure, and its culture. In my experience, I have found that leaders spend considerable time attempting to affect business results, often through changes in organizational structure. Less frequently, leaders focus on the impact they have on the cultures of the companies they lead, whether they intend to or not. They often underestimate the role that culture plays in the business performance of a company and fail to realize that a critical part of the leader's job is cultural definition and development. In fact, as an organization grows in size, the importance of the executive as the visible representation of an increasingly removed or impersonal corporate structure grows accordingly. For leaders of worldwide organizations, the challenges of cultural pluralism and visibility multiply exponentially. Essentially, the leader is responsible for, and sometimes the architect of, several key elements of organizational culture:

- Identifying and communicating the core values and principles that guide organizational behavior and decision making

- Specifying behaviors that exemplify the company's values or principles (and, by inference, those that do not) and leading by example

- Developing a method by which individuals can receive feedback on their performance in both business-financial and behavioral terms

- Ensuring that the reward or reinforcement systems, whether they are monetary, such as compensation, or less tangible, such as inclusion and access, are consistent with organizational values and principles, recognize and promote desirable behaviors, and punish undesirable behaviors

- Personally assuming the responsibility of championing the desired culture and recognizing the need for redundancy and reinforcement concerning what is expected and what is not negotiable

To advance these elements effectively, the leader must create a common notion of what the company is trying to accomplish. This focus involves the establishment of shared agreed-upon objectives, implementation of a consistent approach to management, and embodiment of a strong performance orientation throughout the organization. Dramatic changes in culture may be required when the current culture is significantly out of alignment with the business objectives of the company or when significant inconsistencies exist between key elements (for example, the organization says it values X but rewards Y). These cultural crises normally arise from a series of incremental changes that, taken in isolation, seem relatively inconsequential and that most often occur in an environment of benign neglect by a leadership that chooses to focus on what are thought to be more pressing business issues. A critical step in leading organizations is to recognize that organizational culture *is* a pressing business issue and that shaping it is a principal senior leadership responsibility, rather than one to be delegated to human resources or some other function. History has shown that organizations that fail to address and respond proactively to these climatic changes run the risk of going the way of the dinosaur, only much more quickly.

Another ongoing challenge for the leader of a large company is to build and sustain an appropriate level of positive creative tension. Clearly, building consensus is increasingly a critical leadership skill, because leadership through influence is demonstrably more effective in building commitment and sustained performance than leadership through positional authority or outright fear and intimidation. However, consensus without constructive creative tension is extremely dangerous and manifests itself in several ways.

- Dissent will occur outside meetings rather than inside them.

- The gap between consensus (agreement on decisions) and perceived consensus (the belief that people are in agreement regarding decisions) will widen.

- Difficulties will be exacerbated when decisions are implemented, due to sustained passive resistance.

- Direct conflict will be perceived to be dysfunctional,
  and the ability to read nuances will become the key to
  individual survival and advancement.

Positive creative tension is also the context in which continuous improvement becomes a natural approach to everyday work and a fundamental part of an organization's culture. It normalizes change in noncrisis periods, maintains focus on both what gets done and the way it is accomplished, and ensures openness and responsiveness to feedback from employees and external customers.

The Importance of Consistent Execution

Clearly, a theme inherent in the leader's role as cultural architect is consistent attention and focus. Leaders are both architects and general contractors, and they should be judged not only by the elegance of their plans, but also by the quality of implementation and maintenance of the design. Basically, I think that leaders can and should leverage the power of the "Hawthorne effect" to ensure that constructive change, appropriately paced, occurs in times of both relative stability and rapid change.

The series of studies conducted over sixty years ago at the Western Electric plant in Hawthorne, Illinois, still has a great deal of relevance to executive officers. Although the research initially sought to determine the impact of lighting on productivity, it ultimately taught us a great deal about the importance of involvement and consistent execution. Significant gains in productivity were observed by the researchers, but lighting was not the cause. Instead, three factors, operating together, produced the performance improvement.

1. Change (the lighting level was varied)
2. Attention (employees knew their performance was being observed)

3. Measurement (productivity metrics were clearly utilized and visible to employees)

When we, as executives, attempt to make meaningful changes, we readily acknowledge the need for observable change (it shouldn't merely be rhetorical), attention (to demonstrate our interest in and focus on the desired outcome), and measurement (the results of the change, which we hope will be positive). But the key is *sustaining* gains once they are realized. For me, a key insight from the Hawthorne studies was what happened after the research was completed. When the researchers left, improvement ceased, attention was no longer rigorously paid to performance, and productivity regressed to its original levels. In other words, the rather remarkable growth exhibited during the research period was decidedly short term. I suspect that the regression was not an overnight phenomenon but a gradual one, probably so subtle that hardly anyone noticed, least of all plant management.

This phenomenon, I believe, is all too frequently repeated in large corporations through a myriad of well-intentioned change efforts. In my view, the absence of frequent, consistent follow-up (that is, ongoing attention and focus) inhibits the sustainability of performance improvement or constructive cultural change. A key part of the leader's role is to ensure that appropriate monitoring and follow-up systems are in place to remind the organization of its key priorities. When employees can see and feel that management is focused, attentive, and caring, as demonstrated by persistence and follow-up, the sort of constructive tension is provided that results in long-term change and continuous improvement.

The Role of the Leader in the Future

I think that the leader of the future in large corporations will discover that his or her role has markedly changed; as a consequence, the leader's behavior must also change. In my opinion, this has at least three implications for leadership.

First, the leader of the future must be more flexible, with a broader variety of experiences. The days of an individual's rising through a single functional discipline to the top of a large corporation, particularly a global one, are nearly over. A cross-disciplinary background, from a systems perspective, will be increasingly necessary to address the complexities of change.

Second, the leader of the future will view her or his "ceremonial" or "spiritual" responsibilities as the organization's head to be a necessary and critical function, not a trivial one that must be endured or delegated to someone else. Cultural leaders who fail to recognize or handle effectively the visibility and accessibility issues inherent in senior leadership limit the openness of the culture and restrict their ability to lead through knowledge and personal influence, forcing leadership to be exercised through position or hierarchy. Interestingly, at a time when technology seems to be shortening distances between people, demands for visibility and face-to-face contact with the CEO seem to be rising. My personal hypothesis is that it is becoming easier *not* to travel; thus, making the effort is an affirmation of the importance of people in the field. As our organization continues to grow internationally, my desire to be in the field—to listen, absorb, and learn as well as to communicate the vision and direction of the company—is actually increasing dramatically. The sanctity of the corporate tower has never been more alluring, nor more dangerous.

Third, in a related way, attendant global business issues have become so complex that decision making cannot be effectively centered at the top. For me or any senior management team to be *the* decision-making body for all significant corporate matters would be overwhelming at best and could foster bad business practices. The trend toward increasingly empowered organizations addresses the need to move decision making to lower levels, creates the necessary development opportunities for future leaders, and simultaneously creates an experience base to draw on in times of crisis. Although this movement may be frightening to some who grew up in an environment where CEOs were the final decision makers in nearly all matters and prided themselves on their ability to control events and outcomes, those of us who fill leadership roles can no longer do that. We must increasingly rely on others to share in these responsibilities, and we can facilitate their success by exercising our leadership through the culture of the organization.

We control and influence the organization by setting the cultural framework in which decisions are made: by championing and demonstrating noble values and purposes, by clearly articulating a sense of purpose and business direction, and by embracing the symbolic responsibilities of office as well as the financial ones. Ultimately, we must overcome the risks of isolation and create a global climate that helps us to see and listen. What we see and hear warns us of impending risks in times of calm and becomes our foundation to provide stability and focus in times of crisis.

28 WILLIAM N. PLAMONDON

Energy and Leadership

William N. Plamondon is president and CEO of Budget Rent a Car Corporation. He serves on the board of directors of the American Car Rental Association (ACRA), Northern Central College in Naperville, Illinois, and the Florida-based "Give Kids the World"—for which he also actively volunteers. Plamondon is active in the International Franchise Association, the White House Council on Travel and Tourism Issues Task Force, and the World Travel and Tourism Council.

From his earliest days as a manager, Plamondon turned to his front-line employees to learn the inner workings of the organization. Today, he continues to seek and rely on the insights of the company's service workers. He wants all employees to "aim high, play it straight, and make it fun."

When we think of management gurus, the name Albert Einstein does not spring to mind. But the revered theoretical physicist can teach us volumes about how to lead an organization into the twenty-first century. Like Einstein, leaders of the future must know the elements they are working with, have high aspirations and ideals, and understand the dynamics of movement and how they create energy.

Energy is an organization's capacity for action and accomplishment. It propels the organization forward, maintains its balance, and keeps it focused during downturns, transitions, and crises. It is not enough for leaders simply to possess energy; their job is to help others in the company generate their own energy and pass it on. If we apply Einstein's famous statement of the mass-energy relationship, $E = mc^2$ (energy equals mass times the speed of light squared), to an organization, we could say that energy (E) is created by leaders who inspire the members of their organizations (m) to anticipate and respond at high velocity (c^2).

Applied to physics, Einstein's special theory of relativity reflects a positive correlation between mass and energy. Applied to organizations, the inverse tends to be true. Large organizations can get bogged down in bureaucracy and rules that frustrate and demotivate their members. Processes they may have instituted to help employees make responsible decisions can become ends unto themselves— until the way things are done supersedes getting them done. Leaders of these organizations often believe that if they build enough procedural protection, no mistakes will be made and the right decisions will be ensured. But they accomplish the opposite. Decisions, if they are made at all, are made by default. And no one is accountable, because no individual or group takes responsibility.

Not taking responsibility becomes institutionalized in layers of rules, forms, and unproductive meetings. Bureaucracy and a fear of making mistakes indicate that the organization's management structure and business processes have ceased to be effective; it's time to reengineer them to support an environment that breeds energy. What does such an environment look like? It is one where:

- The organization is open to environmental information from customers, employees, competitors, and the marketplace.

- The team is aware of its strengths and weaknesses compared to the strengths and weaknesses of the competition and plays within them.

- Employees have a sense of purpose beyond just making money, which is guided by a core ideology as well as compelling and challenging performance goals.

- Authority and accountability are decentralized so that the organization becomes a collection of small, interchangeable units working toward a common goal.

- There are many leaders.

Stay Open to Environmental Information

An organization is more than the sum of its people, products, and capital. It's organic. It has a life of its own. If it is to stay healthy and grow, its leaders need to keep it open to the environment and attuned to the signals of the market. This ensures that the company and the systems within it stay resilient and organized around customer requirements. Consistent and frequent communication with customers and employees is critical to that openness. Customers and employees are the best gauge of how a company is faring against competitors and need to be involved in the process of developing new products and services to help guard against isolation.

When it comes to communicating with employees, I have never viewed communication as merely sharing information but as sharing responsibility. Rather than telling people what to do, I ask them what needs to be done and then do my best to remove any obstacles in their way. This not only generates the best ideas but also gives people a stake in the success of an effort. One of our customer service representatives put it best when she said, "If you want me to be there for the crash landing, you'd better invite me to the launch!"

Inviting this kind of participation means giving up some of what we traditionally think of as control, but the end result is one of lasting value, because people become energized to achieve more when given authority and responsibility.

Know the Team's Strengths and Weaknesses and Play Within Them

In addition to listening to customers and employees and staying abreast of current industry and market trends, a leader must know history—world history, the country's history, the company's history, and his or her own history. If you don't know history you won't be able to understand the future.

A sense of history gives you greater perspective on your organization's and your team's strengths and weaknesses. It lets you stand back from an issue and see its broader implications. You will begin to see the inevitable cycles of your business and recognize the things you can do to prolong the upswing of the cycle as well as ways to make the most of the downtimes without turning the organization against itself or wearing employees out.

Knowing history also enables you to recognize opportunities when they arise. The leader of the future will be able to see these opportunities, even when they appear to be obstacles. One of our company's pioneers, Bick Bickson, had this capacity to triumph in the face of what others saw as adversity. He was managing our Hawaiian operations when an airline that delivered 54 percent of the islands' inbound visitors went on strike. While every one of his competitors reduced their fleets and laid off employees, he went the other way. He bought full-page ads in the major papers and slashed the rates on his rental fleet. His employees rallied, volunteering to take one day off a week without pay and using the slow periods to offer extra services free of charge. The strike lasted sixty-three days, and Bickson's Hawaiian operations broke all market-share records and grossed more revenue than they had during the two previous years.

Leaders who are flexible when confronted with obstacles recharge the energy of their employees rather than consume it and keep the organization moving ahead.

Have a Sense of Purpose and a Higher Goal

A successful leader understands that an organization is held together by shared values, beliefs, and commitments. This is what enables it to rise above cyclical hardships and gives it its tone, fiber, integrity, and capacity to endure. The first step to ensuring that your organization is committed to its core values is to find the right people. This starts with the recruiting process. People can't be trained to buy into your company's value system. In selecting new employees—especially for customer-contact positions—it's wisest to hire for attitude and train for skills.

Once employees embrace and understand the organization's core values, the most effective way to unify the company and create momentum is to commit to a clear and compelling goal that anticipates market needs and is aligned with what the organization stands for, a goal that stimulates energy because it is tangible, resonant, and highly focused and is so compelling that it doesn't need a professional phrasemaker to make it sound so. Einstein's theories have a simplicity and elegance that he thought fitting for an interpretation of the universe. If he could explain gravitation, electromagnetism, and subatomic phenomena simply, surely we can express our organizations' goals with brevity and clarity and in such a way that the mass will begin to move at a greater velocity, creating more and more energy.

Leaders need to help set the standards to which the organization aspires, to challenge its members with a lofty goal, and to make sure that everyone understands the goal and what he or she must do to attain it. It is the leaders' responsibility to communicate this goal in a clear and compelling way that inspires the organization to move to new heights and at faster speeds than it would ordinarily attain on its own.

Decentralize Authority and Accountability

Earlier I referred to the inertia that results when rules replace thinking, meetings replace doing, and processes replace responsibility. In today's fast-moving environment, organizations must learn to become small entities within larger ones, combining the resources and economies of scale of a large corporation with the speed and agility of a start-up company. Both have the same mass, but the group of small entities is infinitely faster and easier to steer.

Hire and reward the right people; instill in them the core values of the organization; give them a clear goal, accountability, and responsibility; and then get out of their way. They can't be energized if they aren't given the leeway to make decisions and act without getting a dozen approvals first. As former secretary of labor Arthur Goldberg, in an apocryphal story, observed, "If Columbus had had an advisory committee, he would probably still be at the dock." Push decision making down to those who are closest to the customer or activity and who know the market firsthand. Decentralize authority. Quick decision making is vital in order to compete and win.

Will mistakes be made? Of course. The faster you go, the more chance there is of stubbing your toe, but the more chance you have of getting somewhere. It is well worth risking a blunder or two in pursuit of an energized organization, because in an energized organization, employees usually blunder forward.

Create Many Leaders

The last, and most important, element of an environment that breeds energy is the presence of many leaders. The cloak of leadership is heavy and needs to be shared. No one person can lead or energize an organization. As more people become leaders, the organization will be able to grow, respond, and move faster and faster, thus creating more energy: $E = mc^2$.

The relationship between managers and workers has been permanently altered, and the lines will continue to blur. Revolutionary changes continue to sweep through American business, and organizations must adapt to survive. The leader of the future will need to shepherd the organization through these changes. And whether that leader is in a boardroom or on the plant floor, the skills he or she will be called to draw upon will often intersect with the Einsteinian qualities of wisdom, vision, the ability to create energy, and the realization that a leader's first responsibility is to serve.

Among the many lessons we can learn from Einstein is that all energy should be directed toward the good of the organization and its people. All leaders can find inspiration in his words:

> Each of us comes for a short visit, not knowing why yet sometimes seeming to divine a purpose. From the standpoint of daily life, however, there is one thing we do know: that man is here for the sake of other men—above all for those upon whose smile and well-being our own happiness depends, and also for the countless unknown souls with whose fate we are connected by a bond of sympathy. Many times a day I realize how much my own outer and inner life is built upon the labors of my fellow men, both living and dead, and how earnestly I must exert myself in order to give in return as much as I have received [Albert Einstein, *The World as I See It: Ideas and Opinions*, 1954, p. 8].

29 STEVEN M. BORNSTEIN
ANTHONY F. SMITH

The Puzzles of Leadership

*Steven M. Bornstein is president and CEO of ESPN
and has led the company through its most active
growth period in its fourteen-year history. In March
1993, he was named a corporate vice president of
Capital Cities/ABC, ESPN's parent company. He
serves on the boards of directors of several organizations, including the National Cable Television Association, the National Academy of Cable Programming,
the Cabletelevision Advertising Bureau, Eurosport,
Cable in the Classroom, The V Foundation, the
Walter Kaitz Foundation, Hampton (Virginia)
University, and ESPN.*

*Anthony F. Smith is a director of Keilty, Gold-
smith & Company, an international consulting firm
based in San Diego, California. He has served on the
teaching and research faculties of several universities,
including the University of California at San Diego,
and the European School of Management at Oxford
University. He has also been an active consultant for
over ten years, specializing in organizational change
and leadership development. His clients include the*

American Express Company, McKinsey & Co.,
General Electric, and the National Geographical
Society. Additionally, he has worked with ESPN
since 1988.

Research and writing on leadership over the last twenty years has raised our level of understanding and practice to a new level. Moreover, organizations throughout the world have spent billions to educate employees in leadership by focusing on such topics as influence, organizational change, empowerment, motivation, and teamwork, clearly embracing the notion that leadership is much more than single acts of greatness carried out by a visionary CEO. Leadership is now understood by many to imply *collective* action, orchestrated in such a way as to bring about significant change while raising the competencies and motivation of all those involved—that is, action where more than one individual influences the process.

Given the fundamental changes that have occurred in the world, particularly in our institutions and organizations, it was imperative that leadership thinking move beyond the old theories; however, leaders must be careful not to forget the fact that although leadership is a process that involves many people at various levels, the process most often begins with one person. Therefore, in this chapter, we will not only review the central tenets of leadership from a *process* point of view but will also focus on the central *person* of the process, the leader. Finally, we will attempt to describe the challenging *puzzles* that the leader of the future must resolve.

The Process

Leadership has traditionally been thought of as the result of gifted people with preferred traits influencing followers to do what is necessary to achieve organizational and societal goals. This view, we believe, reflects the leadership of the past or, as Joseph Rost calls it, the "industrial paradigm of leadership." Although truths and insights may be gained from the industrial paradigm, it falls significantly short in explaining and predicting leadership for the future. We submit that leadership in the future will more closely reflect a process whereby a leader pursues his or her vision by intentionally seeking to influence others and the conditions in which they work, allowing them to perform to their full potential and thus both increasing the probability of realizing the vision and maximizing the organizational and personal development of all parties involved.

Although at first glance, this definition may not appear to be a major departure from the industrial paradigm, it has some very significant differences. To begin with, leadership is *an ongoing process*—not an event, not the implementation of a program, and not simply the articulation or inspiration of a great idea. And given the fact that it occurs only when people intentionally seek to influence others, it must be understood to be *an episodic process*. Moreover, the process is *driven by a vision*—typically, the vision of the leader.

Those attempting to understand and practice leadership within today's changing environment must keep in mind that the leadership process is both intentional and based on influence—a process far different from positional power, manipulation, or coercion. Rather, with intentional influence, individuals rely on personal power and credibility to change and affect people and their environments. Real leadership occurs when followers *choose* to follow their leaders—out of a belief in them and their articulated vision. The research on credibility suggests that when one individual attempts to influence another, the potential follower engages in both conscious and unconscious evaluation of the potential leader and will follow, striving to perform at his or her full potential, only the leader deemed to be credible. Credibility is based on six criteria that we call the Six C's of Leadership Credibility:

1. *Conviction:* the passion and commitment the person demonstrates toward his or her vision

2. *Character*: consistent demonstration of integrity, honesty, respect, and trust

3. *Care*: demonstration of concern for the personal and professional well-being of others

4. *Courage*: willingness to stand up for one's beliefs, challenge others, admit mistakes, and change one's own behavior when necessary

5. *Composure*: consistent display of appropriate emotional reactions, particularly in tough or crisis situations

6. *Competence*: proficiency in hard skills, such as technical, functional, and content expertise skills, and soft skills, such as interpersonal, communication, team, and organizational skills

The degree to which leaders are seen as credible is the degree to which potential followers will allow themselves to be influenced. Although the criteria are not equally weighted (one or more selected criteria may be more important than others in any given situation), it is clear that if any one of the six components is noticeably deficient, the overall credibility of the leader will be seriously diminished. The complicating factor is that in order for an individual to exercise leadership, she or he must first be perceived as credible, which is usually established through the exercise of effective leadership. This is just one of many dilemmas and circular puzzles that leaders must face when attempting to lead in the future.

The Person

Although it is true that leadership is a process that involves many people working toward a common vision, we believe that much of the focus on the *process* of leadership has clouded, if not discounted, the importance and centrality of the leader. The process of leadership does not just happen or emerge from groups of people who simultaneously recognize their need to follow a vision. In most cases, one individual either creates or recognizes a need and influences others to work together to pursue that vision. We do not want to oversimplify the multivariate aspects of leadership; dozens, if not hundreds, of factors converge to create its opportunities and realities. But we have found several frameworks to be useful in trying to exercise, as well as in helping others to exercise, the process of leadership.

Leaders are currently facing many puzzles and challenges and certainly will face others that will be even greater in the future. The one dominant puzzle that leaders will need to solve in the future is the *doubt-versus-power* puzzle. Mastering this puzzle will provide great insight into two other puzzles—the *question-versus-answer* puzzle and the *balance-versus-reality* puzzle.

The Doubt-Versus-Power Puzzle

The future is uncertain for current and potential leaders, and for followers, this uncertainty is magnified many times over. Never in history has so much change occurred so fast in our organizations. It is not surprising that employees in most organizations, including ESPN, desire more direction and overall guidance from their leaders. Combined with the uncertainty of change is the fact that employees are no longer guaranteed lifelong employment. Because of more demanding and expanded performance standards created by growth or downsizing, they are feeling as doubtful as ever. In addition, leaders are learning that their organizations need to become flatter, faster, and less hierarchical to allow people the confidence and empowerment to make decisions on their own—in short, to become leaders themselves. As a result, leaders are trying to listen to their employees more intently, and the message the employees are sending is that they need more structure, direction, coaching, and guidance. So not only are followers plagued with doubt; the very leaders to whom they are looking for direction are preoccupied with trying to resolve the doubts in their own lives while simultaneously attending to the multiplicity of needs of their followers. This is a very challenging puzzle to solve. We would argue that the solution begins with understanding the various levels of doubt that leaders and followers face.

To be sure, every human being has some degree of doubt. And the greater the doubt, the more tentative one feels. But leaders and followers cannot afford to be too tentative when they are competing in a global environment. Leaders who are clearly struggling with personal or professional doubt will ultimately lose credibility with their followers and constituents. Followers who are plagued with doubt cannot perform at their highest potential. Charles Garfield, author of *Peak Performance*, and others who have studied this topic, have clearly indicated that doubt is one of the most powerful impediments to human performance. Additionally, if followers are constantly battling with their doubts, they are not thinking about the leader's vision or acting in accordance with it. Figure 29.1 illustrates the various stages of doubt that individuals face in their organizations.

It should be noted that placing the personal fulfillment and satisfaction level at the base of the pyramid is meant to imply that human beings are people first. If they are preoccupied with doubt in their personal lives, they limit their capacity to focus on their tasks or projects at work; they will perform their job out of professional obligation and for job security but not to their full potential. Therefore, assuming that organizational leaders can do little to intervene in anyone's personal world, we will focus on the eight levels of organizational doubt.

Effective leaders are constantly reducing doubt in themselves and their followers. If the followers are doubtful about performing at the *task* level, an effective leader will try to provide the necessary training and support to ensure that they become masters at their tasks. Once followers work out all their doubts at the task level, they will begin questioning and doubting the competence of their team, particularly its leader. They will come to realize that although *their*

Figure 29.1. The Hierarchy of Doubt.

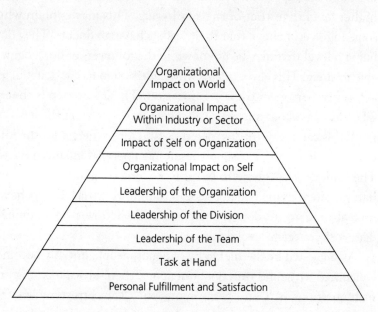

responsibilities on a project may be completed and performed competently, success will not be guaranteed unless others on the team also perform competently; this becomes the source of a new level of doubt. The process is analogous to climbing a mountain. Climbers become concerned and doubtful about the level that lies before them, and only when they have mastered this level, whether it is intellectual or strategic, will they begin to address their doubts concerning the level ahead. It is true that some people will always worry and be doubtful about the highest peak before they have mastered the first step. Leaders need to educate and encourage such followers to focus on the task at hand and trust the leaders of the organization to worry about the highest peak: having an impact on the world.

If every human being has some level of doubt, the key to leadership is to influence people to work at resolving their doubts, thus raising them to higher levels of thinking and behaving. Leaders must also attempt to do the same thing in their own lives, but at a higher level than that of their followers. This may explain why some followers believe that their leaders have no doubts. They do, but at a level that may be unknown to the followers or unrecognizable by them. This also explains why leaders often feel as doubtful as any other person in their organization. The difference is that a CEO's doubts about missing a call reflect the fact that at the leader's level, this can mean the loss of a thousand jobs, whereas for the follower, missing a call may simply result in a poor performance review. The leader's doubts tend to be far more long term and strategic in nature, often giving the impression to followers that leaders have no real-time urgent doubts compared to the followers' own immediate task- or team-level doubts.

As suggested by the hierarchy of doubt, people initially become concerned with, and thus doubtful about, themselves, focusing on such questions as "Can I perform my job?" "Can I trust my leaders in the team, division, or organization?" "If I choose to stay in this organization, how will it affect my life and career?" It is our contention that once individuals have resolved these questions, they will become less concerned with personal fulfillment and satisfaction and far more concerned with affecting others, the organization, and the world.

Now one might ask, "If every employee or member of an organization was working to resolve the highest level of doubt, would the organization be more productive and competitive?" We believe that the answer is clear: productive and competitive organizations are marked by confident people performing as leaders at various levels throughout the organization. This is why we suggest that effective leaders need to work constantly on dissolving doubts within themselves and providing an environment in which their followers have the support and resources to resolve their own doubts. The bottom line is that power and performance are inversely correlated with one's degree of doubt.

The Question-Versus-Answer Puzzle

The hierarchy of doubt implies that leaders need to help their followers resolve their doubts at a number of levels. This is possible when the leader has both the time and the knowledge to do so. As we all know, leaders never have enough time to do everything they should, but more problematic is the fact that leaders do not have all the answers to the questions the followers are asking. Herein lies the second puzzle that leaders must solve in the future: knowing that the followers have questions, that questions reflect doubt, and that doubt impedes performance, leaders feel compelled to answer questions to which they may not have the answers.

We believe that the solution involves two dimensions: *honesty* and *empowerment*. Honesty is fundamental to a leader's credibility, in that it drives perceptions of Character, one of the Six C's. Leaders must communicate to their followers and educate them in what they know and what they do not know. In many cases, followers will not believe leaders who claim that they do not have the answer or information on some given issue. This typically happens because the leader lacks credibility; perhaps in the past, he or she did not reveal the truth and the followers never forgot the dishonesty. Therefore, leaders must sometimes use the response, "I cannot reveal that information now because of the following reasons," and then provide the reasons; this still may not be easy for some followers to hear. Leaders need to know whether their followers are informed enough to understand the rationale behind such decisions. If they are not, the leaders must educate them on such matters. It is important to keep in mind that great leaders do not always seek to please their followers, but rather seek to build their own credibility and earn trust and respect. Such trust demands Courage, another of the Six C's. Leaders who do not believe that such practices will serve them in the end take a huge risk if they attempt instead to use manipulation and deceit to influence their followers.

Related to courage and honesty is the very popular notion of *empowerment*. Empowerment in its most simple form is sharing decision-making power with others. This is much easier when those who are being empowered are both competent and willing and fully understand the vision of the leader. When this is not the case, the leader must create conditions in which the followers can receive the training, coaching, and feedback necessary to perform responsibly with their newly found power. The mission and values of the organization are also critical guides when power is distributed throughout an organization. When someone truly empowers another person, she or he has, in essence, transferred decision-making power on a particular task to that individual. Although the leader may choose to continue a dialogue concerning the task and may even attempt to influence the person at times, he or she does not exercise any decision-making power. We should note, however, that this restriction justifiably ends when the follower's decisions and/or actions are inconsistent with the organization's mission and values.

As you can see, leaders in the future will need to become more comfortable asking questions of their followers, thoughtful and guided questions it is to be hoped, rather than always providing answers. They must also be willing to be open and honest, to avoid even the appearance of the "know-it-all" leader. The potential risk to the leader's credibility is far less, although it is still a risk, when he or she admits making mistakes and not knowing all the answers, rather than maintaining the appearance of knowing everything and risking that the followers will discover for themselves that the leader was unwilling to expose his or her human side. We believe that the leader of the future will be far more skilled at the art of questioning than the art of answering. Practicing this art demands levels of honesty and empowerment that are unknown in today's organizations. It is through this art that leaders can begin to share the burden of leadership with their followers, increasing the capacity and performance of the organization but also creating the remaining puzzle to be solved, that of balance versus reality.

The Balance-Versus-Reality Puzzle

We would hope that the picture of the leader of the future that is beginning to emerge is of a person who seeks to influence others by resolving doubts and empowering followers to perform at their highest potential, not only to pursue the realization of a vision, but also to become leaders themselves. This may sound exciting and even glamorous to many potential leaders; however, influencing others to become leaders presents a challenging puzzle. How do leaders share their burden of leadership while attempting to help their followers to achieve some reasonable balance in life, knowing that leadership does not typically lend itself to a balanced life-style? It is very apparent that people today are placing a much higher value on maintaining a balanced life-style. As a result, they have become far more demanding in asking their leaders to provide them with an environment in which they can achieve such a balance. It is our belief that given the ever-increasing complexities of modern-day organizations, shared leadership is necessary for survival.

This puzzle is perhaps the most difficult to solve. It is possible that a balanced life-style (a forty- to fifty-hour work week, minimum stress, and maximum fulfillment) and leadership are mutually exclusive. We submit that part of the solution to this puzzle lies in the redefinition of a balanced life-style. It appears to us that the reason a lack of satisfaction (or conviction) exists among people who have chosen not to attempt leadership is that they are unrealistic about the demands *and* the rewards of leading people. Perhaps when individuals assess the potential demands and rewards of leadership, they are factoring into the equation their current baseline work satisfaction and fulfillment. Therefore, additional time, responsibility, and pressure seem to cancel out any additional rewards of money, power, and status they may receive. The bottom line is that if leaders are truly credible and have high conviction, they just do it! Leaders lead because they see no other option to achieving their vision and bringing about what they believe are significant and needed changes. We acknowledge that a balanced leader is probably more effective than an unbalanced one—the caution concerns the standard of measurement and the definition that is used. Although we are not presumptuous enough to define *the* standard, we believe that balance is different for leaders than for followers. In fact, for a leader with conviction, the issue of balance pales in comparison to the power of possibly realizing a significant vision and influencing one's own destiny. The harsh reality is that *leadership is extremely demanding*. If it were easy, far more capable people would be doing it. This is analogous to dieting. Some people who diet continue to search for an easy way to lose weight, but as most dieters will tell you, losing weight is extremely tough, requiring discipline, knowledge, energy, desire, and commitment—just like leadership.

Some Final Thoughts on Leadership

We may have raised some questions in your mind about the discomfort, or even imbalance, inherent in leadership. Although we are both committed to encouraging all people to exercise leadership, from the receptionist to the CEO, we in no way want to glamorize the true realities of this arduous process. Leadership is demanding and complex. With the current trend toward diversity in the workplace, quantum-leap technological advances, and fierce global competition, the demands and complexity of leadership become even more daunting. Leaders of the future will lead because they just simply need to. Their *Conviction*, their *Character*, their *Care*, and their *Courage* will drive them to at least try. The people who will lead successfully will be those who can maintain their *Composure* while constantly developing their *Competence* throughout the process. The *Credible* leader will be the leader of the future.

30 SARA E. MELÉNDEZ

An "Outsider's" View of Leadership

Sara E. Meléndez is president of INDEPENDENT
SECTOR *and former president of the Center for
Applied Linguistics in Washington, D.C. She has
worked and written extensively on multicultural and
diversity issues, bilingual education, and increased
educational and leadership opportunities for minorities
in America. Meléndez serves as a trustee of the Educational Testing Service and is on the boards of Quality Education for Minorities and the National Puerto
Rican Forum.*

So much has been written about leadership that it is difficult to
talk or write about it with originality or to totally avoid clichés.
I do have a sense that most of us would say, "I know it when I see
it." When I see it, I also think, "That's the kind of leader I would
like to be." Leaders are usually people of vision, effective communicators, effective decision makers, and intelligent; they respect and
value individuals and their dignity; they are committed to service
and to obedience to the unenforceable; they have total honesty and
integrity; they are kind; and they often see themselves as teachers.
I will discuss some of these qualities later.

Leadership, which is observed primarily as a set of behaviors, is influenced, if not determined, by culture and one's life experiences. Everything I am and do is colored or informed by the fact that I am a Puerto Rican woman in a society where I have always been in the minority. All my experiences and observations are filtered through the lenses of ethnic culture, gender, minority status, and poverty. For many people of color, life's experiences do not provide opportunities to exercise or develop leadership skills, even when they may have the necessary qualities of character and talent.

I am still somewhat surprised when I am referred to as a leader. There is no false modesty or coyness in this. It is not too different from my reaction the first time someone called me "Ma'am," the first time I went to a doctor who was younger than I was, or, more recently, the first time a president of the United States was elected who was younger than I was. Each time, I was shocked. Although I had no control over those events, I did accomplish certain things that caused people to begin thinking of me and referring to me as a leader.

One question I am often asked these days, especially by people who see themselves as emerging leaders, is "What did you do to prepare for assuming leadership positions?" In retrospect, it seems that my preparation for leadership consisted of being in a series of situations where I had a strong conviction, I expressed it, and someone asked me to do something about the situation, a version of "Put your money where your mouth is." I guess that I had passion and didn't know enough to say no.

My first leadership experience came about in church. The pastor, who had never read an article or book on leadership, or probably anything else (it was rumored that he only read the Bible), thought that if I could win contests on Bible verses and be the star pupil in Sunday school, I could probably preach. So he asked me to preach, and I did.

In our church, as in many of the informal churches in Puerto Rican neighborhoods that are not affiliated with any large denominational group, anyone who had the inclination and, I suppose, some ability could become a leader. Women, youth, and even children were encouraged and respected for their contributions. I have since met many Puerto Rican and other Latino leaders who had similar experiences in fundamentalist churches. These churches had very little hierarchy and encouraged talent and passion. Flat hierarchies that encourage talent and passion have often been found, in management research, to be effective organizations.

I had other opportunities to exercise leadership in school, although I never thought of it in terms of leadership until many years later. I went to the public schools of New York City at a time when the schools were in demographic transition, with a small but growing number of Puerto Rican students who spoke no English. I was selected to be the interpreter for them and their parents and I found myself, by necessity, being their advocate as well. Prejudice, discrimination, and neglect were common. My advocacy won me supporters among the students and some teachers, but it sometimes got me into trouble with the administration. Later I learned that all leaders run the risk of incurring the displeasure of those who have a vested interest in the status quo.

Many years later, with a freshly minted master's degree in education, I was offered a job administering a federally funded program for inner-city middle school students, about 75 percent of whom were African Americans and Latinos. All the school district administrators were white, and I thought they didn't know enough about the children for whom they were making decisions daily. Believing that we needed more African Americans and Latinos in those decision-making positions, I decided to go back to school to pursue a doctoral program so that I could become a decision maker in education.

Since then, I have met many educational leaders and leaders of nonprofit organizations who understand the need to have representation by minority groups in the ranks of those making decisions and designing programs. They know that to be responsive to the needs of students, clients, and other end users, providers and servers need intimate knowledge of, or at least familiarity with, the experience and reality of the clients.

Frances Hesselbein led the Girl Scouts of the United States on a campaign to bring diversity and inclusiveness to all the programs and councils, at all levels of the organization. Today the Girl Scouts serves a stunningly diverse population and provides a richer experience to all its clients.

Vision

The leaders I admire have a clear vision of how things should be. They are able to communicate that vision so others can share in it, and then get others to work together as a unit, each contributing his or her best toward the achievement of that vision. In order to have a clear vision, it is necessary to see the present clearly as well. Max DePree, in *Leadership Is an Art* (1989), states emphatically, "The first responsibility of a leader is to define reality" (p. 11). My gender and cultural lenses may cause me to define reality differently from individuals who belong to majority groups. And because my reality is different from the majority's, my vision of the future will probably also be different. There is no value judgment in these statements. I believe that the global economy and culture we will live in has room for many realities and visions. The task is to forge a shared vision.

Warren Bennis, in *On Becoming a Leader* (1989), based his ideas about leadership "on the assumption that leaders are people who are able to express themselves fully. . . . They also know what they want, why they want it, and how to communicate what they want to others, in order to gain their cooperation and support" (p. 3). In addition, having a clear definition of current reality and a clear vision about the future should not preclude listening to others and being amenable to negotiating the language and the fine points of either the definition of the present or the vision of the future. It should be possible to do this without losing the centrality of the vision. Indeed, it may be necessary in order to attain acceptance of the big picture by those one would seek to lead.

Vision is the first important characteristic of leadership, and it can present an obstacle for people of color, women, individuals with disabilities, and others who are not cast in the traditional mold. Their ability to communicate their different vision will be their first major challenge. Women and people of color need to have the usual set of characteristics and skills that all leaders must have in some measure, and they must be able to cross barriers of culture and experience to exercise leadership and engage others in their vision. This requires exceptional communication skills that transcend culturally influenced styles of communication.

Leadership and Diversity

In American society on the brink of the twenty-first century, good leaders must be able to see talent and skills in the diverse individuals and groups that comprise the current work force and that will be even more diverse in the work force of the future. Stephen R. Covey, in *Principle-Centered Leadership* (1990), says that one of the eight characteristics of principle-centered leaders is that they believe in other people (p. 35). I would modify that by adding that they believe in other people even when they don't fit into neat categories.

In my professional career, I often found myself in situations where the management or leadership could not see me in anything but the role of a minority. It was difficult to become involved in mainstream issues because I was seen as having expertise, or an interest, only in women's issues or minority issues. Finally, a visionary leader with a good eye for talent, who realized that my skills and knowledge were adaptable and transferable to many other issues, gave me an opportunity. Not allowing all individuals, from whatever background, to contribute their best impoverishes the enterprise and limits us in achieving our full potential as an organization, as individuals, and as a society. Max DePree understood this and expressed it well in *Leadership Is an Art* (1989): "The simple act of recognizing diversity in corporate life helps us to connect the great variety of gifts that people bring to the work and service of the organization. Diversity allows each of us to contribute in a special way, to make our special gift a part of the corporate effort" (p. 9).

As the United States moves rapidly, and apparently inexorably, toward a population in which one-third of the people are of diverse races and colors, leaders for the future will need to be comfortable with diversity. They will have to understand the dynamics of diversity in the workplace, including the basics of cultural differences in worldview, motivation, problem-solving techniques, work styles, and communication styles. The need for leaders to provide equal opportunity to people of color and to improve the cultural climate of the workplace is only part of the reason they should acquire these insights.

The participation of individuals from diverse groups in the work force will grow even faster than the growth in the population, because these individuals tend to be younger than the majority population. For example, Hispanic men have the highest rate of labor force participation of any group in the United States. Leaders and managers will be faced with employees of increasingly diverse backgrounds, regardless of whether the country backs away from affirmative action. It is in the country's minority groups that the workers will be found.

Increasingly, clients of the nonprofit sector will also come from diverse backgrounds. Nonprofit, voluntary sector organizations will need to design culturally and linguistically appropriate programs and strategies targeted to the particular needs of this heterogeneous population. This is not possible without the contributions of members of these communities. Human service providers have been learning this lesson in health services, substance abuse rehabilitation, family planning, and AIDS prevention.

Passion

Effective leaders are passionate about the cause they are promoting and about their commitment to the greater or public good. One of the espoused values of INDEPENDENT SECTOR, a membership organization of foundations and nonprofit organizations established to promote philanthropy and voluntary action, is "commitment beyond the self." The leaders who founded the organization were and are committed to working for positive change and are passionate about their work.

Women and people of color often have to be careful about how they convey their passion and conviction, particularly with what are considered stereotypically female or minority issues. Often expressions of passion in white men are lauded, while similar passion is often seen as emotionalism when it is expressed by women, or confrontation when it is expressed by men of color. I once had my staff tell me that they thought I had already made up my mind about an agenda item at a staff meeting on which I was seeking input. When I asked one of them why he thought I had made up my mind, he said that I sounded very enthusiastic about it. I explained that I was an enthusiastic person, and that my communication style was in congruence with my opinions. It did not mean that I had made up my mind. I was still open to candid feedback and even different opinions.

Leaders for the future must understand that there are culturally influenced differences in communication styles and that all individuals must be able to be themselves—another of the qualities I have observed in effective leaders. Individuals who must play a role and try to be something other than what they are will spend too much energy in playing the role and will have little left for leading.

Clarity of Goals

Along with vision and passion, clarity of goals is important for a leader. Good leaders can usually explain what they are trying to accomplish clearly and simply, and they can make a convincing case for its importance. Having clarity, however, need not be synonymous with being definite and intransigent. Good leaders are good negotiators and compromisers.

Perseverance

Effective leadership requires perseverance. Good leaders learn from failure—they try again, sometimes in a different way. They are also lifelong learners. The art is to utilize the learning and to know when to give up and try something else. Good leaders also understand that the people they lead may sometimes fail and they do not penalize failure. They help their subordinates and the organization learn from failure. Penalizing failure dampens initiative and risk taking, both of which are necessary for effective organizations and leadership.

Kindness

Good leaders treat everyone around them with kindness, respect, and honesty, in the same way that they would like to be treated. In the Latino culture, it is essential that we preserve the dignity of individuals. This has implications for how we communicate, give feedback and instructions, and set up reward systems and incentives. Although it is possible to succeed in leading people toward a particular goal through fear and intimidation, that is not leadership. Good leaders pay attention to the human needs of their colleagues and subordinates.

Honesty and Integrity

Good leaders are people of integrity. This is probably even more important in the nonprofit sector. Our society still regards the nonprofit sector as the "do-good" sector and expects higher levels of integrity from its leaders than it does from those in other sectors. Scrutiny of the sector has increased recently as a result of a few well-publicized incidents of leaders who strayed from the tradition of obedience to the unenforceable. The public's trust of tax exemption and the contributions of Americans of all income levels require that leaders of this sector adhere to the highest levels of integrity and ethics in the operation of their organizations. Their honesty must apply to their dealings with the public, donors, the government, and the media, as well as with colleagues.

Ongoing Renewal

John W. Gardner, in *Self-Renewal* (1981), exhorts leaders to pay attention to renewal, both self-renewal and organizational renewal. He says that not to engage in ongoing, continuous self-renewal allows rot to set in. Leaders in the nonprofit sector must work diligently to help their organizations continually and continuously renew themselves. Individuals doing the same work year after year can become stale. Organizations need to constantly redefine their issues and goals and redesign their strategies to address new problems. Today's solutions may well become tomorrow's problems and effective leaders and organizations are constantly engaged in reflection and self-evaluation.

Leaders as Teachers

Good leaders are good teachers. So much of what the nonprofit sector does involves teaching—teaching the public about the particular issues of an organization, teaching clients, government, the media, donors, and the organization's staff. Good teaching is essentially good communication, one of the most important skills of a good leader. Max DePree, in *Leadership Is an Art*, says, "Communication performs two functions, described by two 'action-prone' words: educate and liberate" (p. 106). Effective leaders communicate with their subordinates in ways that liberate the subordinates and draw from them their best contributions.

A Sense of Humor

Finally, a sense of humor and the ability to throw back their heads and laugh at themselves are essential for leaders. Recently, some corporations have hired consultants to help their staff play and use humor. It's a sad commentary that we need help to be able to do this.

Self-Knowledge

Although all good leaders need self-knowledge and awareness, women and people of color also need to know a lot about the male and majority culture and styles. Outsiders, or members of minority groups seeking entrance and acceptance into a majority culture and domain, need to be very knowledgeable about those who yield power and about the culture in which they will be working to effect change.

The next century will present new and exciting challenges to leaders. More than ever, they will need to be able to live with ambiguity and constant change. For leaders in the nonprofit sector, a constant must be their own moral compass and their commitment beyond the self to the public or greater good.

31 GEORGE B. WEBER

Growing Tomorrow's Leaders

*George B. Weber is secretary-general of the Inter-
national Federation of Red Cross and Red Crescent
Societies, the world's largest humanitarian organization. The International Federation currently has 163
National Society members worldwide, involving 128
million members and volunteers, 274,000 paid staff,
and an operating budget of twenty-three billion Swiss
francs, with an additional twenty-nine National Societies in formation. International Federation–coordi-
nated assistance reaches fifteen to twenty million
people a year, while the National Societies serve hundreds of millions more through their domestic service
activities. Weber has been awarded a number of
international decorations, including the Venezuelan
government's Civil Defense Award–1st Class; the
Canadian government's 125th Anniversary Com-
memorative Medal; Life Member, Bangladesh Red
Crescent Society; Cross of Merit, Netherlands Red
Cross; Golden Order of Merit, Japanese Red Cross
Society; Exceptional Humanitarian Service Award,
Portuguese Red Cross Society; Friendship Medal,*

*Turkish Red Crescent Society; and Vanier Award as
one of Five Outstanding Young Canadians.*

Most of our leadership successors are already among us—still children or students, perhaps, but already forming up. And much of the shape of the future that they will take over from us already exists. But how will we find and grow the best among them to carry on the humanitarian work that we know will be as vital in their time as it is in ours?

World trends are shaping the challenges that future leaders will need to face and cope with. Even as business, communications, and politics are creating single worldwide systems, the historic human habit of being most comfortable in relatively homogeneous groupings is creating a plethora of new nations. This process is violent in many places and profoundly uprooting of people. Millions today are adrift—some displaced by civil conflict in their own countries, others international refugees, a vast number expatriate workers in other lands. The now century-long migration from rural areas to cities all around the world adds additional tens of millions to the world's uprooted and vulnerable people. These millions eke out subsistence livings until a disaster of some sort—civil conflict, a nuclear accident, a flood, an earthquake—strikes, bringing tragedy.

At the same time, the world's prosperous nations are finding themselves overextended in their social and economic obligations and are drawing back from them; thus, the care and rescue of those in distress is falling to the humanitarian organizations at a time when the resources available to those organizations are increasingly being squeezed. Finding ways to provide services for these people will challenge our successors with even greater intensity: theirs probably will be the fateful choice of whether to define compassion more narrowly or learn how to increase resources steeply so that genuine solutions can be found and applied to the profound problems that face the world's vulnerable people.

There is no question of what tomorrow's leaders of compassionate organizations will *want* to do. But what attributes will enable them to successfully pursue solutions? I see two major skill categories as essential to cope with the inevitable challenges and then to effect the continuous change and improvement that will be needed in the years ahead.

First, even to be considered for a leadership post in a major international organization, a leader will need both a superior level of education and the capacity to work in multiple languages. The latter is essential even though English is increasingly the language of international meetings and operations. The international organization's leader of the future will need to have experience working in a broad spectrum of cultures; even though many leaders get by nowadays with a working command of English and perhaps one other major language, there is no substitute for being able to work in depth—either directly or in sensitive collaboration with a good interpreter—in the languages the service clients speak. Obviously, an international organization's leader of the future will not be able to work in every language, but he or she will need sufficient depth in several to qualify as a student of language.

The leader in an international organization of the future will also need to have broad experience in leading and managing a range of functions with increasing levels of responsibility in such areas as serving vast numbers of people, deploying large and diverse staffs, and administering complex budgets. Demonstrated performance and delivery in these areas will be demanded.

Equally important will be clear evidence that the leader not only can deliver the organization's service product effectively but also is clear-sighted about situations and prospects, can make unpopular decisions that sacrifice short-term considerations as needed for the organization's long-term interests and goals, and accepts accountability for his or her decisions.

In addition to these demonstrable abilities, the leader of the future will have to excel in "softer," less measurable areas such as personality and personally held values. The minimum here is clearly to have complete integrity, honesty, loyalty to principles, self-confidence and self-esteem, tenacity, high energy levels, a resilience that enables the leader to maintain spiritual tranquility amid a climate of pressures centered on high urgency and swift change, and the ability to accept and value diversity and harness its potential by unleashing people's creativity in the service of shared goals.

The challenges ahead will require leaders to identify, promote, reinforce, and live as role models of key core values; inspire diverse groups to common, shared action in which they trade some of their autonomy for a long-term greater common good; and give their best efforts in pursuit of that common good. These essential qualities and attributes are not simply values and skills to be *looked for* in leadership candidates. The future organization will not allow us to find our successors, or our successors to find *theirs*, through judgmental, ringside-seat choices. We leaders of today, and the leaders in our organizations who follow us, must become skilled, committed growers of effective leaders, staffs, and governance people. We have no more important task.

"Growing people" is, of course, something of a buzzword nowadays. Many take it as meaning identification of successors, which can be merely the search for one individual. To me, "growing people" is a far broader concept: it is the creation and cultivation of a climate throughout the organization in which people are actively given the opportunity to try out their talents and skills, are deliberately exposed to progressive challenges, are given training and study opportunities that broaden their perspectives and abilities, and, perhaps most important of all, are given management and leadership tasks that permit them and the organization to learn who and what they are in relation to the organization's mission.

Growing people is something that every manager, from the CEO to line supervisors and professional specialists, should do and on which he or she should be evaluated. When you think of growing people in the sense of extending opportunities for them to try themselves out in a positive learning climate, the chances for them to carry out such opportunities can be nearly endless. In the active organization, constant opportunities arise to increase, expand, and test the values that people can add to the organization and to their own experience.

Many of these opportunities are quite small in the organizational scheme. Are promising staff members given an opportunity to serve on task forces and committees where their thinking and judgment can find some expression? Do they take minutes at management meetings or conferences? Are they given tasks that expose them to the entire organization? Do managers take the time to seriously discuss with staff members their thoughts and feelings about their work, what kinds of experiences they would like to have, their career plans?

Is there a process for alternating assignments in the field and at headquarters? Are there ways for professional specialists to obtain general experience in operations, and for field operations staff to become exposed to the specialist areas that today's manager must become familiar with, such as finance, communications, and information systems? In an organization like the International Federation of Red Cross and Red Crescent Societies, a critical element will be the ability to persuade and inspire the member societies to grow people. The International Federation depends on National Societies for most of the delegates through which its international relief and development work is accomplished, as well as for its governance structures—the policy-level groups that set its directions and make its most basic decisions of mission and program.

Much must be balanced wisely and well by tomorrow's leader. He or she must be able to consider both the immediate and the long term in vision, goals, and decision making and to weigh the precise matter at hand against the holistic view and trend of things. This leader will need to be able to recognize and seek to balance, in his or her own endeavors and in the endeavors of others, the aggressive and the accepting, the time to move ahead and the time to maintain position, and the best way to accomplish short-term results without compromising long-term goals and values.

Intuition and the ability to deal with nonverbal signs of communication will also be critical skills for the leader of the future in order to serve diverse work forces, publics, and populations. Other key attributes will be critical thinking and analytic skills. The capacity to cope with the present while keeping a clear focus on strategy and vision for the future will be important, as will the ability to handle the intense pressures that arise both internally and externally in an organization that serves the public. Critical also will be the serenity to maintain one's balance in work that may involve traveling worldwide 50 percent of the time, having a home life that may at times be pushed last in priority, and dealing with events that habitually disrupt schedules and pose issues about which the leader must become informed overnight, show wisdom, and be publicly confident.

In broad summary, then, the successful leader of a diverse, worldwide enterprise in the tomorrow that is fast taking shape today will work through clearly defined purposes and objectives, be a role model both publicly and for the organization, and be a juggler-balancer who likes people and their diversity, displays inner confidence and poise, and does not shrink from making the necessary tough decisions. This leader is appreciated for the value he or she brings to the organization and its people and is followed in the organization's cultures voluntarily, not merely because she or he is boss.

This last may seem nicely desirable. It is, in fact, crucial. We must realize that the historic command-structure organization is dead. Even the best military organizations recognize that today. We are in a time in which we ask our colleagues to take on missions and assignments and to function, as they carry them out, not as bosses or commanders, but as mentors, guides, and cheerleaders. This is not to say that accountability is any less important than it has ever been. What has changed is that we know that empowered people can accomplish far more for the organization than ordered-about people ever could.

Can any one individual have and effectively practice all of the attributes that I have listed here as necessary in a future leader of an organization such as the International Federation I serve? The answer is going to have to be yes: paragons there will be because paragons there must be. But am I setting forth a scenario of expectations that can offer the leader of the future only the prospect of mixed success and failure?

No—because the successful leader of the future must have one more attribute that weighs perhaps as much as all the others on the scale of effectiveness: he or she must be a tireless, inventive, observant, risk-taking, and ever-hopeful builder and enabler of management and leadership teams within and among the organization's constituent parts. Well constructed, these teams will both underpin and fill out the attributes that must mark the organization's top leadership, as well as accomplishing the details and drive of the organization's vision, goals, and purposes. By working together, the teams will accomplish more than their members as individuals ever could, just as the Federation, when its members work together, achieves more than the sum of the individual members' capacities and efforts.

The prescription I write here is no easy one to fill. It takes hard work and sensitivity to be an effective leader of an international organization like mine, and all signs are that the challenges will grow exponentially in the years ahead. I say to anyone who would lead in the international humanitarian service organization of tomorrow: develop every potential that you find in yourself as a leader and manager of events, people, and work and grow yourself as listener, observer, student of human aspiration and achievement, and believer in human worth. Above all, study constantly how to add value to your organization, its people, and all those it seeks to serve.

Index